AF560090

AGRARIAN SYSTEM DURING THE DOGRA REIGN IN KASHMIR (1846–1889)

AGRARIAN SYSTEM DURING THE DOGRA REIGN IN KASHMIR

(1846–1889)

RATTAN LAL HANGLOO

MANOHAR
2025

First published 2025
First eBook edition 2025

ISBN 978-93-6080-450-3 (hardbound)
ISBN 978-93-6080-052-9 (eBook)

Published by
Ajay Kumar Jain *for*
Manohar Publishers & Distributors
4753/23 Ansari Road, Daryaganj
New Delhi 110002

Cover design by Kamal Purna Jammual

Typeset by Ravi Shanker, Delhi 110095

Printed and bound in India

To

my brothers

SHREE MAKHEN LAL HANGLOO

SHREE PYARE LAL HANGLOO

DR. NANAJEE HANGLOO

not only for affording me the opportunity to concentrate upon my research but also for contributing to my understanding of this phenomenon.

Ek to begaar le aur fir us par mazduri naa de,
Marte hain ae zalim, tir bhi talwar bhi.
Yeh tashhaddud kas koi pahunchaye Maharaj Tak,
Haal-e-raiyyat se ho ba khabar sarkar bhi.

We peasants are subjected to unpaid forced labour,
The cruel government does not hesitate in imposing all atrocities upon us.
(We wish that) someone makes maharaja too familiar about our plight,
Send (somebody to) the government make aware our pitiful condition of the subjects.

– *Dewan-i-Fauq* by Mohammaduddin Fauq
published in Lahore in 1909 (Urdu)

Contents

Illustrations

ILLUSTRATIONS

MAP

Tables

Preface

The region of Kashmir stamps us (Kashmiris) with a character by which we are distinguished from the other Indian states and great civilizations of the world. These general contours of Kashmir have seriously influenced its history, culture, polity and economy in every epoch. In the nineteenth century when the rest of South Asia was slowly transcending to modernity, Kashmir was suffering under Dogra Raj. The peasants' lands were consumed by the increasing taxes levied on lands, persons and on all sorts of artisanal and pastoral production. People had no rights, they were subjected to *begar* (forced labour), and their plight was much worse than those serfs who served in Medieval European Feudal Estates. As a historian from Kashmir region, I could not escape excessive preoccupation with these problems that Kashmiris faced under the shadow of the gloomy years of Dogra Raj. It is, there-fore, necessary to study its Rural Economy that predominantly concerns its people in many ways. I have chosen the second half of the nineteenth century because it is a transitional period in Kashmir's history.

Though this book resembles my earlier work on agrarian system in Kashmir in scope, it is in a large measure a new book. I have taken note of findings of the many young and energetic researchers who are amplifying our knowledge and see how new questions are asked or and how old ones are given new answers at rapid rate though not without controversies that are rooted in Kashmir's politics.

For carrying out this work my greatest debt of gratitude goes to Professor Harbans Mukhia for his valuable guidance and suggestions. I have been fortunate to have found such a great *guru* (teacher) and friend. He inspired me intellectually over a long term and afforded me the much-needed opportunity to interact with scholars in a wide range of historical fields at an early stage of my research, at the Center for Historical Studies, Jawaharlal Nehru University.

My grateful thanks are due to Professor Dilbagh Singh, Professor Yogesh Sharma, Professor Ranjan Chakraborty, Professor G. Hargopal, Professor Ashok Aima (former V.C. Jammu Central University), Professor V. Rama Krishna, Professor R.P. Bahuguna, Professor Surajbhan Bhardwaj, Professor Tabir Kalam and Dr. Nazrul Bari. I owe much gratitude to late Shree Shivji Bhat, Mr. Autar Krishen Kaul, Mr. Pyare Lal Pandita, Rajesh Raina and Mr. Vijay Raina for their help and valuable suggestions.

I am thankful to the management of Manohar Publishers & Distributors particularly Mr. Ajay Jain and Mr. Sanjay Kala for bringing out this book. I also record my indebtedness to my students Dr. Fayaz Ahamad Dar, Dr. Mamta Nanda for their much skilful assistance.

I am also grateful to my family members, Shree M.L. Hangloo, Shree P.L. Hangloo, Dr. Nanajee Hangloo and my all sisters, Ms. Kishni, Ms. Santosha, Ms. Teja, Ms. Sarla, Ms. Sushma for their love and care. My grateful thanks are also due to my in-laws Professor O.N. Kaul, Mr. Rajinder Kaul, Ms. Swani Kaul, Mr. Komal Kaul and Mr. Saiesh Kaul for the various kindnesses offered during the preparation of the book. My children Arkaprateem, Akanksha, Arkapravah and Akhil Bhat also deserve my gratitude.

Special thanks are due to my grandchild Shehjar Bhat who always refreshed me with his intoxicating smile and demanded very little time as and when I was assigned his care taking during my visit to the family at Philadelphia, USA.

My principal debt in the writing this book has been to my wife Sharika Kaul Hangloo for cheerfully tolerating my absences and absent-mindedness, while pursuing her own goals and helping to raise a family, she has found the time to improve all of my writings with her valuable interventions. Without her good cheer and her assistance at every stage of its preparation I would certainly not have completed the work.

Jammu
6 January 2023

RATTAN LAL HANGLOO

CHAPTER 1

Introduction

A study of the agrarian system of Kashmir during the second half of the nineteenth century hardly needs any explicit justification in view of the predominantly rural character of the region. Specialists will have their own explanations as to why the studies of regional patterns of such aspects were not paid adequate attention after the collapse of British colonialism and the end of Dogra Raj in Jammu & Kashmir. To establish a coherent understanding of the nature of the agrarian society of any region may well turn out to be beneficial for establishing a new framework for understanding the nature of that region's society in totality.

Agriculture in Kashmir has always been an exceptionally important aspect of the people's lives, straddling as it does even today, the highland and low land zones, extensive forests and waste land.Though the agrarian history of ancient and mediaeval India in general and of some regions in particular has been examined for quite a long time, little attention has been paid to the study of this problem in Kashmir's history. It is only a thorough examination of various historical issues at the regional level from epoch to epoch that will allow scholars to make broad generalizations about the character of the Indian economy and society as a whole. The character of the ancient and the medieval economy of India has been the subject of intense controversy amongst historians. Thus while D.D. Kosambi and R.S. Sharma have argued for the characterization of a long period of Indian history as feudal, Irfan Habib has questioned the utility of this notion for Indian history. Harbans Mukhia has made a detailed critique of the concept of feudalism and has suggested the notion of a free peasant economy in medieval India, a notion defined very differently from the ones already in circulation. However, it is evident that there would be considerable regional variations in the pattern of development and that a careful analysis of the economy of each region is necessary for an evaluation of agrarian economy of the country as a whole for any period.[1] With this objective in view, I have taken up Rural Economy of Kashmir under Dogras for study in this book.

Unfortunately, most of the works dealing with the history of Kashmir for the above-mentioned period appear to be somewhat unsatisfactory from the point of view of our problem. The first among such works was *Gulab Nama,* written in 1865 by Dewan Kripa Ram, the then Prime Minister of Kashmir.[2] It was written under the supervision of Maharaja Ranbir Singh, the son and successor of Maharaja Gulab Singh. Dewan Kripa Ram hailed from the eminent Dewan family of Aminabad. They had, from the commencement of Maharaja Gulab Singh's reign, practically monopolized the office of the Dewan. He became the Dewan of Maharaja Ranbir Singh at the age of 24 in 1857 and held the office of Dewan till his death in 1876. He wrote *Gulab Nama* in the typically ornate Persian style of the nineteenth century. The author mainly extolled the virtues of Gulab Singh in the book. The economic aspects and their impact on society are brief and completely exogenous to the political events. There is no interaction between politics of those times with the economic conditions despite the fact that the deteriorating conditions of Kashmiri peasantry was the direct consequence of the political events during the Dogra Raj. Dogra Raj was the darkest period in Kashmir's economic history because it increasingly asserted control over people and the region and was very effective in the collection of revenue and other taxes. These were also collected via negotiated contracts (*ijaradari*). Since the transport system was of primitive nature it resulted in inefficient use of resources. Besides this there was no institutionalized form of resistance on the part of the peasantry, which allowed the exploitation of Dogra Raj to persist for a long period.

Likewise, the other works written on Maharaja Gulab Singh and Maharaja Ranbir Singh's period (AD 1846-85) are either biographical or, by and large, political in nature. Seldom, if ever, is there a reference of any social and economic problems of the time in them.[3] We have bulk of official correspondence and record, gazetteers of the region, accounts of European adventurers, travellers and officials connected with the enforcement and reinforcement of colonial authority in the region. Taken together they do not sketch the contours for our research because they have all operated their logic. The colonial officials were partly party to the ill fate of the agrarian community because they were using Kashmiri peasants worst than slaves when supplied by Dogra Raj for rendering *begar* (forced labour). Therefore many of them have focused on especially case studies. None of these works set out to be statistical data for reference work. Some of them, such as Walter Roper Lawrence, have tables but no systematic listing exist. Gazetteers and accounts of adventurers do not use chronological exposition which make the reading difficult for they were themselves unfamiliar with the places, system and events. For example, for constructing the historical details of the peasant population and their holdings areawise, or for comprehending the volume of trade, it is very frustrating. Inconsistencies are common even in such ostensibly standard a series as successive decadewise censuses and records.

During Maharaja Pratap Singh's reign, W.R. Lawrence produced a detailed work on the socio-economic and political aspects of Kashmir's history from the early times to his day, but in his work the exposition of basic concepts is not sufficiently clear and accurate to enable us to use them in considering the agrarian and rural problems of the region.[4] W.R. Lawrence took over as the Land Settlement Commissioner of Kashmir from Mr. Wingate in the year 1889, who could not continue due to varied reasons.[5] Lawrence undertook the land reforms at the time when the Indians in all provinces were demanding radical agrarian reforms and modernization of agriculture. But the utmost honesty that was required to make the settlement a success did not exist. Being an agent of the colonial regime, he tried to relieve the peasantry of Kashmir of the problems of poverty and settlement of their holdings but the exploitative Dogra Raj disallowed any broadbased reform in the agrarian sector. Besides this, his sudden departure from Kashmir in 1895 to join as Secretary to Lord Curzon also left the settlement of holdings incomplete. Some of the effects of his work were ambivalent. Instead of exploring the nature of agrarian economy, functioning of institutional framework and measures that could mitigate poverty at different social levels, Lawrence conceals everything under the umbrella of Dogra bureaucracy's exploitation.

While one finds his arguments persuasive, the comparison and re-examination of his evidence is frequently more suggestive than conclusive. The complex nature of economic data and the frequent gaps make analysis difficult. Lawrence, like any other colonial functionary believed in British supremacy and most probably expected that the success of his survey and settlement would encourage Kashmiri peasantry to legitimize British residents functioning in Kashmir.

Another work is that of M.L. Kapoor, 'A Study in the Socio-Economic Life of the People during Maharaja Pratap Singh's Period (AD 1885-1925)'. But the agrarian system of the state of Kashmir finds no place in it. In the treatment of socio-economic history, the author has not gone beyond the traditional method of giving a general description of the masses. In dealing with the society, he has confined himself to a description of only their dress, food, and pastimes. Social stratification has been discussed in terms of differences in people's dress, food, and habits. He does not explain why the peasant poverty and inequality tended to rise constantly during the Dogra Raj. It is puzzling that the author does not situate the wide-ranging debates about agrarian question or economic history that were in circulation in academic circles at that time. The author has not made use of any Persian and Urdu sources of the time, perhaps that also explains the reasons for the limited scope of this work.[6]

In early 1974, Mohammad Ishaq Khan published a valuable work on the history of Srinagar. Though the author does not offer the reader an analysis of the socio-economic problems of Kashmir as a whole, he has made a penetrating analysis of many problems of the city of Srinagar. The varied problems studied therein appear to have determined the direction of the evolution of the social and economic structure of the city as also the formation of various economic units and their relationship with the various classes of Kashmir's agrarian society from time to time.[7] After Irfan Habib's *Agrarian System of the Mughals* and Indu Banga's *Agrarian System of the Sikhs* we cannot decry the lack of methodological work in this field. Indu Banga in her work, *Agrarian System of the Sikhs: Late Eighteenth and Early Nineteenth Century* has identified more than twelve Sikh *sardars* and a number of non-Sikh independent principalities who ruled over Punjab after the decline of the Mughal and Afghan Empire.[8] There is now substantial body of literature on this issue. With the growth of the Marxist approach there has been a clear orientation for understanding the agrarian issues, peasant problems, agricultural production and distribution, the role of various intermediaries and the attitude of government both in terms of theoretical generalization and historical particularity.

In order to understand the evolution of society, one must examine this process at its lowest end. One must, in other words, carefully examine what changes, if any, occurred in the manner in which the peasants cultivated their field and the manner in which their produce was distributed among various sections of the society. It is this aspect which the recent historical research has thrown up as the most important, I have taken it up in the context of Kashmir's history under Dogra Raj (1846-1947).

The people inhabiting the territory of Kashmir have played an important role in its history from earliest times and survived the conditions imposed upon them by the countries of both the East and the West. The strategic position of Kashmir and its geographical location as well as the nature of political intervention by the region's ruling class had made her development extremely slow till the end of first half of the twentieth century.

In the ancient and early medieval period, the situation in Kashmir was particularly bad. The people had suffered under the Hindu and Muslim rulers when a large number of them had been annihilated. There was no regular system of assessment and collection. The usual political feuds among nobles exposed the valley to menacing neighbours like the Turks and the Mughals. This led to more and more economic decline of the valley, political fragmentation of the nobility and ultimately in 1586, the valley fell into the hands of the Mughal rulers. As early as 1586, Kashmir was linked to the Mughal Empire. The establishment of the Mughal rule in the conquered province of Kashmir was an event of great significance since it brought certain basic changes in the economic relations amongst the various classes of the agricultural community.[9]

The new rules and regulations regarding the land revenue system of Kashmir were implemented by Emperor Akbar.[10] But before his successors could achieve the economic and political objects of their rule, symptoms of decay had began to manifest at the centre, and ultimately, the valley was taken over by the Afghan rulers in AD 1753.[11]

The chief concern of the Afghan rulers too, remained the grasping and realization by quick and oppressive methods of as much of the agricultural produce as possible. No new regulations were introduced, and the old ones were kept intact. There followed a complete breach of law and a violation of the scheduled revenue rates in Kashmir. In course of time, the disintegration of the central administration took place, and the provincial governors appointed by the Afghans became independent.[12] Taking advantage of the weakness at the centre, various intermediaries also engaged in a scramble to obtain territorial possession and control over their respective areas.[13] The already dissatisfied masses were ready to embrace any political shift that could replace Afghan rule (AD 1753-1819). A group of nobility headed by Beer Bal Dhar broke away from the Afghans and settled matters with the Sikh rulers in Punjab in the second decade of the nineteenth century.[14]

It was, therefore, in 1819 that the doubly oppressed subjects of the territory of Kashmir passed into the hands of Maharaja Ranjit Singh. There was a change in the administrative structure of Kashmir, which also led to a change in the land-based relations between various classes of the society.[15] Maharaja Ranjit Singh's reign was very simple as there were no elaborate budget estimates prepared in advance by his government. The Maharaja himself, as we all know, was the centre of the entire governmental system and was assisted by a Chief Minister, few ministers and a number of *dewans, toshakhanias* and *munshis* who administered different departments of the State. The departments like Revenue and Central Secretariat were given by the Maharaja to those astute Hindus whose family members had in the past occupied ministerial posts in the Muslim Court of Delhi and under the Kabul Government also. The finances of the Sikh kingdom were regulated on the principle of keeping the expenditure within the limits of revenue and if the revenue of the kingdom declined owing to some unexpected circumstances, the expenses of the state were also curtailed proportionately.[16] However, these changes did not affect the methods of cultivation, nor did they lead to an economic renaissance, though they did change the condition of the Kashmiri peasantry for the worse. By and large, the Mughal system was followed. The Sikh administrative system did not prove worthy of its expectations. The administration at the hands of the Sikh governors became quite lax.

Like their Afghan predecessors, they did not miss any opportunity to misappropriate revenue.[17] Many additional *abwabs* (taxes) and cesses were allowed to be imposed besides the usual revenue.[18] The intermediaries considered themselves free to impose any cesses on the peasants without the concurrence of the state.[19] Large portions of the peasants' income were taken away by way of rent, high interest charges, and taxes. Unfair terms of price exchange also left the peasants with such little subsistence that it was neither possible for them to improve their farms nor to raise their living standards. Whether the increase in various taxes meant a real rise in the tax burden upon the peasantry is no doubt a difficult question to answer because the sources do not provide us with income data. However, an attempt has been made to measure the incidence of the taxes levied.

In the first half of the nineteenth century, the British colonial masters became more conscious of the mounting danger of Russia from the north-western side of their Indian colony. As a result, they began to think in terms of the liquidation of the Sikh Empire, which could not only transfer to them the economic resources of the Sikh Empire but also provide them with some of the important borders which were indispensable for safeguarding their Indian colony. This attitude of the British was expressed by M.B. Bayley to Hob House in the letter dated January 1841:

> Even if the holding of a force in Afghanistan should be necessary for their maintenance, we should find in the resources of Punjab, resources necessary for their maintenance, we should reinforce them without any difficulty and with Kashmere on our flank and the whole line of Indus in our possession, we might defy all attacks whether from European or Asiatic enemies.[20]

In course of time, the Sikh principalities between the rivers Sutlej and Jamuna passed under the protection and care of the British. The Anglo-Sikh wars followed in 1845-6 in which the British came out victorious and, in the process of settling the political future of the occupied territories and their autonomous vassals and chiefs, they handed over Jammu & Kashmir to Maharaja Gulab Singh as their vassal in 1846.[21] In course of time, the Sikh principalities between river Sutlej and Jammu passed under the protection and care of the British. It appears that there was no money in the treasury for the payment of Rs. 150,000 to the Sikh soldiers. Hardinge declared the annexation of Kashmir to the Company but when Gulab Singh offered to pay the money, Kashmir was made over to him. This was how Hardinge paid the war expenses to the troops of the Khalsa Army at the cost of destroying the lives of Kashmiris and Kashmir region.[22] As the Government of Sikhs was simple at that time, the system introduced by Dewan Bhawani Das seems to have been quite elaborate. Dewan Bhawani Das set up separate treasuries at important district headquarters such as Lahore, Amritsar and Jalandhar. They were required to maintain a regular account of all incomes and expenditures. In 1815, the old division of major and minor heads of accounts was discontinued and the exchequer department was reorganized. According to James Douie, 'the revenue system of Ranjit Singh was an organized system of pillage, for the country was farmed to contractors (*ijaradars*) who were bound to pay a certain sum into the state treasury, and were permitted to collect as much as possible for themselves'.[23] After 1834, when there was a considerable increase in military budget, the ineffective nature of the *kankut* system (the system of revenue assessment) became apparent to Maharaja Ranjit Singh.[24] He started encouraging the practice of farming out revenues of large areas particularly of irrigable lands to the highest bidder for a period extending from three to six years. Under this system the cultivator or a big zamindar or a big state official entered into a contract with the state agreeing to pay the amount stated in the contract deed. The contractor was called *ijaradar* and such contracts eliminated the middle man, and cultivators in village land were allowed full advantage of reaping the fruits of their labour. With the object of getting a sure and fixed estimate of annual income, the Maharaja promoted the practice of farming out large areas of lands and even districts to *ijaradars* who agreed to make the payment of state share regularly.

Although the year 1846 also brought about a change in the administration as a result of the establishment of Jammu & Kashmir state under Maharaja Gulab Singh, the condition of Kashmiris continued to be as it had been under the Sikhs.[25] Though during this period frequent land settlements were carried out in other parts of the country and it was understood that the settlement would lead to more rapid accumulation of capital in agriculture and its consequent improvement, but Kashmir was still passing through a traditional economic order due to its geographical isolation from the rest of India.

There was an increasing neglect of the rural economic infrastructure, transport, irrigation, and flood control systems through corrupt and inept bureaucratic management under the Dogra Raj. All these developments interacted to produce rather alarming consequences for the agrarian economy and peasantry of Kashmir. Land distribution became increasingly unequal, putting pressure on peasants in Kashmir to migrate, and landless peasants became an almost limitless source of manpower for landlords and state officials, carrying out *begar* (corvee).[26]

Thus, the agrarian structure of the period under review was a matter of comprehensive interest, affecting all sections of society. There were competing interests among *jagirdars, pattadars, chakdars, zamindars* and other segments of the peasantry who made up all social classes in a variety of ways.

No pure and simple landlord class existed, and the land assignees and grantees were numerous. Although high officials and the Maharaja agreed that the greatest rewards in society must go to the agriculturalists, they concerned themselves more with the raising of taxes. All the Dogra Maharajas appear to have been too preoccupied with Western penetration to introduce anything new in the field of agriculture.[27]

Consequently, none in the peasantry class could escape the distress and depression due to their mounting indebtedness, forced labour, and the rising number of landless peasants and workers.

Hence, the study of the agrarian structure of Kashmir involves a number of aspects. These include:

1. The impact of the environment on the agrarian economy of Kashmir.
2. The extent of cultivation and the changes, if any, in the cropping pattern.
3. Agricultural production for use and for sale.
4. The nature of agricultural technology.

5. The nature and extent of revenue assignments, grants, and the position of assignees and grantees in rural society.
6. The nature of revenue administration, its organization and functioning.
7. The magnitude of the land revenue demand and its impact on the condition of the peasantry.
8. Other subsidiary occupations of the peasantry which supplemented their income.[28]

All these aspects are closely related and require a detailed study. However, after an examination of the sources, it has not been possible at present to answer all these questions satisfactorily. The paucity of statistical data regarding population, production, and holdings involved a great deal of difficulty in making some generalizations which could prove fruitful.

Therefore, the burden of the present study is to identify purely and in a descriptive manner, the agricultural production of Kashmir; the nature of the cropping pattern and the technology used; the methods of assessment and collection; the magnitude of land revenue demand; and the revenue machinery, its nature and functioning. In addition, attention has also been focused on the land revenue assignees and land grantees. The condition of the peasantry and the pattern of trade have also been kept within the purview of this study.

Like all descriptive works, this book also suffers from inevitable shortcomings. It is only a step towards a fuller understanding of the agrarian economy of Kashmir in all its comprehensiveness. In fact, I had intended to do much further research on this subject before publishing it but the crisis which overtook Kashmir from 1990 made that impossible. The study must, therefore, stand as it is, with only minimal changes, in the hope that in spite of its imperfections it will be of use to future scholars, and stimulate them to carry on, with much vigour, where I left off.

NOTES

1. See D.D. Kosambi, *Introduction to the Study of Indian History*, Popular Book Depot, Bombay 1956, pp. 296-405. R.S. Sharma, *Indian Feudalism*, University of Calcutta, Calcutta, 1965, Irfan Habib, 'The

Social Distribution of Landed Property in pre-British India', *Indian Society, Historical Probing's*, edited by R.S. Sharma, People's Publishing House, Delhi, 1974, pp. 264-316. Harbans Mukhia, 'Was There Feudalism in Indian History', *Journal of Peasant Studies*, vol. VIII, no. 3, Sage, New Delhi, April 1981, pp. 273-310.

2. L.H. Griffin, *The Punjab Chiefs*, Chronicle Press, Lahore, 1865, pp. 227-31.
3. The other works include Pandit Salig Ram Kaul, *Biography of Maharaja Gulab Singh*, Srinagar, 1923: Sardar K.M. Panikar, *Gulab Singh, the founder of Jammu and Kashmir State*, Martin Hopkinson Ltd, London, 1930; A.N. Sapru, *The Building of Jammu and Kashmir State being an Achievement of Maharaja Gulab Singh*, Punjab Record Office, Lahore 1931; S.S. Bawa, *The Jammu Fox, a Biography of Maharaja Gulab Singh*, Southern Illinois University Press; London and Amsterdam; Feffer and Simons, London, 1974; Dewan Narsingdas Nargis, *Maharaja Ranbir Singh* (a vernacular biography), Jammu, 1921; idem, *Tarikh-i-Dogradesh* (Urdu), Jammu, 1967. Fazal Hussain, *Kashmir-aur-Dogra Raj* (Urdu), Gulshan Publishers, Srinagar, 1979. A recent work is by Phool Pyari Mam, 'Maharaja Gulab Singh' (unpublished Ph.D. thesis submitted in 1977 to Kashmir University. But she has also failed to examine some of the important aspects of economic development like agriculture, trade, and industry during Maharaja Gulab Singh's period.
4. For details see W.R. Lawrence, *Valley of Kashmir*, Oxford University Press, London, 1895.
5. A. Wingate, *Land Settlement Report 1889* (unpublished document) Jammu Archives.
6. M.L. Kapoor, 'Social and Economic History of Jammu and Kashmir from 1885-1925 A.D.', an unpublished Ph.D. thesis approved by Jammu University in 1974.
7. M.I. Khan, *History of Srinagar*. Aamir Publications, Srinagar, 1978.
8. Indu Banga, *Agrarian System of the Sikhs: Late Eighteenth and Early Nineteenth Century*, Manohar, Delhi, 1978, pp. 11-60. Much before the rise of Ranjit Singh into power, Punjab was divided into a large number of independent political units. Among them, there were not twelve but fifty-six principalities under the Sikh rulers in the upper *doabs* of Punjab. More than thirty Muslim chiefs were in the lower *doabs* of Punjab, whereas in the hills of Punjab, there were thirty-eight Hindu and Muslim principalities. Majority of the hill states belonged to Hindu Rajput rulers. The combined number of Hindu and Muslim rulers in Punjab during the late eighteenth century was larger than that of Sikh chiefs.

The Sikh and non-Sikh chiefs of the eighteenth century came from different political background. The Sikh chiefs, who established themselves in Punjab plains, had come to power after a long struggle with the Mughals and later the Afghans. They were ordinary people belonging to cultivating class. With the help of institutions like *gurmata, dal khalsa, rakhi* and the *misl,* which they evolved during their period of struggle, they could establish themselves as independent chiefs. Veena Sachdeva, *Mastery of the Province of Lahore,* in T.R. Sharma (ed.), *Ranjit Singh: Ruler and Warrior*, Chandigarh: Publication Bureau, Panjab University, 2005, pp. 6, 63 and 143.

9. *Baharistan-i-Shahi* (Anonymous), Unpublished Persian Manuscript, Srinagar Research Department Library, folios 182b and 183b (henceforth ff. for folios). Suka and Prajayabhata, *Rajvalipatika,* Sanskrit Ms., English tr. by J.C. Dutt under the title *Kings of Kashmira* (3 vols.), printed by S.K. Sham, Calcutta, 1898; Atlantic Publishers & Distributors, Delhi, 1993, vol. III, p. 407.
10. Abul Fazl, *Ain-i-Akbari,* Persian, 3 vols. The original Persian text was translated into English in three volumes. The first volume, translated by Heinrich Blochmann (1873) consisted of Books I and II. The second volume, translated by Col. Henry Sullivan Jarrett (1891), Asiatic Society of Calcutta as a part of their *Bibliotheca Indica* series, vol. II, 3rd edn. 1978, p. 366. See Vol. I, p. 347.
11. Ramjudhar, *Kaifiat-i-Intizam-i-mulk-i-Kashmir,* Persian (unpublished Ms.), Research Department Library, Srinagar, ff. 3-4.
12. Ibid., see also, Lawrence, *Valley,* op. cit., p. 196. R.K. Parmu, *A History of Muslim Rule in Kashmir (1320-1819),* People's Publishing House, Bombay, 1969, pp. 352-3.
13. Ramjudhar, op. cit., f. 4.
14. Parmu, op. cit., pp. 385-7.
15. Dewan Krishen Lal's *Account of Kashmir,* Foreign Secret Consultation, 31 March 1848, file no. 68, National Archives of India (henceforth NAI).
16. Hari Ram Gupta, *History of the Sikhs: The Sikh Loin of Lahore,* vol. V, Munshiram Manoharlal, New Delhi: 1991, p. 356.
17. H.M. Lawrence, *Transfer of Government to Maharaja Gulab Singh,* Section C, 28 January 1848, file nos. 33-4, Jammu Archives.
18. Ibid.
19. Ibid.
20. Charles Hardinge, *Viscount Hardinge,* Clarendon Press, Oxford, 1900, p. 133. See also *Letters from Sir Henry Hardinge to Queen Victoria,*

18 February 1846, Foreign and Political Department, file no. 66, NAI. Hardinge entered the diplomatic service in 1880. He was appointed the first Secretary at Tehran in 1896, and the first Secretary at Saint Petersburg in 1898, when he was promoted over the heads of seventeen of his seniors. While in Russia, he acted as chargé d'affaires in the ambassador's absence (including in late 1902). After a brief tenure as Assistant Under-Secretary for Foreign Affairs, he became Ambassador to Russia in 1904. In 1906, he was promoted to the position of Permanent Under-Secretary at the Foreign Office, where despite his own conservatism, he worked closely with Liberal Foreign Secretary Sir Edward Grey. In 1907, he declined the post of Ambassador to the United States. In 1910, Hardinge was raised to the peerage as Baron Hardinge of Penshurst, in the county of Kent, and appointed by the Asquith government as Viceroy of India, Hardinge and his wife Winifred during his term as Viceroy of India, *c.* 1910-16. His tenure was a memorable one and included the visit of King George V and the Delhi Durbar of 1911, as well as the move of the capital from Calcutta to New Delhi in 1911. Although Hardinge was the target of assassination attempts with bomb attack by the Indian nationalists Rashbehari Bose and Sachin Sanyal, his tenure included an improvement of relations between the British administration and the nationalists, as a consequence of the implementation of the Morley-Minto reforms of 1909, and of Hardinge's own admiration for Mahatma Gandhi and criticism of the South African government's anti-Indian immigration policies. See also Francis Young Husband, *Kashmir*, Adam and Charles Black, London, 1909, rpt., New Delhi: Asian Educational Services, 1996, pp. 168-72. S.S. Bawa, *The Jammu Fox*, London, 1974, p. 88. Karl Marx, *Notes on Indian History*, Foreign Languages Publishing House, Moscow, 1988 (rpt.), p. 142.

21. Lawrence, op. cit.
22. Ibid. Karl Marx also mentions that when British army entered Lahore in triumph on 20 February1846. Marx, op. cit., p. 142.
23. James Douie, *Punjab Settlement Manual*, Superintendent, Government Printing, Punjab, 1899, 1930 New Delhi, rpt. Daya Publishing House, Delhi, 1985, p. 19.
24. Ibid.
25. Sir Francis Edward Younghusband, *Kashmir (1863-1942.)* Adam and Clarles Black, London, 1909; Indian rpt. Asian Educational Services New Delhi, pp. 175-9.
26. Mirza Saif-ud-Din, *Akhbarat*, 13 vols. (unpublished Persian Ms.) Research Department Library, Srinagar, Kashmir, vol. I, f. 74.

27. A.P. Nicholson, *Scrapes of Paper, India's Broken Treaties, Her Princes and Her Problem*, Ernest Benn Ltd, London, 1930, pp. 88-90.
28. The study of the abovementioned aspects is confined to the agrarian system of Kashmir valley only and not the erstwhile state of Jammu & Kashmir as a whole. The state of Jammu & Kashmir consists of three regions, Jammu, Kashmir and Ladakh which have little in common more than a mere political destiny. From August 2019 the status of statehood has been withdrawn to Jammu & Kashmir state and Article 370 of Indian Constitution that granted special status to it has been abolished. The state has been bifurcated and the regions of Jammu and Kashmir have become one Union Territory and the Ladakh has been separated from the state and it has also become another Union Territory. However this reorganizational step has neither enhanced the regions integrating relationship with rest of India nor ensured the regions development.

CHAPTER 2

Agricultural Production

The geographical features of Jammu & Kashmir state, which are almost entirely mountainous, occupy a unique position in the topography of the Indian subcontinent. They vary in height from hillocks on the Punjab border to great mountains in the north. They together constitute the sources of water and lend a peculiar scenic beauty to Kashmir. But whereas they ensure the defence of Kashmir they also have been the cause of its problems. Among these mountains, the valley of Kashmir is a level plain.[1] The sources are generally silent about the details of the total cultivable area and the area under cultivation during the period under study. However, there are scattered references in different accounts. Dewan Krishen Lal who wrote during the mid-nineteenth century, observes that in 1848 the total area of land in Kashmir was 7,50,000 acres out of which 2,00,000 acres was under water, 1,50,000 acres under forest and hills, 50,000 acres under the roads and 3,50,000 acres was cultivable.[2]

The *Majmui* (administrative) *Reports* of a little later period also mention the following details of land under cultivation in Kashmir in the last few years of the nineteenth century:

TABLE 2.1: YEAR WISE AREA IN ACRES FROM 1887 TO 1891

Year	*1887*	*1888*	*1889*	*1890*	*1891*
Area	2,73,737	6,73,739	6,26,968	7,05,139	5,48,989

Source: Majmui Reports (in Urdu) for the years from 1887 to 1891, Ranbir Govt. Press, Jammu & Kashmir Archives, Srinagar.
Note: The area in the table is given in acres.[3]

The physiography of the area that we are dealing with in this work was appropriately characterized by Walter Roper Lawrence, the nineteenth-century expert on Kashmir's agriculture, in the following words:

> This is a celebrated valley, perched securely among the Himalayas at an average height of 6000 feet above the sea. It is appropriately 84 miles in length and 20 to 25 miles in breadth. [In the] North, east and west range after range of mountains guard the valley from [the] outer world, while in the south it is cut off from Punjab by rocky barriers, 50 to 75 miles in width.... As one descends the mountains and leaves the woodland glades, cultivation commences immediately and right up to the fringe of the forests, maize is grown and walnut trees abound. A little lower down, at an elevation of about 7,000 feet, rice of a hardy and stunted growth is found and shady plains trees appear. Lower still superior rice are grown, and the watercourses are edged with willows. The side valleys which lead off from the vale of Kashmir, though possessing distinct charms of their own, have certain features in common. At the mouth of the valley lies the wide delta of fertile soil on which rice with its varying colours, the plain trees, mulberries and willows grow luxuriantly; a little higher up the land was terraced, and rice still grows and the slopes are ablaze with wild indigo, till about 6,000 feet the plain tree gives place to walnut, and rice to millets. On the left bank of [the] mountain river endless forests stretch from the bottom of the valley to the peaks; and on the right bank, wherever its nook and corner is sheltered from the sun and [the] hot breeze of India, pines and firs establish themselves. Farther up the valley, the river already a roaring torrent becomes a veritable waterfall dashing down between lofty cliffs, whose bases are fringed with maples and horsechestnuts, white and pink, and millets are replaced by buckwheat and Tibetan barley. Soon after this the useful birch tree appears, and then come grass and glaciers, the country of shepherds. Where the mountains cease to be steep, fan like projections with flat arid tops and bare trees run out towards the valley. They are known as Karewa.[4]

Despite the fact that the area of land under cultivation in Kashmir valley has been very small due to its mountainous nature, the character of the rural economy has remained agrarian throughout the period of our study.[5]

Crop Pattern

The peculiar physical character and the climate have, from times past, been a serious handicap to intensive farming and diversification of crops in the valley. The land remains under snow for four to five months a year when no cultivation is possible at all. As a result, rice was the main *kharif* crop, but after its harvest in late September and early October, there was very little time left to sow another crop. Every year from March to September ploughing, transplantation, weeding and harvesting took place and it was during this period that peasants were often taken away from their lands for *begar* (forced labour) by the officials of the Dogra Raj for the states' needs and their personal services and as a result lands were not tilled properly.[6] Of all the *rabi* crops, only such crops were sown after the *kharif* season, whose germination took place before the snowfall and the plants started growing after the snow had melted, in the months of March and April. The *rabi* crops, which take four to five months to mature in other parts of the country, took five to six months in the valley of Kashmir.[7] Since *kharif* was harvested by September and early October, i.e. on the eve of snowfall, and since there was little time to prepare the soil for the next crops, *rabi* seeds were sown only in such fields as had not been cultivated during the *kharif* season.[8]

Rabi crops took longer to mature in Kashmir, there was no time for *kharif* crops. In effect, therefore, Kashmir's peasants had to subsist on a one-crop economy, either *rabi* or *kharif*, and supplement their sustenance by depending on pastoralism, craft making or by migrating to neighboring Punjab to work as labourers.

The important *kharif* and *rabi* crops are given in Table 2.2.[9]

In spite of the obvious advantages of the system of crop rotation, farmers generally preferred the cultivation of rice when adequate irrigation facilities were available. They allowed the land to remain lea in times of a deficiency of irrigation and knew that their labour would not be repaid if they sowed other crops that included cotton, varieties of pulses, barley and maize.[10] Furthermore, the small quantities of commercial crops such as, cotton, oilseeds, saffron, etc., grown in the state afforded little scope for agro-based industries.

The Kashmiri peasants believed that the notes of the cuckoo heralded the time of snow. For rice, peasants practiced two systems of cultivation. Under the first, rice was broadcast; under the second, rice was first sown in a nursery and then the saplings (*dan thal*) transplanted.[11] The broadcast system involved much labour because

TABLE 2.2: LIST OF *KHARIF* AND *RABI* CROPS

Kharif crops	*Rabi crops*
Rice	Wheat
Maize	Barley
Cotton	Tibet barley
Saffron	Opium, poppy
Tobacco	Rape
Millet	Flax
Amaranthus	Beans (*Viciafaba*)
Buckwheat	
Pulses	
Sesame	

Source: W.R. Lawrence, *Valley of Kashmir*, London, 1895, pp. 325-30.

it required more ploughing than the nursery system and was unproductive. The nursery system was thus more popular. Besides in this system the peasants of each village voluntarily rendered mutual help in transplantation of rice saplings (*thaejkad*).[12] In the broadcast system, rice had to be sown earlier and required more watering, more weeding, and was labour intensive. The chief problem in weeding arose from the automatic germination of seeds left behind from the previous harvest. The difficulty was overcome by alternately growing rice of green and other coloured straws, so that any left out rice plant could be easily detected and pulled out.[13]

Regular weeding was carried out in case of rice cultivation, maize and cotton crops.[14] Both men and women did the transplantation, but the ploughing operations, broadcast sowing, reaping, and weeding operations were carried out by men alone.

This fact is borne out by a drawing of the mid-nineteenth century Kashmir.[15]

Though the *British Empire Exhibition* states that the transplantation was carried out by women alone and the men used to distribute seedlings but the painting exhibits both men and women transplanting seedlings.

In rice cultivation, weeding was done with hands and feet. There were no special implements. During the weeding operations, the peasants suffered from eruption (*khaz*) caused by the continual

Illustration 2.1: Different techniques involved in paddy cultivation in Kashmir *Source:* Harbans Mukhia's Collection of Pictures from India Office Library, London.

immersion of the parts of their body in water. Their ankles and wrists were affected but hands and feet escaped relatively undamaged owing to the protection provided by mud. The peasants used to apply *kelmtil*, (a type of oil) which was extracted from pine and mixed with ghee, to the affected parts of the body.[16] In the case of maize it was done with hands and hoe.[17] In the case of weeding, the peasants were very alert and kept strict watch over certain insects which caused havoc to the young plants of rice.[18] Agriculture in Kashmir depended largely on the timely arrival of monsoon and, due to the uncertainty of weather, there was considerable seasonal variation in production levels.[19] However, in the scheme of agriculture, food occupied the most significant place. Moreover, cultivation was not possible for the greater part of the year due to the climate, which rendered double cropping pattern more difficult. In order to evaluate the significance of agriculture in the economy of Kashmir, we discuss below some of the most important crops which were cultivated.

(a) *Rice*

Being the staple food of the inhabitants, it was the principal crop cultivated in Kashmir. It accounted for three-fourths of the cultivable area during the Sikh period. It was the chief article of revenue to the state. In total, 75 varieties of rice were produced in Kashmir of varying yields.[20] *Basmati*, *Katichan* and *Sukudas* were considered as the best quality. As per the contemporary sources 3,50,000 acres of land were under paddy cultivation.[21] The production was 7 *kharwars* per acre of land and therefore the total production stands at (3,50,000 × 7) = 24,50,000 *kharwars*. The state claim was half, i.e. 12,25,000 *kharwars* as its share. Besides this, the peasants had to deposit to the government four *traks* additional per *kharwar* of revenue.[22]

There was no systematic method of measuring land. In Kashmir land was measured according to the quantity of seeds sown per acre and the extent of ground which required one *kharwar* of seed. As a unit of land, one *kharwar* of land was equal to 32 *canals* or 4 acres.[23]

However, rice cultivation was confined to the flat portion of the valley with alluvial soil, where water could be reached with ease and was in plenty. It required a warm, moist climate, which was characteristic of this region.[24] The quantity of seeds sown per acre was 20 to 24 *seers* and the outturn varied from 5 to 30 *kharwars*. *Seer* and *kharwar* were standard measures of weight then in vogue. One *seer* was of 21 *chhataks* and one *kharwar* of 16 *traks*; one *trak* was equal to 5 *seers*.[25] In hilly areas where rice was grown, the outturn was of a lower order and the rice was also of inferior quality. Ninety-four rice varieties were grown in Kashmir. Some of them were as follows: *Larbyol, Mushkabudji, Lolianzun, Reban, Yimbirzal, Pothibrar, Sukhdas, Basmat, Shalkav, Braz, Zag-Dattyi, Rani, Kunji-Dani, Gurukoen, Chogul, Mokhtahal, Lachahal, Shahguzu Guru Tanzi, Lal Krahna, Kenu Puthau, Nur, Karhana Shesher, Suirmal, Chatabraz, Kamad, Tachitachee, Mukhtabraz, Dudhakrid, Nekabeyol, Barenbezol, Nihali, Bud Braz, Malwar, Chatazaz, Gurah, Ghunder, Chatanewar, Kawhamah, Maitarahel, Babeer, Mohiwan, Kawa Krihna, Keoziv, Moglubeyol, Chandahal, Sukal, Mohiaznun, Munkahashahd, Shalanzun, Oozulkrid, Baidanzun, Karalanzun, Bathal, Nekanzun Lenahzag, Nekahzag, Kranahzag, Basma, Zazid Zekahtatar,* and *Talaibyol.*[26] Among all these varieties *Kunjidanyi*, *Basmat* and *Chogul* were considered the best. *Chogul* was grown in *pargana* Pakh.[27] Almost all rice-growing lands produced only one crop per year and remained fallow during the winter, when no cultivation was possible.[28] Relatively speaking, rice was the most important crop in terms of value among food grains. The most extensive paddy cultivation was likely to have been carried out on the lands near deltas and streams, which had sufficient slope to facilitate rapid drainage.[29]

(b) *Maize*

In order of priority, maize came next to rice. On the slopes, the uplands, and all those areas in the mountains where some amount of cultivation was possible, maize and pulses were grown. The most favourable lands for maize cultivation were the *karewa* lands and river bank lands. It is not dependent much on irrigation and also does not require manure. The only essential condition for better and fair crop of maize was fortnightly or occasional rains. According to Moorcroft the maize cultivation was also carried out on the plains of northern area of the valley (*maraz* region).[30] It was the staple food of people living on hilly areas and was cultivated during spring season. According to *Kashmir Crop Report of 1837*, the total area under maize production was 89,217 acres.[31] The contemporary sources are silent about the per unit productivity of maize. Therefore, we have to rely on Walter Roper Lawrence. He says that per acre of land under cultivation produced 3.5 *kharwars* of maize.[32] Therefore, the total production was (89,217 × 3.5) = 3,12,259.5 *kharwars*. The state took one-half as well as four *traks* per *kharwars* of total revenue realized. In general, reclaimed swamps and peaty soils are ideal for cultivation. Besides the shepherds, cowherds, and Gujjars, it was consumed by large sections of the population in regions where little paddy was grown.[33] It needed no regular irrigation; timely rains could help in growing this crop. Maize was mostly consumed by the poorer sections of the peasantry including the small peasants because they could not afford to take rice regularly.[34] First, the peasant themselves were left with very little by the state, and second, in times of need, the peasants had to sell their rice and subsisted on maize. And if at all the peasant retained a little rice, he had to exchange it for tea, salt, clothes, etc.[35] He had also to share his portion with the *pandit* (village priest)and the *pir/sayyid* (muslim priest) as the case might be and with the moneylender, the blacksmith, the barber and other village artisans. There was a reverence for the priestly Brahmans and *pirs/sayyids* in Kashmiri society of that period. It traversed through the whole social as well as religious life of peasants in Kashmir and acquired the form of either cash offering or food. It was also customary to hand over a portion of the produce to the artisans of the village comprising the barbers, carpenters, porters, tailors, basket makers, blacksmiths, weavers, shepherds and others. They took a portion of the produce in lieu of their assistance offered to the peasants in the form of iron implements, pottery and so on. These artisans extracted their share irrespective of help offered to the peasants and gradually it became a custom. Besides, these artisans claimed payment for any service rendered other than the customary share of produce from each peasant household.[36]

Maize was not eagerly accepted in exchange, and even in charity, where paddy was available but in *kandi illakas* (hilly areas) where maize alone was grown there was hardly any choice.[37] Apart from this, pounded maize was given as fodder to the cattle. Thus in the agrarian economy of Kashmir, generally speaking, maize too possessed considerable significance for it sustained a large section of the population. Though it was not commercially as important as rice as a staple food of the peasants and the landless labourers it had a significant social role to play. The maize-eating people often boiled maize like rice and ate it in the form of what they called *wat* a sort of maize jelly.[38]

In the complete absence of rain, crops would wither away. The soil and climate did not present much difficulty in its cultivation. The average production of maize per *kharwar* of land was 24 *kharwars.*[39]

(c) *Wheat*

Topographically, Kashmir did not and still does not belong to the wheat-growing regions of the subcontinent.[40] Nonetheless, it did grow

TABLE 2.3: LIST OF SOME CROPS OF KASHMIR WITH THE AMOUNT OF SEEDS SOWN PER ACRE, AND THE OUT-TURN PER ACRE IN THE FAVOURABLE YEARS

Name of the crops in Kashmiri	*Name of the crops in Urdu*	*Seeds sown per acre local weight* seers	*Maximum Produce*	
			Per kharwar= *4 acres* kharwar	*Per acre* kharwar
Ushka	Jaw	24	16	4
Kanak	Gehun	27	8	2
Tilgogal	Loriya	6	16	4
Masur	Masoor	12	6	1½
Kapas	Kapas	36	6	1½
Mung	Mung	12	10	2½
Mah	Mash	12	10	2½
Rajahmah	Lobia	12	10	2½
Dhan	Shali	22-4	10-60 mds	15
Makai	Makki	18	24	6
Tromba	Daraw	24	24	6
Ganhar	Swal	6	49	6

Sources: Gazetteer of Kashmir and Ladakh, Calcutta, 1890. C.E. Bates, *A Gazetteer of Kashmir and Adjoining Districts of Kishtwar, Badarwah, Jammu, Naoshera, Punch and the Valley of Kishen Ganga,* Calcutta, 1873. W.R. Lawrence, *Valley of Kashmir,* London, 1895 and see also *Imperial Gazetteer of India, Provincial Series Jammu and Kashmir,* Calcutta, 1909.

a considerable amount of wheat, second in importance only to maize. Certain specific areas were reserved for wheat cultivation. Its cultivation in Kashmir was mostly confined to Dachanpara and Khourpara *parganas*.[41] It requires a climate that is neither too warm nor too cold. Moreover, it does not need any atmospheric pressure or a great deal of water for its cultivation. One *kharwar* of land could produce 8 *kharwars* of wheat.[42]

(d) *Barley*

Barley was grown throughout the valley on *barani* lands, which were dependent on seasonal rain for moisture. The average production per *kharwar* of land was 16 *kharwars*.[43] Another variety, known as Tibetan barley, was also cultivated mostly in *kandi ilaqas* (hilly tracts) of Kashmir. But it was cut before ripening and was used as fodder for cattle.[44]

(e) *Buckwheat* (Tromba in Kashmiri)

It was grown in the hilly tracts and depended very little on irrigation. One type of buckwheat is known as 'sweet tromba' and the other is white or slightly pinkish in colour.[45] The latter was often grown as a substitute for rice in areas where water was scarce. It was mostly consumed in the form of porridge by the people inhabiting *kandi ilaqas*.[46]

(f) *Amaranthus* (Ganhar in Kashmiri)

Amaranthus was grown in cotton fields and also in maize-growing plots. It needed no irrigation or manure, and with timely rains, a large out-turn was harvested. It was generally consumed by the Hindu population on their days of fasting and on festive occasions.[47]

(g) *Kangni* (*Staria italica* in English)

Kangni is a useful grain and is husked like rice, but the people of Kashmir did not make much use of it because of its heating properties.[48] During the years when an adequate amount of water was not available, most of the land was sown with *kangni*. A good harvest of *kangni* needs two to four ploughings and careful weeding.[49] It was of two varieties, one small and the other big. The former was generally consumed by the peasants, and the latter was used for feeding cattle. Nothing at present is known about the seeds sown per acre but the outturn was 3 maunds (nearly 30 kg).[50]

(h) *Pulses*

In some parts of Kashmir, the cultivation of pulses co-existed with other crops, including paddy and maize. The most popular pulses cultivated were *mong*, *moth* (Phaseolus conitifolius a variety soya bean), *mash* (Phaseolus roxburghii) a variety of *blackgram* and *rajmash* (kindey beans).[51] *Mong* (greengram) is a *kharif* crop and is entirely dependent on rain. The *banjar* lands could produce large quantities of this crop.[52]

(i) *Moth* (Phaseolus conitifolius)

Among the pulses, *moth* was considered inferior and was generally used as fodder for cattle during winter.[53]

(j) *Mash* (Phaseolus roxburghii)

Its cultivation was extensively carried out in hilly areas. It is of two varieties: black and green. Both were consumed by the people. The last mentioned of the pulses *rajmash* are of different varieties and was cultivated almost in every *pargana*. However, the consumption of pulses within the valley was not of the same order as in other parts of India.[54]

Besides the above mentioned crops, Kashmir also produced a large quantity of water-chestnuts and cash crops such as cotton, tobacco, hemp, oilseeds, and saffron.

(k) *Singhara* (Water chestnut)

William Moorcroft, who visited Kashmir in the early period of Sikh rule, says that the average production of water chestnuts was about nine million, six hundred and twenty thousand tons, and the total sale of *singharas* was worth about Rs. 3,00,000 a year. Moorcroft commenced his journey towards the end of 1819. He found no difficulty in obtaining Ranjit Singh's permission to travel throughout his kingdom. May be his project to visit Ladakh led Ranjit Singh to launch subsequently a parallel military project to bring under his political domination all the eastern trans-Himalayan territories including Ladakh, Baltistan and Garo. Soon after the expedition was given practical shape by Dhian Singh and his brother Gulab Singh when they commissioned Zorawar Singh to conquer this region. Proceeding to Ladakh via Kullu Manali and Bisahar, Moorcroft entered Kashmir in September-October 1822, after staying in Ladakh for about two years (1820-2). In Srinagar, he married and had a son also. He left Kashmir in 1823, accompanied by Khwaja Mohammad Shah Naqshband, a Turanian affluent merchant and a cavalcade of 300 porters and horses[55] Ganeshi Lal, who visited Kashmir during the initial period of Dogra rule, observes that Rs. 25,000 was annually contributed to the government revenue as cess on *singharas*.[56] Thus, it is clear that *singharas* were an important horticultural produce of Kashmir. In 1849, Gagra Kotwal and Gulshah were the contractors of water chestnuts produced in Kashmir. Their records state that 81,000 *kharwars* was the average yield.[57]

It was mostly procured from the Wular Lake, the largest lake in the valley. It lies at an elevation of 5,180 ft. above sea level and occupies an area of 12.5 sq. miles in normal condition. During floods the lake extends to 100 sq. miles. It gives the semblance of a small sea of blue water, besides its navigational advantages for the inhabitants of adjoining areas. During the period under study it produced a large quantity of water chestnuts.[58] It was a big trading concern to the state. In 1856 water chestnuts in Srinagar, were sold at the rate of Re. 1 a maund (slightly less than 30 kg.).[59] The state exported water chestnuts to Rawalpindi (now in Pakistan) in exchange of rock salt during Maharaja Gulab Singh's reign (AD 1846-57).[60] The total produce of water chestnuts for the year 1856-7 was 22,000 *kharwars*. It was dried and then ground into flour; cakes were then made, which the richer classes consumed with salt, ghee and meat. The pandits used to take it on the occasions of fasts and festivals. The poor peasants simply boiled it for eating. [61] In 1871-2 it contributed Rs. 35,615 to the state revenues.[62] Hence it appears to have contributed a handsome amount to the state exchequer and was also as a means of employment to peasants, boatmen and officials.[63]

(k) *Cotton*

Cotton was grown to a small extent all over the valley. Its cultivation was carried out on *karewas* and low-lying lands. According to the *Kashmir's Crop Report of 1937,* the total area under cotton production was 19,200 acres. According to Moorcroft, the Sikh rulers introduced brown cotton in Kashmir from Yarkand, but the climatic conditions didn't favour it and it failed and turned white on its third sowing.[64] The average production per acre of land was 1.5 *kharwars.* Therefore, the total production was (19,200 × 1.5) = 28,800 *kharwars.* The state claimed half of the produce.[65] Thirty-six *seers* were sown per acre for the return of a product of 1½ *kharwars,* 124 *seers* and 8 *chhataks* per acre.[66]

(l) *Tobacco*

It was cultivated in most parts of the valley. The best tobacco was grown near Srinagar town. The limited nature of its produce is borne out by the fact that, annually, large quantities of tobacco are imported from other countries.[67] In 1890 Lawrence provides us information that the total revenue realized from tobacco was worth Rs. 40,840 *chilki.*[68]

(m) *Hop*

Hop cultivation was carried out only in Sopore. The hop field at Dobgam Sopore was nearly 119 acres in extent. In Barzulla too, 58 acres were devoted to its cultivation.[69] But until the nineteenth century, hop cultivation appears to have been on an experimental stage. Even as late as AD 1895, the total annual income from its produce was only Rs. 6,000.[70]

(o) *Oil Seeds*

These were largely grown in Kashmir, and the principal among these oil seeds was rapeseed, of which there were three varieties. The first, *tilogoglu,* was sown at the rate of 6 *seers* per acre and the outturn was 4 *kharwars.*[71] The other varieties *sarshaf* and *sandji* yielded a small amount of oil. Besides these, large quantities of linseed were also produced, of which an average crop would be 2 *maunds* (maund was slightly less than 30 kg) per acre.[72] Rapeseed provided the best oil for lighting purposes and linseed for eating. Moreover, oil was also extracted from walnuts and apricots for use in cooking.[73]

(p) *Saffron*

Saffron cultivation of Kashmir deserves a special mention because Kashmir was and is the only state in India where saffron is grown. It is grown in two localities, namely Pampore *wudar* (*karewas*) at a distance of 15 miles from Srinagar near Pampore, and on a fairly limited scale in Kishtwar.[74] The methods of cultivation of saffron at both places were different. In Kishtwar, owing to the low rainfall and fear of saffron being eaten up by porcupines, it was grown in flat fields, planted in rows at a depth of about 18 inches from the surface.[75] In the Kashmir Valley, the saffron fields were divided into 5 sq. ft. beds, surrounded by a 6-inch deep drainage channel, and saffron was planted on these beds at a depth of 4 inches from the surface.[76] These saffron fields remained under cultivation for about ten years, during which period the number of corns was almost doubled.[77] After Saffron cultivation for about a decade the land was left lea or was ploughed for crops like barley.[78] Ganeshi Lal says, 'These fields are not watered with any stream or rivulet and are dependent on the rain water alone.'[79] During Maharaja Gulab Singh's time, many attempts were made to extend the cultivation of saffron but none of the soils except those of Pampore responded to the experiments of the Maharaja and his saffron contractor Pandit Lachman Dhar.[80] In 1871 the total saffron produce amounted to 200 *kharwars.*[81]

(q) *Pulses*

Pulses were of course consumed by the people now and then, particularly during winter months when no leafy vegetables were available. Pulses as agricultural products do not appear to have been important as they had been and still are grown in the Indian plains. In Kashmir, unlike in the plains, they formed no part of the regular diet, but were meant only for consumption during the scarcity of green vegetables in winters.[82]

Among the fruits common in Kashmir were apples, pears, peaches, cherries, apricots, almonds, walnuts, and grapes. The last three varieties of fruits were of great economic value, although produced on a very limited scale.[83]

(r) *Grapes*

This forms an important item in the agrarian economy of Kashmir, There can be no doubt that grape production was encouraged during Maharaja Ranbir Singh's and Maharaja Pratap Singh's time because among all the fruits grapes proved of great financial value to the state. During Maharaja Gulab Singh's time there neither existed any system of turning grapes into wine nor did Maharaja Gulab Singh take any steps in this direction to make it commercial. It was only during Maharaja Ranbir Singh's reign that for the first time a wine plant was established in Srinagar and due attention was paid to the cultivation of grapes.[84] A large portion of the produce was used for making wine. However, during Maharaja Ranbir Singh's time there was a general decline in its production, which is evident from the fact that in 1870, the number of *kharwars* produced was 245, in 1877 it was 163, and in 1878 only 160 *kharwars* were produced.[85] Perhaps this could be attributed to certain natural calamities that befell the people during the period under consideration, such as famines, floods and fires and earthquakes which occurred in Kashmir in 1863, 1872, 1875, 1877, 1878 and 1879. Political disturbances as a result of Shia-Sunni conflicts might have also contributed to the decline in the production of grapes.[86] In 1889-90, Monsieur Peychand was deputed to examine the wineyards of Kashmir. He stated that the average production per 100 acres of land was 36,000 bottles of wine and the cost of cultivation per acre was Rs. 20.[87] In 1895 the total production used for the said purpose, was 164 *kharwars*. Ten thousand four hundred thirty-eight bottles were manufactured out of this produce.[88]

Tables 2.4, 2.5, 2.6 and 2.7 give details of the variety of grapes and wine manufactured.

The following tables show the quantity of grapes used for manufacturing different kinds of wines and the total number of bottles manufactured in the Gupkar distillery from 1882 to 1895.[89]

Apart from the food crops, cash crops and fruits Kashmir possesses an extensive and valuable forest produce comprising *deodars*, *firs*, *blue pines*, *santonian*, *lac*, *kuth* and other medicinal plants and flowers whose extraction provided some amount of essential oils.

TABLE 2.4: VARIETY OF GRAPES AND THE VOLUME OF PRODUCTION

Kind of Grapes	*Black & Red*	*White*	*Total*
Kharwars 1st class	131	16	147
K.T. Seers	15	2	17
K. *Kharwars* second class	2	0	2
Total	16	-	16
K.T. Seers	14	-	14
	3	-	3
	138	16	154
	13	2	15
	5	0	5
Quantity manufactured bottles	9,396	1,042	10,438

Source: Pandit Bhagram, *Annual Administrative Report 1885-86*, Jammu Archives.

TABLE 2.5: VARIETY OF GRAPES AND THE NUMBER OF BOTTLES OF WINE MANUFACTURED

Kind of grapes	*Kharwars 1st class K.T. Seers*			*Kharwars 2nd class K.T. Seers*			*Total K.T. Seers*			*Quantity manufactured Bottles*
Black & Red	131	15	2	16	14	3	138	13	5	9,396
White	16	2	0				16	2	0	1,042
TOTAL	147	17	2	16	14	3	154	15	5	10,438

Source: Pandit Bhagram, *Annual Administrative Report 1885-86*, Jammu Archives.

TABLE 2.6: AMOUNT OF GRAPES AND THE QUANTITY OF WINE MANUFACTURED

(*Figures in* kharwars)

	Kinds of grapes used				*No. of* kharwars *make 100 bottles of wine*	*No. of* kharwars *Apples 100 bottles*
Year	*White*	*Black*	*Total*	*Apple used in*		
1882	119	60	179	4,598	1-4	–
1883	173	87	260	1,781	2-0	–
1884	293	147	440	61	1-13	–
1885	219	109	328	-	1-13	–
1886	283	142	425	-	2-11	–
1887	258	412	670	-	1-15	–
1888	168	33	201	-	2-10	–
1889	102	26	128	-	3-11	–
1890	67	41	108	100	2-8	–
1891	195	118	313	-	1-8	–
1892	55	30	85	422	1-8	9-15
1893	184	142	326	1,442	1-10	4-8
1894	104	95	199	2,440	1-11	4-5
1895	16	149	165	1,979	1-9	5-0
TOTAL	2,336	1,491	3,827	12,623	-	-

Source: Pandit Bhagram, *Annual Administrative Report 1882-95*, Jammu Archives.

(s) *Deodar*

Deodar is a valuable forest product and is found between 5,000 and 9,000 ft. above the sea level. The largest area occupied by this deodars is in Uttar Machipora tehsil in Kamraj *wazarat* of Baramulla.[90] Even as late as the third decade of the twentieth century very little amount of this wood had been exploited for commercial purpose. The chief obstacle in its exploitation was the absence of transport facilities.[91]

It was mostly used for construction works. Lack of transport presented a great deal of difficulty in making this tree a viable

TABLE 2.7: MANUFACTURED QUANTITY OF WINE AND BRANDY AND OTHER ITEMS IN KASHMIR

Quantity Manufactured[89]									
White wine	*Red wine*	*Grape Brandy No. 1*	*Grape Brandy No. 2*	*Apple Brandy*	*Vinegar*	*Methyllated spirit*	*Cider*	*Champane*	*Total no. of bottle manufactured*
5,700	3,900	352	1,446	53,515	132				65,045
6,300	4,500	300	150	25,594		4,556			41,490
9,750	10,500		645	31,891		4,392			57,178
7,155	10,685	2	1,080	3,900		2,560			25,386
6,679	13,780		304	684	509				21,956
13,230	21,600		540	600					35,970
3,240	36	1,350				120			4,746
2,736	36		150		960				3,882
2,700	1,620		72						4,392
13,645	6,729		168		199				20,741
3,317	1,095		276	7,079		2	3,554		11,769
11,580	7,774	334	533	20,436	181	43	1,261	15	44,435
6,089	3,247	579	359	30,859	1,317	223			43,949
1,205	9,397	1,153	192	21,738	53	63	4,815	15	33,801
93,326	94,989	4,070	5,919	1,96,296	3,351	11,959			4,14,740

Source: Pandit Bhagram, *Annual Administrative Report 1880-95*, Jammu Archives.

commercial proposition. At that time wood for different uses was carried by coolies to the nearest waterways where it was floated to other areas. In some areas these logs were carried by bullocks, but the local bullocks were not strong enough to carry them over long distances, the floating of wood could be done only in the summer and spring months when the snow melted.[92]

(t) *Blue Pine*

It appears at a height of 6,000 ft. and extends upto 10,000 ft.[93] Its finest specimens are found in the deodar area of forestry.[94] Trees of 15 ft. in girth and 150 ft. in height are not uncommon though their life is far shorter than that of the deodar.

(u) Silver Fir

It occupied a zone between 8,000 and 11,000 ft. above sea level. Owing to its thin high altitude, it was cumbersome to fell the timber. Its timber was mostly used as firewood by the local population on a very limited scale. In comparison to deodar and blue pine, it lacked strength and fineness. The trees were generally 100 ft. long and 16 ft. in girth.[95]

(v) *Santonian*

It is a very costly drug, though its mother plant is most abundantly found in the forests of Kashmir. During the reign of Maharaja Pratap Singh, experiments were made to extract santonian and it was established, following an analysis of the plant, that the collection be made sometime between July and August, when it contained a fair percentage of santonian, i.e. between 4 and 9 per cent.[96] It added a sum of Rs. 2.5 lakh per annum to the state revenue.[97]

(w) *Lac*

It was during the Dogra period that the existence of natural lac on black trees was noticed for the first time, but owing to the lack of transport, its exploitation on scientific lines could not be undertaken.

However, during the reign of Maharaja Pratap Singh, a proposal was made for the deputation of forest officers of the Central Provinces for acquiring training in lac culture.[98] Many other plants yielding medicinal drugs such as *dizitails*, *hoscymus*, *bellodona*, *menthol* and *podophyllum* were also found and were to be paid a special attention as important commercial products.[99]

(x) *Kuth* (Saussureal Alappa)

It is known as Saussureal Alappa, it grows extensively in Kashmir forests but is abundant in Wangat and Sind valleys. It is a highly valuable drug and its chief market was in China. It is of four varieties: *kuth*, *drankhar*, *poshkar*, and *kar*. Kashmiris used *kuth* for purposes such as an application on ulcers, a hair wash, a medicine for cholera and also for preserving clothes against the ravages of pests.[100] In AD 1894 the income from this product was Rs. 24,000.[101] For a long time in the past, the government realized only a small amount of money from the sale of this valuable product. Later on, the *kuth* market was studied and investigations were made with regard to its use. During the period of our study the price generally averaged Rs. 216 per maund.[102] Today, the revenue generated from this product is between Rs. 2.5 lakh and 14 lakh.[103]

Apart from this, experiments were conducted for the extraction of essential oils from wild roses, thyme and *Skimmial anreola* found in the forest of Kashmir.

Notwithstanding these experiments, till the close of the nineteenth century, the natural resources of Kashmir had not been fully exploited. The reasons for this are pretty obvious. First, the local demand for forest produce and mineral products was limited. Second, there was a lack of skilled labour and technical knowhow was also absent. Over and above all these factors, Kashmir was a mountain-locked country. There was a communication barrier with other parts of the country arising from the fact that the transport system was poorly developed. As a result, Kashmiri people remained unaware of the economic advancement taking place beyond these mountains.[104]

Technology and Irrigation

Technically, agriculture in the valley was practiced along traditional lines. Agricultural implements were few and simple. There were variety of plough made from various woods like mulberry, ash and apple.[105] The plough used for the first ploughing was tipped with an iron blade and was worked using a pair of oxen. This plough was sharply designed. Subsequently, the clods were ploughed and broken with wooden mallets (*yetaphur*), also known in some parts of the valley as *yabchot* (a wooden hammer with long handle). Women mostly did this work. All the fields were turned into smooth earth before they were again ploughed (known locally *ala*), this time using a plough with an iron tip. This plough was a little broad so that it could help smoothen the soil.[106] After distributing manure evenly, the fields were irrigated and again ploughed. This time a simple plough (known locally as *heege*) without the iron tip was used. A willow ring (*kanivaer*) was put around the tip of the plough so that the plough did not go deep into the soil.[107]

The entire process is depicted in Illustration 2.2.

To quote Lambert, 'They (peasants) are very primitive in their habits. One often sees their wooden plough being dragged by an ox and a donkey. All their implements are of the most inferior description'.[108] The peasants practised two systems of rice cultivation. Under the first system, seeds were grown broadcast while under the second system, seeds were first sown in the nursery and then saplings transplanted.[109] The second system is a later development. The broadcast system involved much labour because seeds were sown earlier and required more watering and weeding. It needed more ploughing than the nursery system and was fairly unproductive. In comparison, the nursery system was in greater vogue.[110] There were two methods of preparing the soils, namely *tao* (dry) and *kenlu* (wet). Under the *tao* system, the soil was made absolutely dry to eliminate any moisture before sowing the seeds. According to the *kenlu* method the field was allowed to remain wet.[111] Agriculture in the valley depended largely on the timely arrival of the monsoon and due to the uncertainty of the weather there was a considerable variation in production levels. The valley received precipitation during two periods—the cold season

Illustration 2.2: Preparation of fields for paddy cultivation.
Source: Harbans Mukhia's Collection of Pictures from India Office Library, London.

(from December to April) and the southwest monsoon period from June to September. Rainfall in October and November was lowest. November was generally the driest month of the year.[112]

For average rainfall in Kashmir see Table 2.8.

TABLE 2.8: AVERAGE RAINFALL IN INCHES FOR 29 YEARS, ENDING 1905

Month	*Jan.*	*Feb.*	*Mar.*	*Apr.*	*May*	*June*	
Srinagar	3.13	2.24	3.58	3.29	2.93	1.67	
Month	*July*	*Aug.*	*Sep.*	*Oct.*	*Nov.*	*Dec.*	*Total*
Srinagar	3.03	2.26	1.64	1.12	0.47	1.34	26.70

Note: The total rainfall is 26.70 inches.[113]

The cold season precipitation from December to March was chiefly due to storms which advanced from Iran and Baluchistan across northern India. These western disturbances occasionally resulted in very stormy weather in Kashmir with violent winds on higher elevations and much snow. Snowfall was heavy on the Pir Panjal range, the heaviest being in January and February.[114] In the valley and in the mountain ranges to the north and east this was the chief precipitation of the year and it was very heavy on the first line of permanent snow; it rapidly decreased eastwards towards the Karakoram Range. Srinagar, Dras and Anantnag in the region received the largest amount of snowfall. In April and May, occasional thunder storms occurred in the valley and the surrounding hills, resulting in light to moderate showers. This hot season rainfall was of considerable importance for cultivation in the valley.[115]

Generally, the cultivation of *kharif* crops began around Noaroz in the month of March and in some areas in early April. Rice fields were ploughed four times while wheat, barley and maize fields were ploughed only twice. In March, the rice fields which remained uncultivated since the last rice crop was cut in September, with the result that sometimes the soil became hard and stiff. The soil was softened by the frost and snow but if sometimes there was less or no snowfall it was difficult to plough these lands. Therefore, special type of irrigation was carried out before the ploughing season commenced. In contrast, in some other villages, the soil was so damp that ploughing was done perforce while the soil was wet and such lands were not very productive.[116] Zain-ul-Abidin endowed the revenues of Khuyhama Pargana (*pargana* was an administrative unit) to a department entrusted with the task of stopping soil erosion.[117]

For obtaining a good rice harvest, heavy snowfall on the mountains in winter is necessary in order to fill up the streams in summer. Besides, the timely rains in March and early April and clear skies and bright warm days in May, June, July and August, with an occasional shower in September, are essential. Kashmiri cultivators believed that a good rice harvest depended on the cold dew which penetrated the outer husk and helped in the swelling, hardening and the formation of the grain.[118]

The non-use of soil inverting ploughs—generally used in the west—in the hot climatic areas of India is justified but it is surprising that these soil-inverting ploughs were not in use in Kashmir even though it had a European climate.[119] If this indicates that the cultivator in Kashmir was aware of the advantages of storing nitrogen in the soil which would have got oxidized by deep ploughing, then the cultivation of rice as the main food crop year after year defies the principle of dependence of rice crops on the nitrogen preserved in the soil. The cultivable lands in Kashmir have the highest fertility compared to the Indian mainland. Besides, the soil in Kashmir carry a large fertility silt as a reserve. These reserves are carried in the upper layer of the soil in the form of humus. The humus got mixed with the upper layer of soil automatically because of the activities of burrowing earthworms and a variety of other insects.[120]

The three sources of nitrogen: first, the nitrogen which exists as gas in the atmosphere, known as uncombined nitrogen or free nitrogen; second, the nitrogen existing as organic compounds either in decaying matter in the soil or in animal waste; and third, the nitrogen contained in inorganic compounds resulting from the final breakdowns of these two materials. Both the last forms of nitrogen are usually referred to as 'combined nitrogen' because they exist in combination with other

Illustration 2.3: Ploughing operation in the paddy fields.
Source: Harbans Mukhia' Collection of Pictures from India Office Library, London.

materials. Plants have some difficulty in assimilating any of this nitrogen. Therefore, the soil has to wait for soil flora to break down the organic wastes and wait further for the soil solution to dissolve the products thus procured. Only when all this has been done can the soil use these food materials.[121] My discussions with some of the peasants and their oral testimonies also revealed that if the soil was deeply ploughed there was always a chance of seeds and small rice plants rotting in the water and hence no deep ploughing was permitted.[122] In the last quarter of the nineteenth century, the area of cultivation per plough in Karnah tahsil was less than 4 acres.[123] However, when the *heege* (third ploughing after the fields were watered) was over, the fields were subjected to combing (*danth*), which removed the dry leftovers of the previous crop and other bushy items which would have come to the surface of the soil after ploughing. The *danth* of the Kashmiri cultivator was what *Tuhafat-i Punjab* mentions as *dandal* in the context of Punjab.[124] The difference was that in Kashmir it was driven by two oxen while in the Punjab it was driven by four. But the more important task of *danth* was to help close (*wodere*) the rat holes. Also if these holes were left open and unattended they would result in water drainage from the fields. The comb was made of a wooden log, slightly curved and approximately 6 ft. long and 3 ft. in girth. This log was yoked to a pair of oxen. If some of the earthen clods remained uneven till then, a simple wooden log (*mond*) driven by two oxen was used in the irrigated fields to level the fields before the sowing of rice crops.[125]

The rice seeds were carefully selected at threshing time and were stored in grass bags (*vethren*). Jute bags were also used but it was a later addition because it was unaffordable for the peasants. Before sowing, the seed was tested by winnowing and then dried, and immediately afterwards was soaked in water while it was warm. After this, the grass bags were immersed in water until the process of germination of seeds commenced. The seeds were kept in big earthen vessels (*mache* or *kye*) for nearly 40 days for sprouting before they were sown. In some areas, fresh walnut tree leaves were also used for covering these grass bags and pots full of paddy seeds. The walnut leaves had a heating property which speeded up the process of sprouting. Every day, after sunset, water was drained out from these clay pots using grass rings which disallowed the rice seeds to move out with the water. Again, every morning, fresh water was poured into the clay pots. At night, these clay pots and grass bags with the seeds were kept in a warm place, generally in the cow shed (*gupangan*). Once the seeds sprouted, they were broadcast. Up to the late nineteenth and even early twentieth centuries, the broadcast method (*wotur*) was used.[126]

Rice was grown up to an altitude of 7,000 ft. In higher altitudes it was convenient to sow earlier than in the lower regions, and as the winters came early and it was essential to harvest the crop before snowfall. In slopes and steppes, terrace cultivation was a common feature because it also prevented the soil from being completely washed away.[127] Even in certain lower altitude villages, where it was the custom to sow rice earlier than usual, the outturn was always heavy. After the rice crops grew upto 8 to 10 cm, the operation of weeding (*lath dein* or *wubhat*) out the tender grass (*aiev ta sol*) that grew along with the rice plants, as also the practice of placing the rice plants almost evenly in the fields, were taken up. This exercise was carried out by men with two sticks in both hands and sometimes women also joined in depending on the availability of labour of each peasant family.[128]

This painting shows ploughing being carried out by a man and women breaking the clods of earth with mallets after the first ploughing.

This practice was also known as *khushaba* for which there is no English equivalent. It was very essential for the broadcast system. It involved putting the rice plants in the right place and pressing the soft mud gently around the green seedlings. A novice could not do this work, therefore, it always involved experts who could detect counterfeit grasses which looked exactly like rice. In Kashmir this practice was known as *goadrove* or taking out the plants from thickly

Illustration 2.4: Agricultural operations carried out by peasants.
Source: Harbans Mukhia's Collection of Pictures from India Office Library, London.

sown areas and re-planting them in a vacant space in the field. Generally, this task was assigned to women. One of the reasons for this almost even adjustment was that the plants would never be starved of nitrogen. In the soil there is always a struggle between plants to obtain nitrogen.[129]

The practice of *khushaba* was learnt from a young age by watching. This operation was performed with hands but was also done using the feet. Sometimes it was carried out using animal labour, like cattle splashing up and down the wet fields (*gupannend* or *huel*). The weeds usually grew back in the fields within a month and the next weeding (*nendeh*) commenced.[130] In case of broadcast rice crop, weeding was generally carried out four times because in these fields the growth of weeds (*hama*) was quick. Once the weeds got ahead of the rice it became extremely difficult to repair the damage and uproot the grasses which only experts could detect. However, the uprooted weeds too were not wasted; these were folded and placed beneath the soil to rot and become manure.

In the transplantation system only three weeding operations were required. Weeding of rice crop was very painful and labour intensive.[131] In 1888, A. Wingate, after carefully observing the behaviour of Kashmiri cultivators, noticed that the cultivator in Kashmir was not an early riser as he did not begin any real work before 7 a.m., though he boasted of rising with the cock's crow when the weeding of the rice fields commenced.[132] There were no special implements used for weeding as it was done with the hands and feet. While carrying out weeding in the rice fields, the peasants had to remain constantly postured on their knees with their backs bent with 1 ft. backwards and one foot forward in the wet fields till the end of the operation with very brief intervals for rest. Sometimes, when the crop was 2 ft. high, the entire field was ploughed up. This operation was known as *sele*.[133]

During the weeding operation, particularly of rice crops, the peasants suffered from frequent eruptions (*khaez*) caused by the constant immersion of their legs and hands in water. Water was drained out, though not totally, during all these operations so that the plants did not root out of the soil and flow away with the water. Their legs and wrists were specially affected by *khaez* though their hands and feet remained relatively undamaged owing to the protection provided by the mud. The peasants usually applied pine pitch (*kelmteel*), a kind of oil which was extracted from pine, and applied it to the affected parts of the body for relief.[134]

Both men and women did transplantation but the ploughing operations and broadcast sowing and weeding operations were done by the men. When rice crop bloomed and the grains began to form, water was drained off the fields. This process was known as *rabe dadeh,* and a little before harvest a final watering (*paph sag*) was given which helped the crop's ears to swell. Before the harvesting of rice crops in September the little rainfall which usually took place was considered beneficial. Such rains were known as *kambarkah* and were welcome. They not only improved the rice crops but also enabled the cultivator to sow the spring crops.[135]

The annual produce of rice in the time of Zain-ul-Abidin was 77 lakh *kharwars.*[136] In 1822–3, Moorcroft states that the total rice production was 20 lakh *kharwars*. Civil war and consequent Mughal occupation following Zain-ul-Abidin's death diverted attention from the maintenance of canals, causing them to enter into a state of dysfunction as the elements of nature wrought havoc on them. None of the rulers after him focused attention in this direction, as a result of which rice cultivation remained confined only to the flat portion of the valley where water could reach with ease and in plenty. Second, rising taxes drove the peasants away and rendered it impossible for them to attend to the renovation and upkeep of the canals.[137] This is also specifically attested by A. Wingate, the First Land Settlement Commissioner who visited Kashmir in the second half of the nineteenth century. He recommended to the Maharaja that irrigation be treated as an issue of prime importance and that it was heavily dependent on the tanks and diversion of various water courses that required immense amount of human labour as they had fallen into disrepair.[138]

In 1861, when a rice exhibition was held in Lahore, the Kashmiri authorities sent only three varieties of rice—*Chogul*, *Kunj danya*, and *Basmati danya*—to be displayed there.

The outturn of rice varied between 10 and 60 maunds per acre but 20 to 40 maunds covered most of the rice lands in the valley. The quantity of seeds sown per acre varied between 20 and 24 *seers.*[139]

However, the process of cultivation of other crops was not as complex as rice. The slopes and uplands which were devoted to the cultivation of maize and pulses required neither regular irrigation nor multiple ploughings. The ploughing for maize and autumn millets was not so meticulously done as for rice. Two or three ploughings were sufficient; the final one covered the seeds. In the case of maize crops, it was done using hands and hoe. The best maize crops were raised in reclaimed swamps and black peaty soils which were found under the banks of the Jhelum.[140]

Generally, as in other parts of the Orient, the practice of mixed cropping was also prevalent in Kashmir. Various crops like maize, beans and a variety of pulses were cultivated in a mixed manner. Sometimes maize and pulses were grown with some other crops barring rice and saffron. According to Howard, this practice of mixed cultivation of crops helped both sets of crops and when the two grew together the character of growth improved.[141]

Wicker baskets and *kanvots* (knight caps) were used by peasants for carrying manure. In between the ploughing and harvesting time, shovels, hoe and rake were used. The shovel was used for digging the corners of the field which the plough could not reach, and for embanking. The hoe was used for loosening the soil and for uprooting the weeds of the previous crops. The rake was used for drawing together straw and for smoothening the soil whenever necessary.[142] The sickle was used at the time of harvesting. It was a very important and integral implement in Kashmiri agriculture but certainly not 'imbued with any community spirit' as understood by Marc Bloch in the case of medieval France.[143]

There was no special arrangement for threshing paddy which could have saved a great deal of labour. In most parts of the valley there were no carts except near the area of Wular Lake, to carry crops to the threshing ground or take home after the sheaves were harvested. For the threshing of paddy, bundles of rice straw were tied against a wooden log in the presence of the *shiqdar*, the supervisor of crops, on the threshing ground. Then commenced the beating of the sheaves of paddy on this wooden log.[144] That was how the grains were detached from the stalk. The straw was carefully stored because it was considered the best fodder for cattle and very useful as thatching material for huts and houses. Rice straw was the most popular fodder in Kashmir. This information is well preserved by Victor Jacquemont. Born in 1801 in Paris, Jacquemont was the son of a noted philosopher and writer. At a very early age he evinced a strong interest in natural history. His unbiased good sense led him to separate the practical from the absurd. Finally, he was instructed to investigate the natural history of India on behalf of the Royal Museum of Natural History of Paris. In pursuance of his mission he arrived in London in 1828 and obtained letters of introduction for all possible assistance in India from the Royal Asiatic Society. When he reached India in 1829, Lord William Bentinck gave him numerous letters of introduction which enabled him to be received and assisted by all those who proved helpful and with whom he became acquainted. Here he studied some important languages and history of the country. About the relations between the Afghans and Sikhs he says the Afghans are 'a warlike nation which has so many times invaded India and can bring thirty thousand cavalry in the field'. Immediately, he adds, 'The days of Mahmud Ghazni and Timour are posts. The Afghans are very inferior to Sikhs and are, at most, just strong enough to do battle from time to time with Ranjeet Singh. He disciplines his army in the European fashion, and almost all his officers are French.' About Kashmiri shawl-weavers in Ludhiana he says, 'There is a numerous colony of Kashmirians here, who manufacture shawls similar to those of their own country, but generally of inferior quality.' Regarding the conquerors of Kashmir and their total effect on the country, he writes elaborately about how the Afghans during the last century having deprived the Mughals of that conquest, and the Sikhs having driven the Afghans from it, a general plunder followed each new conquest; and during the intervals of peace, anarchy and oppression, did their best against labour and industry. The country is now therefore (1831), so completely ruined that the poor Kashmirians seem in despair and have become the most indolent of men.... In Kashmir there is scarcely more chance for getting a supper for him, who being rendered desperate sleeps all day under the shade of a plane-tree. Concluding on the general administration and condition of the masses in 1831, he says that 'India is no longer the poorest country in the world; to me Kashmir exceeds all imaginable poverty'. Finally, about the enterprising habits of Kashmiri traders he says,

'Kashmiri merchant, it is true go about everywhere from Kashmir to Teheran, and even to Meshed; they go through Lahore, Delhi, Bombay, Bushir, Shiraz, etc., without passing through Cabulistan for a very good reason.'[145]

Barley and wheat were harvested and threshed in the months of June and July. The ears were trodden on by cattle or sometimes beaten by sticks, and when there was no wind, a blanket was flapped to winnow the grain (*wapat*). Anything that came with the spring crop was doubly welcome for Kashmiri peasants, who regarded it as a kind of lottery.[146]

For the husking of paddy, a mortar and pestle were generally used. The peasant did not have to receive any special training for using these implements; the techniques came to him from observation and practice from early childhood.[147]

However, in the nineteenth century, there are references to *jindra* or husking machines. While touring Gilgit, Partap Singh noticed that these machines were moved by water. The *jindra* was a large wooden axle to which two large curved wooden arms are affixed in the middle at an interval of some distance and nearly opposite each other. This was being constantly worked by falling water directed through an open pipe over a wooden wheel also affixed to one end of the axle, something akin to a water wheel. The two arms in turn stroked the near end of the machine which worked to husk the paddy at the further end. There were only six such machines in Kashmir in the early nineteenth century.[148]

Owing to the large amount of cattle dung and abundance of wood for fuel, Kashmir was very fortunately placed. Rice fields were manured and improved by the distribution of clods of fresh earth. Both men and women carried the refuse from the village and the farmyard manure to the fields. It was ploughed in or sometimes heaped at a place through which the irrigation duct passed and, after the fields were irrigated, it was then spread over the fields manually.[149] In early April, the turf clods were cut from the banks of streams and irrigation channels and broadcast over the wet fields. However, it sometimes happened that the entire land could not be manured because of the scarcity of labour. This happened when the most hated institution of *begar* took away large number of peasant labour during the cultivation season.[150] This establishes the fact that technology and social problems were very closely interlinked.

Crops suffered in most parts of Kashmir because of the non-availability of the necessary means to minimize the damage done to the crops by external factors. In Kashmir proper, pests like Dadur, Halov, Kril and Mohur were very common. The other factors that damaged the crops were *handur* and *rai*. The first affected a variety of paddy which failed to mature in time. It was due to a disease which usually occurred when there was an early snowfall resulting in cold winds which prevented the ripening of the grain on the plant. As a result, the grain with the husk remained by and large unripe. *Rai* on the contrary was a disease which ate up the substance of the grain.[151] The husk cover of the grain would indeed ripen but there would be no grain in it. This disease usually occurred due to failure of rains. There was an abundance of food plants like *Euryale ferox*, *Nymphaea stellata*, *Nalba, Nelumbium speciosum*, the exquisite pink water lily, *Acorus calamus* and *Typasp*, the reed mace, all of which contributed to the sustenance of the Kashmiris.[152]

The Kashmiri cultivators believed that greater the number of ploughings the larger the outturn of the crop. But, unfortunately, the number of their cattle was small and the holdings large, though not as large as in other parts of India.[153]

In relatively favourable weather conditions, from October to December, the cultivators were busy ploughing dry lands for wheat and barley. By the end of December, though the ploughing operations ceased and the Kashmiris got busy with weaving blankets and other domestic work including the tending of sheep and cattle.[154]

In the fifteenth century, Zain-ul-Abidin experimented with the cultivation of sugar cane in the Martand Pargana, but this endeavour failed because of the climatic conditions. We do not hear of it afterwards.[155] Apart from the aforementioned crops there also were a number of horticultural products such as apples, pears, grapes, mulberry, walnuts, quince, cherry, peach, apricot, raspberry, gooseberry, and strawberry.[156] Mirza Haider, the maternal uncle of Babur, who ruled Kashmir from 1540 to 1550, wrote in 1541, pears, mulberry and cherries are met with but the apples are particularly good. There are other fruits in plenty, sufficient to make one break one's resolution. Among the wonders of Kashmir are the quantities of mulberry trees cultivated for their leaves from which silk is obtained. In season, fruits are so plentiful that it is rarely bought and sold. The owner of the garden as well as the man who has no garden are alike, for the gardens have no walls and it is not usual to hinder any one from plucking fruits.[157]

Small peasant holdings were more numerous in Kashmir. They were generally less rigid and more adaptable to changing situations. Agriculture in Kashmir provided very modest livelihood. It was, therefore, always combined with other occupations like pastoralism, woodcraft, pottery, metal trades, shawl making and other items of artisanal production. In many ways these circumstances continued to shape its historical development.[158]

Crops and their Patterns

Time and again it has been stated that, in India, two crops were cultivated; but as Harbans Mukhia very rightly remarks, 'The fact that Indian soils yielded two crops a year is, of course, true merely as a general statement; understandably there would be considerable regional variation in the degree of soil fertility. Thus, if some regions were capable of yielding three or four crops a year, others evened out nature's largesse by producing more or less one crop and perhaps an insignificant second.'[159] The opinion expressed by Mukhia is very appropriate to the situation in the Kashmir region during our period of study. The agricultural activity in Kashmir revolved mainly around two seasons—autumn (*kharif*) and spring (*rabi*)—with *kharif* being the more important of the two.

The crops cultivated in the *kharif* season were rice, maize, saffron, tobacco, millet, amaranthus, buckwheat, pulses, sesame, and cotton. The *rabi* crops included wheat, barley, Tibetan barley, opium, poppy, rape, flax, and mustard. Of all the *rabi* crops only such crops were sown after the *kharif* season whose germination took place before the snowfall and whose plants started growing once the snow had melted in the month of late March or early April. These *rabi* crops, which took four to five months to mature in other parts of India, took five to six months to mature in the valley of Kashmir.[160] Since the *kharif* crop was harvested by September, or sometimes in early October, i.e. on the eve of snowfall, there was little time left to prepare the soil for the next crop. Therefore, *rabi* seeds were sown in fields which had not been cultivated during the *kharif* season. The crops harvested in the *rabi* season were very insignificant, both in terms of quantity and quality. Besides, not all lands under cultivation except some of the rice lands produced two crops.[161]

The nature and growth of any crop was dependent on climatic conditions but the resistance of a particular crop to frost, cold winds, etc., depended on how the crop was fed. Moreover, cultivation was not possible for the greater part of the year due to the climate which rendered a regular double cropping pattern nearly impossible. Abul Fazl says that chickpea and barley were not found in the Sarkar of Kashmir.[162] Chickpea would have been introduced in later times but there are references regarding the cultivation of barley before the Mughal occupation of the valley in late sixteenth century.[163] Bernier, who visited Kashmir in 1665, mentions vineyards, rice, wheat, hemp, and saffron crops being cultivated in Kashmir.[164] Among fruits he mentions the famous Kashmiri apples, pears, plums, apricots and walnuts, melons, paleques, watermelons, water parsnips, red beet, radishes, and most of the potherbs.[165] The peculiarities of the physical features and the climate that prevailed in Kashmir at that time disallowed intensive farming as well as diversification of crops in the valley. Since the land remained under snow for four to five months in a year, a time when no cultivation was possible, the agrarian economy of Kashmir was generally one crop-based *(yakfasli)*.[166] Rice was the main *kharif* crop and after its harvest in September there was little time left to sow another crop. Abul Fazl mentions that there was no fine variety of rice in the sixteenth century even though he acknowledges plentiful rice crops in the valley. In fact, he had the Indian mainland in view where the finest varieties were produced.[167] In one of the *tahsils* of Kashmir, Lawrence counted 53 varieties of rice. The white rice variety, *basmati*, was considered the best. This and another white variety, *kanyun*, germinated very quickly and ripened more rapidly than any other variety but these varieties were also very delicate and could not stand the harsh cold winds. Therefore, white rice was less popular with the cultivator than red rice which was hardier and gave a larger outturn. Red rice (*zagbata*) could be grown at higher altitudes and was less liable to be damaged by animals.[168]

However, in spite of the obvious advantages of the system of crop rotation, the peasants generally preferred the cultivation of rice when adequate water was available. They allowed the land to remain lea in times of deficiency of water and knew that their labour would not be repaid if they sowed other crops. Further, the small quantities of commercial crops grown in the valley afforded no scope for agrobased industries during the period of our study.

In the high altitude villages and uplands of Kashmir very fine crops of maize were also grown even if rains were delayed. A month after sowing, when the maize was about a foot high, women weeded the fields with a small hoe and loosened the soil about the roots. As a rule, maize was grown on dry land and it was rare to find such lands irrigated. For a really good crop of maize, fortnightly rains are required, but in the swamp lands the natural moisture of the soil produced good crops. Timely rains could help produce bumper crops of maize and pulses.[169] According to nineteenth-century estimates, the average production of maize per *kharwar* (80 *seers*) of land was 24 *kharwars*. (The *kharwar* as a unit of measure of weight was equivalent to 80 *seers*; but a *kharwar* as a unit of measure of land was equivalent to the amount of land where 80 *seers* of seed could be sown.) Some of the maize fields were irrigated but not much manure was added. A large part of the stalk was left to rot in the fields under snow and rains.[170]

Wheat seeds were sown in September and October and the crop ripened in June. The common variety was red wheat with a small hard grain which was considered very inferior in the rest of India.[171] Abul Fazl says this of sixteenth-century Kashmir, 'Wheat is a small grain and black in colour and there is little of it and little consumed.'[172] The Kashmiri cultivators looked down upon wheat and barley crops not only because rice was their staple food but also because the climate was unfavourable for a reasonable harvest of wheat. The ploughings for wheat and barley were very few and very slovenly.

Lawrence found that these fields of wheat and barley were choked with weeds and he never expected to find any crops growing under such conditions even in the nineteenth century. He says that the

Kashmiris were not ignorant of following a spring crop with an autumn crop but rather that the scanty and uncertain rainfall and cold climate were the serious handicaps for production of these crops on a larger scale.[173] Three ploughings for wheat at the most and two ploughings for barley were considered sufficient. Unlike the Indian mainland or Punjab, no labour was spent on weeding or manuring of wheat and barley crops.

Trumba or buckwheat (*Fagopyrum esculentum*) was a useful crop which was sown late in almost any soil which did not have any irrigation facility. Apart from being a feed for poultry and horses, it was also consumed by human beings in some villages in the upper reaches. The variety of pulses included *mong* (*Phaseolus mungo*), *baqla* (*Vicia faba*), *mah* (*Phaseolus radiatus*), *moth* (*Paconitifolius*), and *razmash* (*Phaseolus vulgaris*).[174] In the month of May these pulses were sown in the upland areas and also in those rice lands which were given rest. The pulses did not require much weeding or irrigation. They were mostly dependent on natural rains.[175]

Among the oilseeds, *rape* (*Tilgoglu* or *Brassica campestris*) was the main variety. It was sown in the month of September and October on dry lands, and especially on reclaimed swamps. Its cultivation did not involve any weeding except where wild hemp was very vigorous. Timely rains were required for a good harvest in May and June. The second variety was known as *sarshaf* (*Brassica campestris*) or *taruz*. It was sown in spring and its ripening coincided with *tilgoglu*. The other variety was known as *sandji*. Often, when the rice crop was standing, rapeseed was cast into the wet soil and no ploughing was given and a crop of rapeseed was obtained by the spring season. The harvesting of the rice crop, which was carried out while sitting in the field, facilitated getting into the soil and thus saved a lot of human labour. Its outturn, however, was lower. The average produce per *kharwar* was 16 to 20 *kharwars*.[176] In the lower slopes and mountains linseed was also cultivated. These lands were ploughed twice and a third ploughing was given when the seed was sown in April. The crop was harvested towards the end of July. It required rains in May, failing which it withered.

Of all the oilseeds, *til* (*Sesamum indicum*) was a very common crop. It was sown in April and the land was ploughed four times; a fifth ploughing was done at the time of sowing. *Til* requires a rich soil and no manure and is depended on timely rains. The two varieties were those of white and black *til.*[177] This particular crop was weeded using hands and hoe and deserved more careful attention than any other crop like rice. The *til* crops were harvested after rice. The survey by Lawrence in the nineteenth century reveals that an average yield was 1.5 maunds per acre.[178] The barley cultivated in the valley was not of good quality and the barley fields were neither weeded nor manured. In fact, barley had more of a ritual or medicinal use than as a food crop. In the higher reaches, at an elevation of 7,000 ft., the kind of barley grown was known as Tibetan barley (grim) which was a staple food among the mountain people. It was sown in May and June and ripened in August and September. The average production per *kharwar* of land was 16 *kharwars.*[179]

Cotton was grown in Kashmir up to a certain level of elevation. It was grown on the *karewas* and also in the low-lying land, which was irrigable but required rest from rice. The soil was ploughed three times in quick succession and the clods were pulverised using mallets.[180] The seed was soaked in water and mixed with ash before sowing. The sowing of the cotton crops took place at the end of April and May and the fields often watered afterwards. *Karewas* was best suited for their cultivation. In the late eighteenth century, efforts were made to introduce brown cotton, the Yarkand variety, but it did not grow well because of the nature of the soil even though the climate was not a problem.[181] In the nineteenth century, the average production of cotton per *kharwar* of land was about 6 *kharwars.*

Kangani or *shol* (Italian millet or *Setaria italica*) was a useful crop. A large area of rice lands were also sown with this crop when cultivators realized that water was scarce. The lands were ploughed four times for this crop. This crop was always sown in April and May and was harvested in September.[182] It required only one weeding. The most popular variety was a Chinese one which was known as *ping* or Chinese (*Panicum miliaceum*). Its appearance is like that of rice and it was occasionally weeded.[183]

Ganhar or amaranth was another crop cultivated in Kashmir. It was introduced into India by the Portuguese.[184] It was grown in rows among the cotton fields and along the borders of the maize plots with its gold, coral and crimson colours. It was sown in the month of May and the land was given three ploughings and a large outturn was harvested in September. Apart from its food value, its stalks were used for the extraction of alkaline substances.[185] In the sixteenth century, 10,000 to 12,000 bighas were devoted to saffron (*Crocus sativus*) cultivation. The saffron fields at Pampore extended over about 24 miles (39 km) and at Paraspore, 2 sq. miles (3.2 km).[186]

In the nineteenth century, even though the cultivation of saffron lands was spreading, only 132 acres out of 4,527 acres of land were used to cultivate it. In the sixteenth century, saffron cultivation was a great source of revenue for the state. For seed purposes, a particularly sloping ground was required and it took nearly three years before the bulbs could be planted out in small, square plots where the saffron was grown. These plots remained fallow for eight years and no manure was applied in order to keep the specificity of the quality of the soil intact.[187]

These lands were ploughed in the months of March and April. The saffron fields were rendered soft and spades were used to plant the saffron bulbs in the ground. They sprouted within a month's time and grew until September/October when they reached full maturity, taking at least six months to do so. When the bulbs sprouted to the height of a human finger, they would begin to flower; each bulb produced eight flowers. Each flower had six lilac-tainted petals, among which three were yellow and three ruddy, and it were the last three which yielded saffron. Once the saffron bulb was planted it produced flowers for six years continuously. For the first two years the produce was always less as compared to the third year when the saffron bulb produced the maximum it could.[188]

In the nineteenth century it was noticed that when one bulb was planted in the square it lived for 14 years without any help. It produced new bulbs while the old ones rotted away without any effort from the cultivator. The bulbs were planted in July-August and all that the cultivator had to do was to break up the soil surface gently a few times and ensure proper drainage of the plot by digging a neat trench on all four sides. The flowers appeared around October. In 1871, the total production was 28,800 lbs., i.e. 200 *kharwars*.[189]

Before the nineteenth century people came from various parts to cultivate saffron. In the nineteenth century, however, except a few people from Srinagar, the cultivation of saffron was in the hands of the local cultivators in Pampore. Once the flowers were collected, the real work of extracting saffron commenced. The flowers were dried in the sun and the three long stigmas picked up by hand. The stigma had a red tip and this tip formed what was called *Shahi Zafran*, the first quality saffron.[190] The long white base of the stigma also made saffron but it was considered of inferior quality. The article thus collected in a dry condition was known to traders as *mongla* and sold for Re. 1 a *tola*. When the *mongla* saffron was extracted, the sun-dried flowers were beaten lightly with sticks and winnowed. Then, the whole mass was thrown into the water where the petals swam and the essential parts of the flower (*niwal*) sank and were collected and those which rose to the top were dried again and again, beaten with sticks and then immersed into the water. The process was repeated three times and each time the *niwal* became poorer. One form of adulteration was to mix the *niwal* of the third class with the *niwal* of the first. The saffron obtained in this way was lighter in colour and fainter in scent than the *mongla*.[191]

Tobacco was also grown in Kashmir, mostly in and around Srinagar and other towns. In India tobacco was introduced during the last years of Akbar's reign, in AD 1600, in coastal Andhra Pradesh.[192] It was known as *brewari* (*Nicotiana tabacum*). The finer tobacco was that of the *chilasi* variety. It was sown in April and harvested in August. It required very fertile soil and was irrigated using the pot and lever system. In addition to these crops, a number of vegetables and fruits were also grown in abundance. The produce of the Digar Abi area in Ich Nagam Pargana was poor in 1861. Some of the villages were productive and the rice producing area was a little over 3 per cent.[193]

Table 2.9 shows the percentage of the various *rabi* and *kharif* crops. Hops began to be cultivated from the late nineteenth century.[194]

Quite a number of implements were used for preparing the soil, right from ploughing to sowing. The plough was the most important implement used in the cultivation of land. But the ploughshare would leave many clods unbroken. A wooden hammer was, therefore, used for breaking them.[195] The third stage arrived when the soil was reploughed. This time the ploughshare used was slightly smaller and

TABLE 2.9: PERCENTAGE OF *RABI* AND *KHARIF* CROPS

Rabi Crops	*% of Cultivation*	*Kharif Crops*	*% of Cultivation*
Wheat	17	Rice	30
Barley	5	Maize	2
Ong	1	Kanganichina	2
Vegetables	1	Vegetables	2
Sarshaf and Tilgoglu	1	Cotton	4
Oilseeds	10	Fallow land for the year	4

Source: W.R. Lawrence, *Valley of Kashmir*, London, 1895.

its tip was of wood and not iron.[196] After this was done, the fields were watered, and when water had soaked in the soil a little, it was supposed to be ready for the fourth or final stage of preparation of the soil for cultivation.[197] At this stage, use was made of a wooden log approximately 6 ft. long and 3 ft. in girth. This log was yoked to a pair of oxen and served as a roller, levelling the fields and breaking up any clods that had remained in place previously.[198] Use was made of a wicker basket and *kanvot* (nightcap) by the peasants for carrying manure.[199] In between the ploughing and harvesting time, use was often made of shovels, hoes and rakes. Shovels were used for digging the corners of the field which the plough had not reached and for embanking.[200] The hoe was used for loosening the soil and for uprooting the weeds of the previous crops. Rakes were used for drawing together straw and for smoothening the soil wherever necessary.[201]

Illustration 2.5 depiects all the items' peasants made use of.

The use of sickles at the time of harvesting was essential.[202] There was no special arrangement for the crushing of paddy, which could have saved a great amount of labour. For the crushing of paddy, bundles of rice straw were tied against a wooden log in the presence of the *shiqdar*, the supervisor of crops, in the crushing ground, and then commenced the beating of sheaves of paddy on this wooden log.[203]

For husking of paddy, mortar and pestle were generally used but during the early years of Maharaja Pratap Singh's reign we have evidence that for husking of paddy there were husking machines in

Illustration 2.5: Traditional technique of raising a mud wall and the implements used. *Source:* Harbans Mukhia's Collection of Pictures from India Office Library, London.

some areas. The State had only six husking machines called *gindra*, run by water power. This was a large wooden axle to which in the middle two large curved wooden arms were affixed nearly opposite each other. This was being constantly worked by fall of water directed through an open pipe over a wooden wheel and these two arms in turn rose to strike to husk *sali*.[204]

The peasants did not have to receive any special training in the use of these implements; the technique came to them through observation from early childhood.

Owing to the large amount of manure of cattledung and abundance of wood for fuel, Kashmir was very fortunately placed. Rice fields were manured and improved by distribution of clods of fresh earth. However, it sometimes happened that all land could not be manured because of scarcity of labour.[205]

Another kind of manure was prepared by burning the standing weeds and stubble of the previous crop on peaty soils before the land was ploughed.[206] They provided potash to the soil. Besides ashes in houses were carefully stored for manuring the vegetable fields.[207]

In most parts of Kashmir, crops suffered because of the non-availability of the means of minimizing the damage done to the crops by external factors. In Kashmir proper, pests like *dada*, *halov kiri* and *mohru* were very common.[208] The other factors which damaged the crops were *rai* and *handru*. Handru was the name applied to that variety of paddy which failed to mature in time. It was a disease in the crop which occurred usually when there was early snowfall resulting in cold winds which prevented the ripening of grain on the plant. As a result, the grain with the husk remained by and large green. *Rai*, on the contrary, was the disease that ate up the main substance of the grain. The husk cover of the grain would ripen alright but there would be no grain inside it. This infestation occurred generally due to the failure of rains.[209]

Irrigation

Irrigation was a factor of prime importance in Kashmir because agriculture was largely dependent on it. The almost annual flooding of rivers, which was usually relied on in the exploitation of agricultural resources, appears to have convinced the foreign travellers of the abundance of irrigation. To increase agricultural production, Sultan Zain-ul-Abidin constructed and reconstructed several canals some of which include the Utpalpura canal, the Naidashaila canal, the Avantipura canal, the Lalkul or Pohru canal, the Zaingir canal or Lachman Kol, the Manas canal, and the Mar canal. The Martand canal and Karala canal were constructed earlier but Zain-ul-Abidin reconstructed them.[210] Bernier observed in the seventeenth century that in recent years extensive water works had been carried out with the objective of bringing water to the *karewas*.[211] From the sides of all these mountains innumerable springs and streams of water gushed forth, conducted by means of embanked earthen channels even to the top of the numerous hillocks in the valley, thereby enabling the inhabitants to irrigate their fields of rice.[212]

The river Jhelum has many tributaries. On its right bank it receives the Liddar or Lambodri, which comes down from the everlasting snows that overhang from the head of the Liddar valley and from the mountain lake of Tarsar. Below Srinagar at Shadipur—the place of the marriage of two rivers—the Sind River joins the Jhelum, and beyond lake Wular, the Pohru stream which drains the Lolab valley and merges into a great river. On the left bank the chief tributaries are the Vishav, the Rembiara, the Romshi; the Doodganga joins the Jhelum at the lower end of the city of Srinagar.[213] 'These waters, after separating into a thousand rivulets and producing a thousand cascades through the charming country, at length collect and form a beautiful river, navigable for vessels as large as borne on our Seine … the numberless streams which issue from the mountains maintain the valley and the hillocks in the most delightful verdure,' observes the French traveller, Bernier.[214] He goes on to say,

> The whole kingdom wears the appearance of a fertile and highly cultivated garden. Villages and hamlets are frequently seen through the luxuriant foliage. Meadows and vineyards, fields of rice, wheat, hemp, saffron and many sorts of vegetables, among which are intermingled trenches filled with water, rivulets canals and several small lakes vary the enchanting scene. The whole ground is enamelled with our European flowers and plants and covered with our apple, pear, plum, apricots and walnut trees, all bearing fruit in great abundance. The fruit is certainly inferior to our own, nor is it in such variety;

but this I am satisfied is not attributable to the soil, but merely to the comparative ignorance of the gardeners for they do not understand the culture and the grafting of trees as we do in France.[215]

But the examination of sources leads one to conclude that the existing irrigation system presented a great hazard in carrying out normal agricultural operations. It was adequate only in a few areas. Sultan Zain-ul-Abidin converted depressions in lands into wells and also constructed a lake in Padmapura (Pampore) and named it Zain Sara.[216] In most parts, water canals could not be dug owing to difference in surface levels. The places where the water could be led on to the land were relatively few and there could be no question of involving human labour for raising the water owing to the extreme intensity of labour involved.[217] Jahangir had introduced the system of water distribution. He laid down the rule that the upper villages which had no local spring and the lower villages which received no overflow water from the upper villages were entitled to a share of irrigation from the main channel. The land settlement of 1889 by Lawrence recorded this information.[218] Between the sixteenth and nineteenth centuries there was no substantial increase in population because the number of villages mentioned in the Mughal statistics was the same as in the 1901 census for corresponding districts.[219] For instance, the villages of Vihu Pargana were situated at a great distance from Romshi and Doodganga rivers and much of the land was dependent on Kanchi Kol for irrigation purposes.[220] In 1891, Kanchi Kol was utterly broken and no arrangement was made for improving the same canal.[221] Similarly, the Hari Khul remained in a ruined condition for years together.[222] In 1890-2, the land settlement commissioner laid down that there was much to be done in the area of agricultural technology of the state. Bhag Ram stated, 'In sinking irrigation wells in certain dry localities, in utilising peat as a fuel for steam pumps, to drain the great swamps of the valley and so on I could enumerate several kinds of agricultural improvements which would tend to benefit the state and people.'[223] The problem in irrigating the land was the lack of organization. Even as late as 1889, Wingate, one of the land settlement experts, said, 'I propose to reserve to the Durbar all rights in respect of water because in Kashmir nothing is so important or stands so much in need of control and organization. There is abundance of water but the tail villages, unless very strong in men and so able to send up contingent to fight for it, cannot get it and much water runs to waste and much irrigable land is dry.[224]

In Kandi *illaqas* irrigation was difficult except where small water channels were taken along the hillside. Although water was easily found from 70 to 100 ft. below the surface, wells were very few and the peasants had hardly any money to spend on sinking wells.[225]

The well irrigation system also existed in towns like Srinagar, Anantnag, Baramulla, and Sopore. It was used as lift irrigation for vegetable lands and also in kitchen gardens. For rice cultivation, well irrigation was hardly used. The lift irrigation system (Tolsag system), was operated by means of a long pole to which, half way down, a short pole was attached to form a fork. A piece of wood joined to the upper end of the fork provided the lever for a long pole placed at a right angle to it. The short end of the pole carried a large stone as a counterpoise to the other end where a thick rope hung with a wooded bucket attached to it. The bucket was lowered into the well by pulling the rope and dragging down the pole and as the rope was released the weight of the stone on the other end raised the bucket. This is referred to by James Douie as a bucket well.[226]

The painting as shown in Illustration 2.6 shows the use of this Bucket Well in use for irrigation purposes.

As far as the canal irrigation system was concerned, it was also full of defects almost up to the end of nineteenth century. Some areas depended on spring water for irrigation but this water was very cold and took a lot of time to reach the degree of temperature necessary for rice cultivation. Second, it did not carry the fertile silt with it. 'On the other hand spring water did not contain scum which is considered bad for rice.'[227]

The winter rain enabled the peasants to proceed with the sowings for the spring crop. He also depended upon the occasional recurrence of such showers during the following three months for the harvest, which the increasing warmth of the months of March and April were sure to bring on well if the rains were fairly plentiful.[228] The Pir Panjal range was served by its various streams and there was an enormous amount of water, some of which was utilized for irrigation. But there

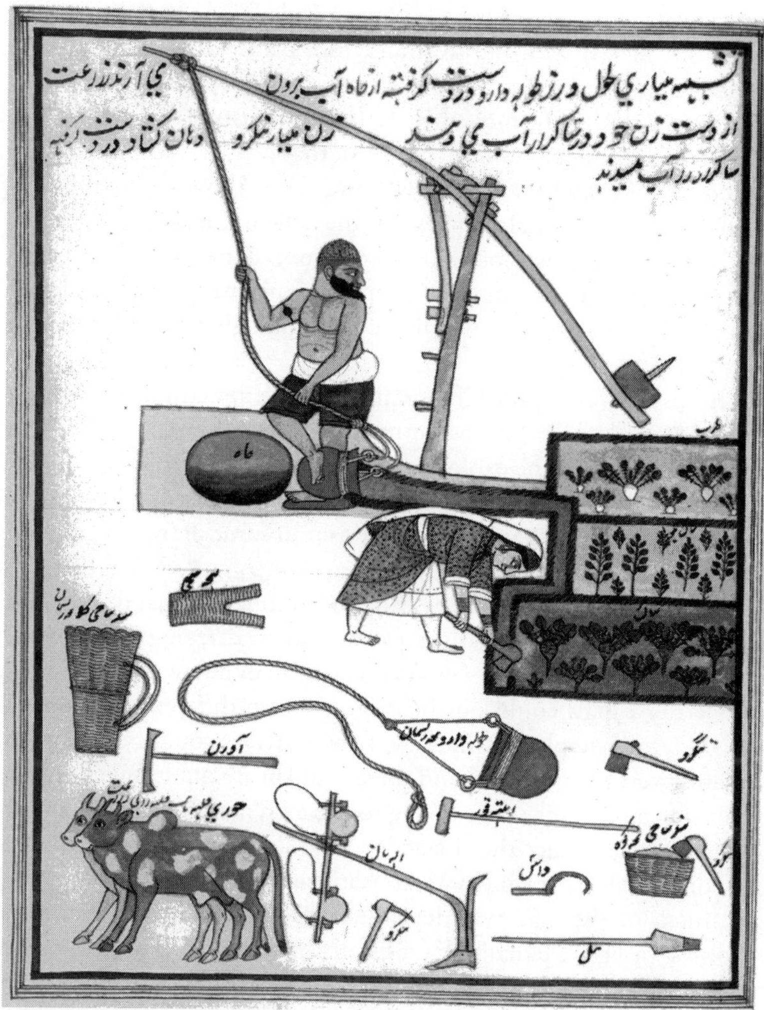

Illustration 2.6: Traditional system of irrigation. *Source:* Harbans Mukhia's Collection of Pictures from India Office Library, London.

was no technology to bring the watercourses over the higher plateaus. As a result, most of lands were dependent on rain water.

The northeastern end of the valley was irrigated by various streams which united with the drainage of the Lolab and Utar to form the river Pohru. This river helped to form a wide low level flat that may almost be classed with the river alluvium plane. This flat made the pargana of Zaingir a fine prosperous region because good crops were only grown with rain moisture. As to the moisture, the valley was intermediately in a position between that which was flooded by periodical rains and that which was arid. Even though enough rains fell on the two mountain ranges, yet the areas of Srinagar, Avantipur and Anantnag were without rain. But the occasional cloud did spread over the whole area and did give a supply of moisture enough to bring down the temperature of the air but not enough to allow a double cropping pattern.[229]

It was a factor of prime importance because agriculture was largely dependent on it. The almost annual flooding of rivers, which was usually relied on in the exploitation of agricultural resources appears to have convinced the foreign travellers of abundance of irrigation.[230] There were plenty of water bodies in Kashmir some of them were used for fishing (Illustration 2.7).

The examination of sources leads one to conclude that the existing irrigation system presented a great hazard in carrying out normal agricultural operations. It was adequate only in a few areas. In most parts water canals could not be dug owing to difference in surface levels.[231] And the places where water from rivers could be led on to the land, were relatively few and there could be no question of human labour for raising the water owing to the extreme intensity of labour involved. For instance the villages of Vihu Pargana were situated at a great distance from the main water channels like Romshi, Doodganga, and much of the land was dependent on Kanchikul for irrigation purposes. In 1891 Kanchikul was utterly broken and no arrangement was made for providing irrigation to these areas.[232] The same was the case with Ullar *illaqa*. The irrigation of the area was insufficient for its agricultural requirements and the only way of increasing the water supply was by constructing tanks. This, however, could not be done due to lack of manpower and as a result, the peasants' lives became more insecure.[233] Wingate who surveyed the valley for the land settlement of 1889 says,

I propose to reserve to the Durbar all rights in respect of water because in Kashmir nothing is so important or stands so much in need of control and

Illustration 2.7: Fishing techniques in Kashmir and the water transport. *Source:* Harbans Mukhia's Collection of Pictures from India Office Library, London.

organization. There is abundance of water but the tail villages unless very strong in men and so able to send up contingent to fight for it, cannot get it and much water runs to waste and much irrigable land is dry.[234]

After the commencement of the land settlement in 1888-9, the state looked after irrigation channels promptly, but this was done by levying an extra irrigation cess. Second, the development activities were concentrated in Jammu and registered very little progress in Kashmir. There was large room for improvement. The old canal near Ashi Mukam, if restored with improved alignment, would have irrigated the important *karewa* of Ranbir Singh Pora and added largely to the state revenue. The Hari-Khul was, for years together, in a ruined condition.[235] In the year 1891-2, Rs. 6,066 was spent for repairing the irrigation works but generally improvement in the irrigation facilities in the valley started only in the fourth decade of the twentieth century. It was only during the years 1931-40 that the irrigation canals like Zaingir Canal, Lal Khul, Martand Canal and new canals which were fed by Jehlum, Vishav and Liddar rivers were constructed.[236]

In fact, in 1890-2, the land settlement commissioner laid down that there was much to be done by the way of agricultural improvement of the state. 'In sinking irrigation wells in certain dry localities, in utilizing peat as a fuel for steam pumps, to drain the great swamps of the valley, and so on. I could enumerate several kinds of agricultural improvement which would tend to benefit the state and the people. But, for the time being, I believe that these schemes are premature, and that taking up and measuring agricultural improvement is pointless until the land settlement is completed.'[237]

In Kandi *illaqas* irrigation was difficult except in case of small water channels flowing along the hillside.[238]

Although water was easily found from 70 to 100 ft. below the surface, wells were very few and the peasants had hardly any money to spend over constructing wells.[239] In some tracts, temporary wells were constructed to provide water to the main channels. These channels were often taken over by the edges of *karewa* lands, which was a far more difficult process of irrigating land.[240] The well irrigation system also existed in towns like Srinagar, Anantnag, Baramulla and Sopore. It was used as a lift irrigation for vegetable lands and also in kitchen gardens and extensive vegetable cultivation around the Dal Lake and Chattabal in Srinagar.[241]

The lift irrigation system (*tolsag*) was carried out by means of a long pole, to which half way down a short pole was attached to form a fork. A piece of wood attached to the upper and lower ends of the fork served as the lever for a long pole positioned at right angles to it. The short end of the pole carried a large stone as a counterpoise, to the other end where a thick rope hung with an earthed bucket attached to it. The bucket was lowered into the well by pulling the rope and dragging down the pole as the rope was released the height of the stone on the other hand raised the bucket.[242]

So far as the canal irrigation system was concerned, it was also negligible and no less defective even up to the end of the nineteenth century. The river Jhelum was also not used for extensive irrigation within the valley. No new canals were constructed during the period of our study. The newly constructed canals, Nandi and Dandi, are attributed to Maharaja Pratap Singh, which proved to be excellent sources of irrigation, but actually those canals were built in the third and fourth decades of the twentieth century. The construction of these two canals was an extension and reconstruction of a canal built by the local peasants, the takeoff of which was defective and the distribution inadequate.[243]

The natural resources of irrigation too were uncertain and sometimes insuffîcent. Capt. Knight who visited Kashmir in early 1862 observes, 'No rain having fallen as yet, the springs and rivers were all dry.'[244] The chief danger arose from the excessive rains with floods in the alluvial plateaus injured by prolonged moisture and early snow and uncertain rainfall.[245] In 1854 the rains caused floods and destroyed the entire harvest in the lowlying areas.[246] In 1855 when the harvest had not been collected the valley witnessed early snowfall.[247]

Hassan says, 'During Samvat 1934 and Hijra 1294, i.e. AD 1877 in the month of Katak (i.e. September/October), when Maharaja Ranbir Singh was ill and administration was in the hands of Wazir Punoo, it rained continuously for two and a half months.' The river Jhelum was in spate and the Wular Lake too was flooded; consequently, the entire crop was destroyed. The administration had not give thought

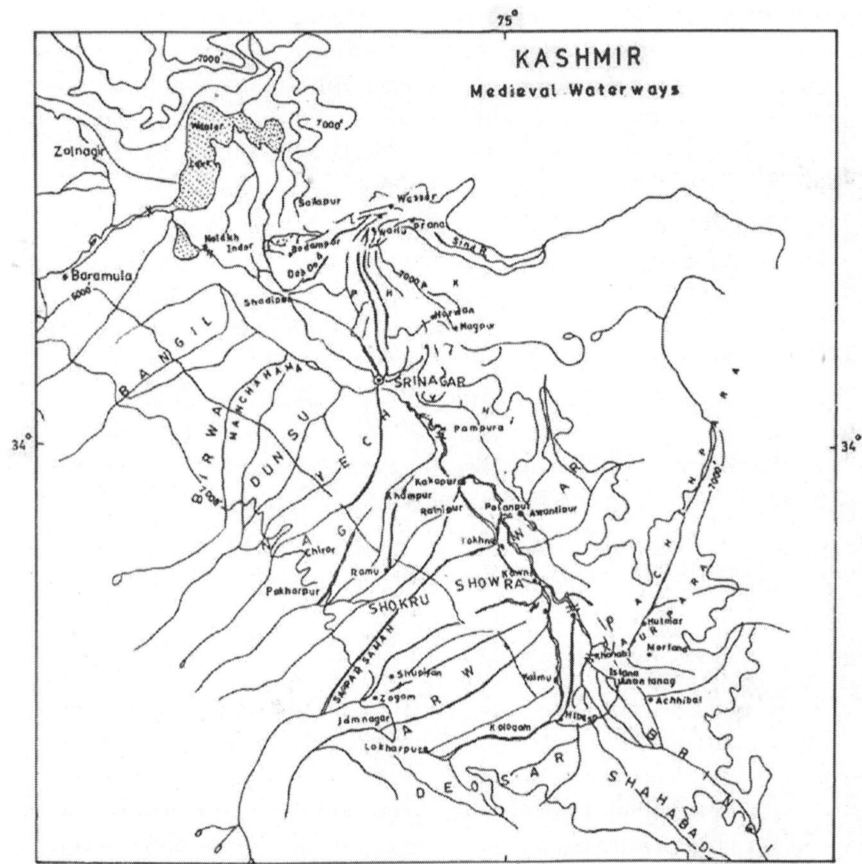

Map 1: River system in Kashmir. *Source:* Map drawn by Anant Rao on the basis of information provided to him from various texts on Kashmir.

to the impending famine. However, Wazir Punoo issued two lakh *kharwars* of *Shali* from the reserved stock with a view to putting off this symptomatic appearance of famine till the next spring.[248] In 1896, heavy snowfall prevented the usual area of land being brought under cultivation. It was followed by heavy rainfall, and the peasant's condition deteriorated further. The State did not fail to collect the irrigation cess even though ever since 1880 when a cash assessment had been made, the peasants had to attend to irrigation themselves.[249]

Some areas depended on spring water for irrigation but this water was ice cold and took much time to reach a certain degree of temperature necessary for rice cultivation. Second, it did not carry the fertility of silt along with it.

NOTES

1. M.A. Stein, *Ancient Geography of Kashmir*, Baptist Mission Press, Calcutta, 1899, pp. 24-7. C.E. Bates, *Gazetteer of Kashmir and Adjacent Districts of Kishtwar, Badrawah, Jammu and Nowshera, Punch and the Valley of Kishen Ganga*, Office of the Superintendent of Government Printing, Calcutta, 1873, rpt. Light & Life Publishers, New Delhi, 1980, pp. 1-3. F. Drew, *Jammu and Kashmir Territories*, Edward Stanford edn., London, 1875, pp. 9-13. Peer Hassan Shah, *Tarikh-i-Hasan* (Persian), vol. I, State Government Press, Srinagar, 1885, pp. 3-7. A.N. Raina, *Geography of Jammu and Kashmir State*, India Book House, Bombay, 1971, rpt. National Book Trust, Delhi, 1977, pp. 1-24. It is the most comprehensive and coherent of all the indigenous Persian sources of Kashmir. It was compiled by Ghulam Hasan Khoihami and contains historical literature from the earliest times to AD 1885. The work is in four volumes. Volume one deals with the geology of Kashmir, its fauna and flora, archaeological remains, internal and external trade, sources of irrigation, agricultural and horticultural produce, revenue of Kashmir under the Mughals and the Afghans, bridges, gardens, shawl trade, etc. Volume two narrates political history from the earliest times. This volume in particular and other volumes in general depict information on various aspects of agrarian system of Kashmir. Volumes three and four are devoted to describing the life of the saints, scholars and poets who lived during the rule of the Sultans and the Mughals in Kashmir. Its first, second and third volumes are published. Its second volume has been translated into Urdu by Moulvi Ibrahim in 1957.

2. Dewan Krishen Lal, *Account of Kashmir*, Foreign Deptt. Secret Correspondence, 31 March 1848, file nos. 66-77, National Archives of India.
3. *Majmui* Reports (in Urdu) for the years from 1887 to 1891, Ranbir Government Press, Jammu & Kashmir Archives in Srinagar.
4. Lawrence, *Imperial Gazetteer of India*, vol. XV (*From Karachi to Kottayam*), The Clarendon Press, Oxford, London, 1909 (rpt.), Rima Publishing House, Delhi, 1985, pp. 5–6.
5. See *Foreign Dept. Sec. 31st March 1848*, file nos. 60-77, unpublished National Archives of India (NAI).
6. See Mirza Saif-ud-Din, *Akhbarat* (Persian Ms.) (AD 1846-57), vol. IV, ff. 61, 78, 84. Research Department Library, Srinagar, Kashmir. See also Charles Girdlestone, *Memorandum on Kashmir*, Foreign Department Press, Calcutta, 1973, p. 35.
7. W.R. Lawrence, *Valley of Kashmir*, London, 1895, pp. 325-30; *Imperial Gazetteer of India*, vol. XV (*From Karachi to Kottayam*), Oxford, 1908, pp. 115-17.
8. F. Drew, *The Northern Barrier of India*, E. Stanford, London, 1877, pp. 172-3. See Lawrence, *Valley*, pp. 325-30. See *A Note on Jammu and Kashmir* (published by Jammu and Kashmir State), Ranbir Press, Jammu, 1928, pp. 27-9.
9. Lawrence, *Valley*, op. cit., pp. 325-30.
10. F. Younghusband, op. cit., p. 78. See also W.R. Lawrence, *Assessment Report of Uri-Tehsil*, Jammu, Ranbir Press, 1898, p. 4. W.R. Lawrence, *Assessment Report of Baramulla Tehsil*, Ranbir Press, Jammu, 1905, p. 9.
11. Report of British Entire Exhibition, Jammu and Kashmir, Fleetway Press, Holborn, London, 1924, pp. 20-3.
12. *Mahan Singh, Tarikh-i-Kalan* (unpublished Persian Ms., Punjab), Archives Patiala, M/1004, f. 201. The manuscript is listed as Annonymous but lately it was established by many scholars that it was written by Mahan Singh. See W.W.H. Greatheds, Impressions about Kashmir as contained in an extract from a letter dated 26 October 1871 from National Archives of India, also cited in Charles Girdleston, *Memorandum on Kashmir*, Appendix D, Fleetway Press, Holborn, 1863, London.
13. Lawrence, *Valley*, pp. 325-7. *A Note on Jammu and Kashmir*, State Archives, Srinagar, p. 28.
14. G.T. Vigne, *Travels in Kashmir, Ladakh, Iskardu Countries Adjoining the Mountain Course of Indus and Himalayan, North of Punjab*, vol. I, Henry Colburn, Publisher, London, 1842, p. 310. See E.F. Neve, *Beyond the*

Pirpanjal, Church Missionary Society, London 1915, pp. 59-60. Hargopal Khasta Koul, *Guldasta-i-Kashmir* (Urdu), Lahore 1883, p. 79. 'Lion of Kashmir', Hargopal Khasta Koul, 1847-1923, was a resident of Nawakadal. He was the son of Ram Chander Koul who had four sons, Kanjinath, Har Krishan, Shivnath and Salig Ram. His paternal grandfather Gwasha Koul and great grandfather Mahadeo Koul were exiled during tyranical rule of Pandit Birbal Kak Dhar. They were from Rayiteng, Rainawari. His maternal grandfather 'Rayees e Kashmir' was Vaid Ram Matoo during tyranical Afghan Muslim occupational era. He started *Bidya Bilas* in 1886, which happened to be first newspaper from Jammu & Kashmir, in Urdu and Hindi. From Kashmir, the first newspaper, later on *Tohfa-e-Kashmir,* was started by Munshi Harsukh Rai in 1875. The eight page weekly was published on Saturdays from Maharaj Ganj, Srinagar. Major P.D. Hinderson C.S.E. helped him to get a job in Dogra adminstration. He asked his friend Kernel Henry, who was first Resident for Kashmir to consider both Hargopal and Salig Ram as administors in residency office. In 1894, Hargopal Khasta formed an association namely Samaj Sudhakar, which had its object of the heralder of social reforms, and Pandit Suraj Kak Mattoo was the pioneer of this organization. Girls' education and widow re-marraige used to be taboo those days. Only a section of elite Karkun pandits were enlightened enough to excel in Education. Pandit clergy like their contemporary Muslim clegymen were against modern education. He started girls primary schools in the city, that bought him wrath of priestly pandits. He was also pioneer in the field of modern education in Kashmir, he founded a Hindu school for boys, which has played commendable role in modern education in Kashmir which was later on upgraded as Sri Partap College by Christian missionary Annie Besant. He was among first to talk about widow remarriage of Pandit women along with his pupil Kashap Bandhoo. He established 7 schools for girls education. His daughter Padmavati presided over the chain of schools. She was a widow and he tried to get her remarried but Pandit Clergy warned him of ex-communication. So he dropped the idea but he never stopped to educate Pandit fraternity about this issue Jai-Kashmir & Sher i Kashmir. The revolutionary Kaul Brothers, Hargopal Kaul (Khasta), Salig Ram Kaul, Janki Nath Kaul and Hari Krishan Kaul were the first agitators who challenged the autocracy and raised the banner of revolt against the strong and powerful ruler, Maharaja Ranbir Singh. In 1887, under the governorship Wazir Pannu and Pandit Raj Kak Dhar, when a famine struck the state and many officers, taking advantage of the abnormal situation begun to flee and left the helpless Kashmiris but Pandit Hargopal couldn't stand with such a situation. Pandit Raj Kak Dhar, Subhan Chak and Wazir Pannu: the trio used to fleece people like anything, everything was taxed except air and water, even dogras taxed night soil as well. Lacs of Kashmiris died: Exorbitant taxes and famine led to martyrdom of lacs of Kashmiris. There were reports that Pandit Raj Kak Dhar along with his *dag shawl* accomplices Subhan Chak dumped 1000s of dead bodies in Wular Lake. Pandit Hargopal and Salig Ram raised the voice against Ranbir Singh's adminstration and accused him of starving Kashmiris to death. Pandit Hargopal was arrested by Dogras. During his confinement in prison at Bahu-fort Prison, Jammu, Hargopal wrote his famous Masnavi 'Gopal Nama' in which he versified the condition of Kashmir and exposed the court intrigues. He also composed a poem entitled 'Narsingh Autar' which is a satire on the political system.He wrote for Ranbir Singh:

Na Kar moo kaala apna badi se
Badi aakhir badi hai aur badi hai
(Do not blacken your face,
Evil is evil after all and evil)

Reports were there that his brother Salig Ram was killed in the custody. Under pressure from local agitation, Dogra regime released Pandit Hargopal to return to his innate place and people of all the shades conferred him a stimulating reception only to substantiate his sobriquet of 'Lion of Kashmir', which afterwards was conferred to Sheikh Mohammed Abdullah.

15. This drawing is in India Office Library, London. Professor Harbans Mukhia of Jawaharlal Nehru University, New Delhi, has been kind enough to provide me this and some other illustrations for my use from his collection of the photographs of the drawings.
16. C.E. Bates, *A Gazeteer of Kashmir and the adjacent districts of Kishtwar, Badrawar, Jammu, Naoshera, Punch, and the Valley of the Kishen Ganga*: 1873. Indian reprint. Light & Life Publishers, 1980, pp. 14-18.
17. Dewan Kripa Ram, *Gulzar-i-Kashmir* (Persian), Lahore, 1870, p. 486. The original manuscript is available in the National Archives, New Delhi. Lawrence, *Valley*, op. cit., pp. 325-7.
18. See, *A Note on Jammu and Kashmir*, p. 28.
19. W.R. Lawrence, *Imperial Gazetteer of India Provincial Series Jammu and Kashmir*, Vol. XV, Oxford, 1908, rpt. Calcutta, 1909, p. 20.
Guy Hunter, *Modernizing Peasant Societies*, Oxford University Press,

London, 1968, p. 87. F. Drew, *Northern Barrier of India*, Stanford, London, 1877, pp. 170-3.

20. *Tarikh-i-Kalan,* op. cit., f.133. Mahan Singh, *Tarikh-i-Kalan* (unpublished Persian Ms., Punjab Archives Patiala M/1004 Punjab Archives Patiala, f. 201 The manuscript is listed as Anonymous but lately it was established by many scholars that it was written by Mahan Singh.
مزرعه های شالیزار برای دولت مایه اصل برای مالیات به شمار می رفت.در ایالت کشمیر غالباً هفتاد و پنج نوع از برنج اعم از محصول مختلف به دست می آمد.باسمتی ،کانی چن و سک داس در آنها بهترین نوع برنج محسوب می شدند.بنابه گفته یکی از اثر معاصر ۵۳،۰۰۰ هکتار زمین برای کاشت شالیزار مخصوص بود.
21. Ibid., f. 65.
22. According to Birbal Kachru it was introduced by the Afghans, and it was done to ensure the liquidation of arrears due from the peasant on account of the seeds and *taqvi* loans provided to them by the state during famines.
مقدار یک خروار شالی که مدت بشتاد و پنج سال ابتدائی عمل را راجه سکه جیون بصیغه تخم و تقاری در زیر رعایائی پرگنات بنابر کومک کشت زار زیر باقی بود و بر سال عمال بر مجال از آنہا باز یافت می نمودند و بسب درازی مدت زر اکثر جا وزنی موجود دور بعض مکان بعوض تلف آمده وجود نداشت.از پخته مردم ذراعت بخش را تصدیق در حمت باید حال در افزائیش حاصل قصور رفتد راه می یافت باز یافت مقدار نبودموقوف و حصه چہار ترکی بطرف سرکار مقرر ساخته.
23. Godfrey Thomas. Vigne, *Travels in Kashmir*, Ladak, Iskardo, the countries adjoining the mountain-course of the Indus, and the Himalaya, north of the Panjab, 2 vols. Henry Colburn, London, 1842, vol. I, p. 309. Mir Ahmed, *Dastural Amal-i-Kashmir* (unpublished Persian Ms.), M 829, Punjab State Archives, Patiala, f. 133b. Mirza Saif-ud-Din, *Akhbarat*, vol. I, f. 7. See *Diary of R.G. Taylor, Punjab Government Records (1847-9)*, vol. VI, Punjab Government Press, Lahore, 1911-15, p. 31. Dewan Kripa Ram, *Gulzar-i-Kashmir*, op. cit., pp. 256-7.
24. W.R. Lawrence, *Imperial Gazetteer*, pp. 49-50. A.N. Raina, *Geography of Jammu and Kashmir State*, Director, National Book Trust, Delhi, pp. 100-1. See *Techno-Economic Survey of Jammu and Kashmir State,* NCAER, Delhi, 1969, pp. 17-18.
25. Lawrence, *Valley*, op. cit., p. 159. *Gazetteer of Kashmir and Ladakh* compiled under the direction of Quarter Master General in India, the Intelligence Branch, Superintendent of Govt. Printing, Calcutta, 1890, p. 59. Mir Ahmed, op. cit., f. 133 b., Mirza, op. cit., vol. I, f. 7. Dewan Kripa Ram, op. cit., pp. 256-5.

26. Kripa Ram, *Gulzar-i-Kashmir*, p. 278. Charles Girdlestone, op. cit., Appendix C. See *Gazetteer of Kashmir and Ladakh*, p. 57.
27. Hargopal Koul Khasta, *Guldasta-i-Kashmir* (Urdu), Lahore, 1883, pp. 20-2. *Gazetteer of Kashmir and Ladakh*, p. 57. Peer Hassan Shah also says about *Chogul*. 'Chogul—among these is extremely soft and sweet.' See Hasan, *Tarikh-i-Hasan*, op. cit., vol. I, p. 185.
28. F. Drew, *Northern Barrier of India*, pp. 170-3.
29. Dewan Kripa Ram, *Majmu-i-Report of Jammu and Kashmir* (Urdu), Ranbir Government Press, Jammu, 1873-5, Jammu Archives.
30. Ibid.
31. *Kashmir Crop Report of 1837*, NAI.
32. Lawrence, *Valley*, op. cit., p. 37.
33. Ibid., pp. 336-71, Lawrence, *Gazetteer*, op. cit., pp. 49-50. Raina, op. cit., p. 103.
34. Younghusband, *Kashmir*, op. cit., p. 200.
Capt. Cunnigham (*Memo on Kashmir*), Foreign and Sec. C, 31 March 1848, file nos. 60-77, NAI.
35. Dewan Krishen Lal, op. cit.
36. Chief Secretariat Political and General Department File No. 76 of 1896, (unpublished document), Jammu Archives.
37. Ibid.
38. Ibid.
39. *Gazetteer of Kashmir and Ladakh*, pp. 61-2. Hassan, op. cit., vol. I, p. 185.
40. R.L. Singh, *India: A Regional Geography*, National Geographical Society of India,Varanasi, 1971, pp. 347-61. Raina, op. cit., p. 102.
41. *Tarikh-i-Kalan*, op. cit., f. 204.
42. *Gazetteer of Kashmir and Ladakh*, op. cit., p. 61.
43. Ibid., see Lawrence, *Valley*, op. cit., p. 338.
44. Hassan, op. cit., Vol. I, p. 185. Raina, op. cit., p. 102.
45. Lawrence, *Valley*, op. cit., p. 338.
46. Ibid., see also Lawrence, *Gazetteer*, p. 52. *Gazetteer of Kashmir and Ladakh*, op. cit., p. 61.
47. Lawrence, *Valley*, op. cit., p. 338.
48. Ibid., p. 337.
49. Ibid.
50. Ibid., pp. 337-8.
51. Ibid., p. 337.
52. *Gazetteer of Kashmir and Ladakh*, op. cit., pp. 60-4.

53. Dewan Krishen Lal, *Account of Kashmir, Foreign Deptt.* See 31 March 1848 (unpublished document), file nos. 60-7, NAI.
54. Ibid., W.R. Lawrence, see also *Assessment Report of Handwara Tehsil,* Ranbir Press, Jammu, 1922, p. 32.
55. M.M.A. Beg, *Zara-i-Islahat* (Urdu) Jammu & Kashmir Government Press Srinagar, 1950, pp. 8-9. See also W. Moorcroft and G. Trebeck, *Travels in Himalayan Provinces of Hindustan and Punjab, Ladakh and Kashmir,* 2 vols., John Murray, London, 1971, vol. II, p. 350. An account of Moorcroft's itinerary is available in two volumes edited by Professor Horace Hayman Wilson. His notices relating to the life and conditions of Kashmir during the last phase of Afghan rule are very valuable. They also throw light on the system of administration, military security, judicial system, agriculture and revenue system. He also mentions the parganahs, and the relations of the Khakhas and Bombas with Afghan and Sikh rulers. But his clear views of economic and commercial aspects of shawl-wool and shawl industry are most valuable and deserve further study and research.
56. Ganeshi Lal, *Sayahatnama* (Persian) Punjab Government Record Office, June 1846, rpt. 1955. English tr. by V.S. Suri, Chandigarh, 1976, p. 37.
57. Mirza Saif-ud-Din, *Akhbarat,* op. cit., vol. II, f. 86.
58. *The Jammu and Kashmir Yearbook: A Master Document on Jammu & Kashmir, the People and their Life,* Government Press, Jammu, 1972, p. 13.
59. Mirza, op. cit., vol. IV, f. 239.
60. Ibid. See R.H. Davis, *Report on Trade and Resources of the Countries on the North Western Boundary,* printed at the Government Press, vol. LXII, Lahore, 1862, Appendix XVII.
61. Mirza, op. cit., vol. X, f. 44. *Gazetteer of Kashmir and Ladakh,* p. 68. Hasan, *Tarikh-i-Hassan,* vol. I, p. 186.
62. Charles Girdlestone, *Memorandum on Kashmir,* p. 34.
63. Ibid.
64. Moorcroft William, *Travels in the Himalayan Provinces of Hindustan and the Punjab,* p. 152.
65. Ibid.
66. Younghusband, op. cit., p. 202.
67. Lawrence, *Valley,* pp. 393-4.
68. Wingate, *Assessment Report* (unpublished report), Jammu Archives, p. 54.

69. Pandit Bhag Ram, *Annual Administration Report of Jammu and Kashmir* (*1889-90*), Rambir Press, Jammu, 1891, pp. 55-6.
70. Pandit Bhag Ram, *Annual Administration Report of Jammu and Kashmir State* (*1894-95*), Rambir Press, Jammu, 1896, p. 105.
71. Younghusband, op. cit., pp. 200-1.
72. Ibid., p. 201. See also W.R. Lawrence *Assessment Repent of Awantipura,* Rambir Press, Jammu, 1920, p. 19.
73. Lawrence, *Valley*, p. 339. *Report of British Empire Exhibition*, op. cit., pp. 24-5.
74. *A Note on Jammu and Kashmir State*, op. cit., pp. 29-30.
75. Lawrence, *Valley*, pp. 342-3. *Report of British Empire Exhibition*, pp. 24-5.
76. Dewan Krishen Lal, op. cit., Dewan Anant Ram, *Mujmu-i-Report* (Urdu), Rambir Press, Jammu Archives, 1877-8, p. 105.
77. C.E. Bates, *Gazetteer*, p. 44; Lawrence, *Valley*, p. 343.
78. *A Note on Jammu and Kashmir*, pp. 29-30.
79. Ganeshi Lal, *Sayahatnama*, p. 38.
80. Mirza, op. cit., vol. VIII, f. 28.
81. C.E. Bates, op. cit., p. 44. During the last two years of the decade the production declined because of the gradual decay of the bulbs. Charles Girdlestone, *Memorandom on Kashmir*, p. 39.
82. Ibid.
83. Almonds and walnuts are counted among dry fruits. They commanded very little or no price. Orchards had seldom any enclosure, people subsisted on fruits during famines.
84. Andrew Leith Adams, *Wanderings of a Naturalist in India: The Western Himalayas, and Cashmere (1827-82)*, Edinburg, 1867, rpt. Asian Educational Services, Delhi, 2012, p. 305. Dewan Anant Ram, *Majmu-i-Report* (1877-8), pp. 96-7.
85. Dewan Anant Ram, op. cit., pp. 96-7.
86. Besides the natural calamities, i.e. Hassan, op. cit., vol. I, pp. 479-92. Ramju Dhar, *Kaifiat Intizammulk-i-Kashmir* (Per. Ms.) (1886-7) Research Department Library, Srinagar, ff. 7-8.
87. Pandit Bhag Ram, *Annual Administration Report* (*1889-90*), Jammu, 1891, pp. 42-3.
88. Pandit Bhag Ram, *Annual Administration Report* (*1885-6*), Jammu, 1887, pp. 100-6.
89. Ibid., pp. 134-5.
90. *A Note on Jammu and Kashmir State*, p. 35.
91. Ibid., It is an extremely important tree of western Himalayas and of

N.W. India. A tree of deodar was generally of 25 ft. in girth and 200 ft. in height. See *Report of British Empire Exhibition*, pp. 16-17, Lawrence, *Valley*, pp. 78-9.

92. *Report of British Empire Exhibition*, p. 18. See Lawrence, *Valley*, op. cit., p. 80.
93. Lawrence, *Valley*, op. cit., p. 80.
94. Ibid.
95. Girdlestone, op. cit., p. 92.
96. *A Note on Jammu and Kashmir*, p. 34. See *Report British Empire Exhibition*, pp. 18-21.
97. Ibid., p. 22.
98. Ibid., pp. 21-2.
99. *A Note on Jammu and Kashmir*, pp. 34-5.
100. Girdlestone, op. cit., p. 37. *Gazetteer of Kashmir & Ladakh*, p. 53.
101. Pandit Bhag Ram, *Annual Administration Report* (*1894-5*), Jammu, 1896, p. 141.
102. *A Note on Jammu and Kashmir*, p. 35.
103. Ibid., pp. 35-6.
104. Hassan, op. cit., vol. I, pp. 69-81. Lawrence, *Valley*, pp. 14-16.
105. Bamzai, *Socio-Economic History of Kashmir*, pp. 178–9.
106. Lawrence, *Valley of Kashmir*, op. cit., pp. 322-4. See also William Moorcroft, MS. EUR.D.265: 77. Also see Mahd Joo, *Various Trades in Kashmir.* This book contains illustrations of trades in Kashmir with their respective implements. The paintings in the book were all done by a local artist named Mahad Joo.
107. Abdul Wahab Malik, personal interview.
108. C.A. Lambert, *A Trip to Kashmir and Ladakh*, London, 1877, p. 172. From the statement of Lambert, it becomes clear that the use of the donkey was also made for ploughing though not very generally.
109. Lawrence, *Valley of Kashmir*, op. cit., pp. 319-24.
110. Ibid.
111. Ibid., p. 325.
112. Lawrence, *Imperial Gazetteer of India,* pp. 19-22.
113. Ibid., p. 82.
114. Ibid., pp. 14-20.
115. Ibid.
116. Ibid., p. 48.
117. Chadurah, *Tarikh-i Kashmir*, p. 46; see also, Zutshi, *Sultan Zain-ul-Abidin*, p. 143.
118. This argument is based on oral information collected from Kashmiri

cultivators.

119. Howard and Howard, *The Development of Indian Agriculture*, p. 15.
120. For details on the role of earthworms in soils. For details see John Murray, *The Formation of Vegetable Mould Through the Action of Worms, with Observations on their Habits*, London, 1881.
121. Haward, *Earths Green Carpet*, pp. 32-3.
122. Abdul Wahab Malik, oral testimony.
123. *Note on Assessment Report of Karnah Tehsil Muzaffarabad*, p. 6.
124. Harbans Mukhia, 'Agricultural Technology in Medieval North India', *Exploring India's Medieval Centuries*, Aakar Publishing House, Delhi, 2010, pp. 277-306.
125. Abdul Wahab Malik, oral testimony.
126. Ibid. In the hilly areas (*kandi illaqas*) the process of broadcast sowing continued even up to the early 1950s when finally the Chinese varieties of rice known as China and K39 arrived in Kashmir.
127. *A Report of the British Empire Exhibition*, p. 16.
128. Mahad Joo, *Various Trades in Kashmir*.
129. Howard, *The Earth's Green Carpet*, pp. 32-3.
130. Abdul Wahab Malik, personal interview.
131. Ibid.
132. Lawrence, *Impact of New Settlement on the Cultivator of Kashmir*, p. 252.
133. Abdul Wahab Malik, oral testimony.
134. *A Report of British Empire Exhibition*, pp. 23-5. Also, see Bates, Gazetteer, op. cit., p. 14.
135. Rattan Lal Hangloo, 'Agricultural Technology in Kashmir 1600-1900', *The Medieval History Journal 1600-1900*, vol. 11, no. 1, Sage, New Delhi, 2007, pp. 63-71.
136. Jonaraja, *Zaina Rajatarangini*, op. cit., Stanza 974.
137. *Techno- Economic Survey of Jammu and Kashmir State*, National Council of Applied Economic Research, State Government Press, 1969, pp. 17-18.
138. Wingate, *Preliminary Report of Land Settlement in Jammu and Kashmir 1889*, p. 13. Hangloo, 'Agricultural Technology in Kashmir 1600-1900', op. cit., 2007, pp. 63-71.
139. Lawrence, *Provincial Gazetteer*, p. 59; Raina, *Geography of Jammu and Kashmir State*, pp. 100-1.
140. Lawrence, *Valley of Kashmir*, pp. 336-7.
141. Albert Howard, *An Agricultural Testament*, Oxford University Press, London, 1972, p. 9.

142. *A Report of British Empire Exhibition*, pp. 23-5.
143. Marc Bloch, *Technology and Social Evolution*, p. 88.
144. Jacquemont, *Letters from India*, pp. 219-43. *A Report of British Empire Exhibition*, pp. 23-5.
145. Ibid.
146. Ibid.
147. P.N.K. Bamzai, *Socio-Economic History of Kashmir (1846-1925)*, Metropolitan Book Co., New Delhi, 1987, pp. 184-5. See also Joo, *Various Trades in Kashmir*.
148. Singh, *Diary of an Inspection Tour to Gilgit*, pp. 5-7.
149. Vigne, *Travels in Kashmir*, vol. I: p. 309.
150. Mirza, *Akhbarat*, op. cit., vol. I: 29, 62 ff. Also see Lawrence, *Valley*, op. cit., pp. 319-21, and Pearce Grevis, *This is Kashmir*, Cassell & Company Ltd., London, 1954, pp. 57-8; Khoihami, *Tarikh-i Hassan*, vol. II, pp. 869-70.
151. Lawrence, *Assessment Report of Uri Tehsil*, pp. 40-1.
152. Lawrence, *Provincial Gazetteer*, p. 17.
153. Ibid. For details also see *Census of Jammu and Kashmir, 1881*.
154. Abdul Wahab Malik in personal conversation.
155. Jonaraja, *Zaina Rajatarangini*, Stanza 974.
156. *Tarikh-i Kalan*, op. cit., f. 134. See also Francois Bernier, *Travels in the Mughal Empire* (AD *1656-68*), Humphrey Milford, Oxford University Press, London & Bombay, 1916, p. 133; Moorcroft. Ms. EUR D.264, p. 170.
157. Dughlat, *Tarikh-i Rashidi*, p. 425.
158. Girdlestone, *Memorandum on Kashmir*, pp. 29-30. See also Lawrence, *Valley of Kashmir*, p. 388.
159. Mukhia, 'Agricultural Technology in Medieval North India', pp. 214-15.
160. Lawrence, *Valley*, op. cit., pp. 325-30 and Lawrence, *Assessment Report of Baramulla Tehsil*. See also Hangloo, 'Agricultural Technology in Kashmir 1600-1900', op. cit., pp. 63-71.
161. Drew, *The Northern Barrier of India*, pp. 172-3.
162. Abul Fazl, *Ain-i Akbari*, vol. II, pp. 353-4.
163. Kalhana, *Rajatarangini*. Here vol. II, book VII, verse 1864, p. 145 is being referred to. In early texts too the word Yava is used to denote barley even though it did not constitute a food item except for the poorest of the poor. Barley has always been an essential item in most of the rituals of the Kashmiri Pandits.
164. Bernier, *Travels*, pp. 52, 309, 342, 397.

165. Ibid., pp. 396-7.
166. Lawrence, *Valley of Kashmir*, p. 329.
167. Abul Fazl, *Ain-i Akbari,* vol. II, p. 353.
168. Abdul Wahab Malik, oral testimony.
169. Khoihami, *Tarikh-i Hassan,* vol. I, p. 185. Also see Raina, *Geography of Jammu and Kashmir*, 103.
170. *Gazetteer of Kashmir and Ladakh*, pp. 61-2.
171. *Tarikh-i Kalan*, f. 204; also see Raina, *Geography of Jammu and Kashmir*, p. 102.
172. Abul Fazl, *Ain-i Akbari*, vol. II, p. 353.
173. Lawrence, *Provincial Gazetteer*, p. 50.
174. Khoihami, *Tarikh-i Hassan*, vol. I, p. 186.
175. *Gazetteer of Kashmir and Ladakh*, pp. 60-4.
176. Wingate, *Preliminary Report of Land Settlement in Jammu and Kashmir 1889*, p. 64. See also Lawrence, *Valley of Kashmir*, pp. 330-9.
177. *Tarikh-i Kalan*, f.133.
178. Lawrence, *Provincial Gazetteer*, p. 56.
179. Wingate, *Preliminary Report of Land Settlement in Jammu and Kashmir 1889*, p. 64.
180. Younghusband, *Kashmir*, pp. 199-203.
181. Moorcroft, *Travels,* vol. II, p. 260.
182. *Tarikh-i Kalan*, f. 133.
183. Lawrence, *Valley of Kashmir*, p. 339.
184. Randhawa, *A History of Agriculture,* vol. II, p. 184.
185. Younghusband, *Kashmir*, pp. 199-203.
186. Randhawa, *A History of Agriculture*, vol. II, p. 214.
187. Lal, *Sayahatnama*, p. 38. Also see Abul Fazl, *Ain-i Akbari*, vol. II, p. 358.
188. Lal, *Sayahatnama.* See also Lal, *An Account of Kashmir.*
189. Bates, *Gazetteer 1873*, pp. 43-4.
190. Lawrence, *Provincial Gazetteer*, pp. 55-7.
191. Ibid.
192. Randhawa, *A History of Agriculture*, vol. II, p. 280. For details also see Gokhle, *Tobacco in 17th Century India.*
193. Wakefield, *The History of Kashmir and Kashmiris*, p. 139.
194. Lawrence, *Assessment Report of Ich Nagam Pargana*, p. 8.
195. See Illustration no. II, Fig. 1 were it is clear. It has been referred to as *yeta fur* in Persian. Dewan Kripa Ram, op. cit., p. 485.
196. Ibid., p. 486.

197. Ibid.
198. Ibid.
199. Ibid., p. 487. See also *A Report of British Empire Exhibition*, pp. 21-2. See Illustration no. II, p. 36.
200. Dewan Kripa Ram, op. cit., p. 486.
201. Ibid., pp. 486-7.
202. Ibid., p. 487.
203. Victor Jacquemont, *Letters from India*, London, 1936, pp. 219-43. Victor Jacquemont visited Kashmir during the Sikh rule. See Kripa Ram, op. cit., p. 447 and Illustration no. 3.
204. See Pratap Singh, *Diary of an Inspection Tour to Gilgit*, 1893, Jammu Archives, pp. 5-8.
205. G.T. Vigne, *Travels*, vol. I, p. 309, Lawrence, *Valley*, pp. 319-21.
206. Lawrence, *Valley*, op. cit., pp. 319-21.
207. Ibid.
208. W.R. Lawrence, *Assessment Report of Uri Tehsil*, 1891, Jammu Archives, p. 40.
209. Ibid., pp. 40-1.
210. Jonaraja, *Zaina Rajatarangini,* stanzas 863-71, 1330; Kalhana, *Rajatarangini,* vol. I, book III, n. 467; see also vol. I: 474. Srivara, *Rajatarangini,* vol. I, stanzas 53, 55; Sayyid Ali, *Tarikh-i Kashmir*: f.19a.
211. Bernier, *Travels*, p. 412, fn.1.
212. Drew, *Northern Barrier of India*, pp. 172-3.
213. Lawrence, *Provincial Gazetteer*, p. 90.
214. Bernier, *Travels*, pp. 396-7.
215. Ibid., p. 397.
216. Srivara, *Rajatarangini,* verse 1, stanza 1.
217. Raina, *Geography of Jammu and Kashmir*, pp. 69-70.
218. Lawrence, *Valley,* op. cit., p. 324.
219. Irfan Habib, *Agrarian System of Mughal India*, p. 18.
220. Lawrence, *Assessment Report of Vihu Tehsil*, pp. 12-13.
221. Raina, *Geography of Jammu and Kashmir*, pp. 69-70.
222. Pandit Bhag Ram, *Annual Administrative Report of Jammu and Kashmir*, p. 117.
223. Pandit Bhag Ram, *Annual Administrative Report of Jammu and Kashmir (1890–91)*, pp. 66-7.
224. Wingate, *Preliminary Report of Land Settlement in Jammu and Kashmir 1889.*

225. Wreford, *Census of India*, pp. 22-3.
226. James Douie, *The Punjab North Western Frontier Province and Kashmir*, p. 143.
227. Lawrence, *Provincial Gazetteer*, p. 55.
228. Fedric Drew, *Jammu and Kashmir Territories*, p. 41.
229. Sharma, *Kashmir Agriculture and Land Revenue System under Sikh Rule*, p. 19.
230. Ibid., pp. 319-21. Younghusband, *Kashmir*, pp. 222-3.
231. Lawrence, *Valley*, op. cit., p. 323. Charles Girdlesetone, op. cit., p. 35. See R.G. Wreford, *Census of India*, vol. XXII, 1941, Jammu, 1943, p. 22.
232. Raina, *Geography of Jammu & Kashmir*, pp. 69-70.
233. Lawrence, *Assessment Report of Vihu Tehsil*, 1891, Jammu Archives, pp. 12-13.
234. A. Wingate, *Preliminary Report of Land Settlement in Jammu and Kashmir, 1888* (unpublished), Jammu Archives, 1889, p. 36.
235. Pandit Bhag Ram, *Annual Administration Report of Jammu and Kashmir (1895-96)*, Jammu, 1897, p. 117.
236. R.G. Wereford, *Census of India*, vol. XXII, 1941, Jammu, 1943, pp. 22-3.
237. Pandit Bhag Ram, *Annual Administration Report of Jammu and Kashmir, 1890-91*, Jammu, 1892, pp. 66-7.
238. Lawrence, *Gazetteer*, p. 45, see F. Brew, *Northern Barrier of India*, pp. 172-3.
239. Capt. Knight, *Diary of a Pedestrian in Kashmir and Tibet*, London, 1863, p. 42. Girdlestone, op. cit., p. 35.
240. Ibid.
241. Mirza, op. cit., vol. VII, f. 17.
242. See illustration A. Petrocokino, *Kashmere: Three Weeks in a Houseboat*, London, 1920, p. 25. A. Petrocokino, who visited Kashmir most probably in 1917, seems to have been a very keen observer of things and provides one with certain important facts of socio-economic life in Kashmir during his sojourn there.
243. R.G. Wreford, *Census*, 1941, p. 23. These canals irrigated lands between Jhelum and its tributaries, the Vishv River, Liddar, Ranbiara, Sandran and Brangi. M.A. Stein, *Ancient Geography of Kashmir*, pp. 99-102.
244. A. Neve, *Thirty Years in Kashmir*, London, 1913, p. 30.
245. Mirza, op. cit., vol. I, ff. 52-3.
246. Ibid., vol. V, f. 42. See also Ramju Dhar, *Kaifiat-Itizam-Mulk-i- Kashmir* (Persian Ms.), Research Department Library, Srinagar, f. 9.

247. Ibid., vol. VIII, f. 128.
248. Hasan, op. cit., vol. I, pp. 464-5.
249. Pandit Bhag Ram, *Annual Administration Report of Jammu Kashmir*, Jammu, 1893, pp. 66-7.

CHAPTER 3

Land Revenue System

Methods of Assessment

On conclusion of the Second Anglo-Sikh War, which took place several years after the death of Maharaja Ranjit Singh, Gulab Singh played a prominent role in getting the treaty signed between the British and the Sikhs. For his services, Gulab Singh received Kashmir from the British under the treaty of Amritsar in March 1846. The information documented by Kashmiri and non-Kashmiri historians and writers with regard to various shades of Afghan rule in Kashmir stands unorganized and no serious attempt has been made to examine this information available in vernacular literature. Bamzai has characterized the Afghan rule very appropriately when he says,

> Rude was the shock that Kashmiris got when they witnessed the first acts of barbarity at the hands of their new master.... Abdullah Khan Ishaq Aqasi, let loose a reign of terror as soon as he entered the valley. Accustomed to looting and murdering his subjects, his soldiers set themselves to amassing riches by the foulest means possible. The well to do merchants and noblemen of all communities were assembled together in the palace and ordered to surrender all their wealth in lieu of their lives. Those who had the audacity to resist were quickly dispatched with the sword and in many cases their families suffered the same fate.[1]

The land revenue system was extremely ill-organized when Maharaja Gulab Singh acquired Kashmir in AD 1846. Revenue officials behaved in an arbitrary manner with regard to the assessment and collection of land revenue.

During the Mughal period (1586-1753), the method of crop assessment prevalent in Kashmir was crop-sharing under *nasq*. Irfan

Habib very rightly remarked that the *nasq* system of assessment in Kashmir was 'Subordinate to Crop Sharing'.[2]

Under the Afghan rule (1753-1819) the revenue system of Kashmir did not alter significantly except for the introduction of some new *abwabs* which were levied on the peasants in addition to the usual land revenue demand.[3] The 66 years of Afghan rule are characterized by an exemplary official brutality, coercion, economic exploitation, wastage of state resources, decline in agricultural production, drainage of wealth by imposing heavy taxation, mis-governance, and corruption.

The Sikh rulers (1819-46) also allowed the system of crop sharing as the method of assessment in Kashmir.[4] Crop sharing at the best of times leaves considerable loopholes for corruption. In times of uncertainty, when the hand of government control over its officials grows feebler, the officials' arbitrary demands tend to soar. The Sikh *ijaradar* was no mere contractor. The amount of *ijara* was generally close to the revenue due to the government, the margin enabling the *ijaradar* to meet the expense of collection and to save something as a profit. For example, the whole province of Kashmir was given in *ijara* to its Nazim Diwan Chunni Lal for an amount of Rs. 27,50,000 in 1824[5] and to Diwan Kirpa Ram for an amount of Rs. 26 lakh in 1826.[6] Similarly, Shujabad in the suba of Multan was given to Diwan Sawan Mal and as after two years the revenues from this *ilaqa* increased by 50 per cent, the Maharaja gave him Multan also in *ijara*.[7] In 1817, Jhang was given to Sukh Dayal for an amount of Rs. 4,00,000 and again in 1820 for Rs. 4,10,000.[8] Similarly, in 1832 this *ilaka* was given to Diwan Sawal Mal for an amount of Rs. 4,35,000.[9] Diwan Devi Das had taken the country of Ramgarhias on a contract for Rs. 4 lakh.[10] The great seal (*Muhar-i-Kalan*) of Maharaja remained in *ijara* for a long time with Lala Devi Das for Rs. 1,80,000 till 1818 when it was given to Lala Devi Sahai for Rs. 2,25,000.[11] On some occasions some competent high officials of the central offices of the state or some favourite or experienced chiefs like Diwan Bhawani Das would also be commissioned for the purpose. For example, for the year 1817-18, Jammu was farmed out to Diwan Bhawani Das for Rs. 1 lakh.[12] However in a given area, *ijara* could alternate with direct collection. The proportion of revenue collected through *ijara* appears to have been considerable. The *ijardari* system under the Sikhs was not confined to lands alone. Even *sairat* or taxes other than the land revenue were given in *ijara* to important and responsible officials or citizens of the State. For example, Lala Sukh Dyal got the *ijara* of *sairat* for Rs. 13 lakh[13] and similarly the *sairat* of Kashmir were given in *ijara* in 1822.[14] Generally the amount of *ijara* was close to the amount of revenue due to the Government. The *ijaradar* was left with a small margin to meet the expenses incurred in connection with the collection and to get his share of profit. The *mushakhasa* or the assessed amount was generally based on records of collections made in the past. If the revenue of a particular area increased, the amount of *ijara* was also raised and before giving an area in *ijara* to a person the Maharaja obtained the correct information regarding income from the revenue of that area. Diwan Sawan Mal and General Ventura were commanded by the Maharaja to prepare correct estimates of revenue accruing from Dera Ghazi Khan and Jhang before these areas were given in *ijara*.[15] The *ijaradars* were required to submit a detailed statement of the produce of land under them and the amount collected, and before getting the charge of an *ijaradari* he was bound to give a deed of acceptance to the government and the net amount of *ijara* was given in deed along with the crop from which the contract took effect. The *ijaradar* gave an undertaking to report correctly about the amount collected from peasants. Each *ijara* grant was made in writing and invariably contained a reference to the urgency of always keeping in mind the welfare of the cultivators and prosperity of the *ilaqa*. The majority of the *ijaradars* were connected with the government and administration in one way or another. Diwan Devi Das, Bhai Ram Singh, Fakir Nuruddin, Prince Naunihal Singh, Raja Bhupinder Pal of Basoli, Raja Dhian Singh, Raja Fazl Dad Khan, Diwan Sawan Mal, Sham Singh Peshawaria, Sardar Desa Singh Majithia, Sardar Jawand Singh Maukal were all connected with the Government and had been big *ijaradars*.[16]

The total amount of land revenue of Maharaja Ranjit Singh's kingdom was estimated at Rs. 1,24,03,900 annually by Murray.[17] The amount given by Murray includes the income realized from tributes. Shahamat Ali estimated the total revenue from land at Rs. 1,96,57,172.[18] The figures given by Cunningham amounted to Rs. 2,79,00,000.[19]

According to these figures, the total annual revenues from land in the dominions of Maharaja Ranjit Singh ranged between Rs. 2 and 3 crore and on an average they were more than Rs. 2.5 crore. In Kashmir, the average of these figures came to over Rs. 34 lakh a year. Shahamat Ali gives the figure of Rs. 36,75,000 as land revenue in 1838.[20] Cunningham writing in 1844 gives the figure of Rs. 30,00,000 for Kashmir.[21] The average for Multan worked out to about Rs. 41 lakh a year. According to Shahamat Ali, the land revenue of Multan was Rs. 38,98,550 in 1838, however, Cunningham gives the figure as Rs. 45,00,000 for Multan.[22] The average for those parts of five Doabs which were covered by the former Mughal province of Lahore came to over Rs. 95 lakh a year.[23] The average for the three provinces of Kashmir, Multan and Lahore added up to Rs. 1,60,00,000 a year. Dr. William Moorcroft. wrote,

> everywhere the people were in most abject conditions, exorbitantly taxed by the Sikh government and subjected to every kind of extortion and oppression by its officers. The consequence of this system is the gradual de-population of country. No more than one-sixteenth of the cultivable land surface was under cultivation; as a result, starving people had fled in great numbers to India. No fewer than 6,800 patients were on the list at one time, a large proportion of whom were suffering from the most loathesome diseases, brought on by scant and unwholesome food, dark, damp and ill ventilated lodging, excessive dirtiness and gross immorality. Every trade was taxed: butchers, bakers, boatmen, vendors of fuels, public notaries, scavengers, prostitutes as well as the shawl makers, all pay a sort of corporation tax.[24]

Ramjo Dhar in *Kifiyat-i-Mulk-i Kashmir* says that taxation under Sikh rule as compared to the Afghans was very light. He hails Sikh rule as the rule of justice with benevolent character.[25] Many other Sikh historians called this Sikh rule in Kashmir as *Sarkar-i-Khalsa*, i.e. a just rule based upon the commonwealth of Guru Gobind Singh.

Besides land tax, there were some other, though less important sources of revenue to the state exchequer including customs and excise duties. Customs duties were levied on every article, even on fuel wood and vegetables. Griffin mentions that duties were charged on 48 articles.[26] As regards salt tax, Wade told the Maharaja on 25 February 1832, 'in British territory it was customary to take salt from the trader at one place, afterwards he could go anywhere in his country and nobody could interfere with him'. He suggested that the same practice should be adopted in the Sikh kingdom.[27] At the very beginning of Maharaja Gulab Singh's reign, all matters involving the general administration, the land revenue system, and internal and external trade were submitted to him. For his consideration, he did not propose any structural change in the revenue administration. He appears to have more or less adhered to the Sikh system.[28]

The method of assessment during Maharaja Gulab Singh's time was a peculiar system of *batai*.[29] Under this system the estimate of production was made when the grain was in heafs and was divided after threshing as in regular *batai*, because in the *batai* system the division of grains was made on the threshing floors. The other two methods of *batai* were *khet batai* and *lang batai*. Under the former, a certain measured area of standing crop was taken, the produce of which was assumed to represent the share of the entire holding. Under the *lang batai* system, the peasant divided the grain into as many heaps as there were shares and that revenue official took the heap that he liked.[30] The crop was harvested by the peasants and collected in stocks (*gunnies*) consisting of a certain number of *kharwars*.[31]

The government's demand was ascertained after the amount of each man's produce was determined by the *kardar* with the help of the *shiqdar*. The state demand at the time consisted of one-half of the produce. In addition to this, the peasant had to pay about 16 per cent of the produce as *trakee* and *abwabs*. The term *trakee* meant tax. Under this system when all was said and done about the collection of revenue, a *trak* of paddy (of 5 *seers* of 83 *chhataks*) was charged from peasants per *kharwar*. This tax had been introduced in Kashmir by the Afghan rulers. *Abwabs* were the other cesses levied by various revenue officials.[32] The total demand amounted to two-third of the produce and one-third was left for the peasant.[33] Under this particular system then in vogue, the state took a certain number of *kharwars* in kind and the rest in *mobiyah*.[34] The government's demand was ascertained after the amount of each man's produce was determined by the *kardar* with the help of the *shiqdar*. The state demand at the time consisted of one-half of the produce. In addition to this, the peasant had to pay about 16 per cent of the produce as *trakee* and *abwab*.

TABLE 3.1: THE HIGH INCIDENCE OF GOVERNMENTS REVENUE DEMAND

Hardo Hissa (total produce)	90 *kharwars*
Sarkaree Hissa (government share)	45 *kharwars*
Trakee and *Abwab*	15 *kharwars*
The total government demand	60 *kharwars*

Source: H.M. Lawrence, *Transfer of Government to Maharaja Gulab Singh*, 28 January 1848, Section C, File Nos. 33-44, Jammu Archives.

Out of this share the state took in *mobiyah* at various rates 37 *kharwars* and 8 *traks* and remaining 22 *kharwars* and 8 *traks* in kind. The allowance to be deducted for carriage was 2 *kharwars* and 6 *traks* and there remained 20 *kharwars* and 2 *traks*.[35]

In another case, 62.5 per cent of the state share of revenue was commuted into cash on the basis of a price prescribed by the state and 37.5 per cent of the produce was collected in kind.[36]

Out of 37 *kharwars* and 8 *traks* commuted into cash, 22 *kharwars* and 8 *traks* were converted into money at the rate of 1.37 per *kharwar* and the remaining 15 *kharwars* at the rate of 1.25 per *kharwar*.[37]

But this system of assessment was applied to the *sarkasht* lands. However, on *paikasht* and *navabadee* lands, the rates of assessment were slightly less. There were two broad divisions of land in Kashmir—*sarkasht* and *paikasht*. Those lands which were under regular cultivation near the city were called *sarkasht* lands. The lands which were cultivated by the peasants living in other villages were known as *paikasht* lands.[38] Both *rabi* and *kharif* crops were assessed in the same manner. No separate method was adopted for cash crops like cotton, tobacco, oilseeds, etc. The *navabadee* lands were those which were newly brought under cultivation.[39]

This form of *batai* remained the most important and widely applied method of assessment in Kashmir. However, certain other methods of assessment were also experimented with from time to time. The *Akhbarat* of Mirza Saf-ud-Din furnishes us with detailed information on different methods of assessment tried at various stages.[40]

Mirza Saif-ud-Din says that the revenue officials were engaged day and night in preparing a register of assessment in 1846.[41] In that year, Devi Dutta, a Punjabi land revenue expert, was directed by Maharaja Gulab Singh to find out ways and means to increase the assessment as much as possible.[42] Unfortunately, the records do not mention the exact nature of the method of assessment worked out by Devi Dutta of Punjab. All that is known is that he assessed the lands according to *kanals* and the revenue was to be collected from town to town and from village to village at a uniform rate of Rs. 2 a *kanal.* A *kharwar* of land was to be assessed at the rate of Rs. 120.[43]

Again in the winter of 1848, Maharaja Gulab Singh deputed Moulvi Mazhar Ali and Dewan Kanahya to assess the produce of paddy in Pargaha Ich-Nagam.[44]

In 1851 Maharaja Gulab Singh's officials completed the assessment operations in Handwara tahsils and fixed in every two *kharwars* of produce of half *traks* as the share of the cultivator and one *kharwar* and five *traks* as the share of the state and the remaining one *trak* was to meet the demands of the secretariat staff and contingencies. The peasant's share of total produce was further reduced under this assessment system to only 29.5 per cent.[45]

For administrative purposes, in 1852, Maharaja Gulab Singh got the whole of the valley divided into seven divisions and tried to follow the British code, but owing to the incompetent and illiterate Kashmiri revenue staff, this could not succeed. It was in 1846 that the greater part of Punjab came under British land revenue administration. Summary settlements were made and regular settlements commenced. The immediate relief that the regular settlements provided to the people of Punjab appear to have convinced Gulab Singh of the necessity of introducing the British code.[46]

In 1853, some relaxation was made in the assessment of waste lands which had been brought under cultivation. It was agreed that the state would take two-fifths of the produce from these lands, leaving the remaining three-fifths to the peasants.[47] In 1854 the work of assessment and collection was entrusted to military commanding officers. The assigning of the work of assessment and collection to military commanding officers must have taken place most probably because a large amount of revenue was in arrears.[48]

Notwithstanding these experiments, the method of assessment prevalent for most of the time in Kashmir during the reign of Maharaja

Gulab Singh remained *batai,* which he inherited from the Sikh regime. Wingate, who made preliminary arrangements for the land settlement in Kashmir, says that during Maharaja Gulab Singh's time, Sikh procedure was followed and the same is borne out by G.R. Taylor, who visited Kashmir during Maharaja Gulab Singh's period.[49]

During Maharaja Gulab Singh's time, several attempts were made to introduce a satisfactory method of assessment but all of them proved unsatisfactory and also lacked a definite purpose. The failure of these attempts can most probably be attributed to the arbitrariness followed by the revenue staff which met their timely needs.[50]

In 1857 Maharaja Ranbir Singh took over the administration of Kashmir. He annually farmed out the circles of villages to contractors called *kardars.*[51] In 1859, the valley of Kashmir was divided by these *kardars* into several fiscal units for the purpose of assessment, and each unit of land under their charge was further subdivided into three parts. In the two lower parts, rice was allowed to be grown, and in the third part, no rice cultivation was allowed. The third part was generally that portion of land which was on high altitude so the *kardars* did not permit rice cultivation because it could prove a failure.[52] Expectedly, every *kardar* was bent upon collecting as much as he could. Thus, the *kardar* dictated not only the method of assessment of his choice to the peasants but also the crops to be sown by them. In 1860 in the *pargana* divisions of Kashmir expectedly, every *kardar* was bent upon collecting as much as he could. Thus, the *kardar* dictated not only the method of assessment of his choice to the peasants but also the crop to be sown by them. In 1860, the *pargana* divisions of Kashmir were liquidated and they were merged into the *chakladari* system. The *chakla* was usually larger than the *pargana,* and its revenue was formed out of *chakladars.* In this *chakladari* system of assessment, in 1860, the *pargana* divisions of Kashmir were liquidated and they were merged into the *chakladari* system. The *chakla* was usually larger than the *pargana,* and its revenue was formed out of *chakladars.* In this *chakladari* system of assessment, the average collections of five years prior to the *chakladari* system were taken as the basis. This system of assessment was first introduced for three years; later in 1863, at the completion of the first term, the assessment was renewed. Some slight enhancement in revenues took place at this time. Unfortunately, because of the natural calamities that took place during the years 1864-5, the assessment could not be carried out. Again, from 1867, the system worked for some time by demanding one half of *rabi* crops and 60 per cent of the *kharif* harvest as the state share. This system was seriously opposed by the people from Vihu, Nagam, and Shopian *parganas*, and finally the system fell into disuse because the peasants were not ready to carry on with the system of lease for quite some time.[53]

However, by 1869 the practice of contracting with *muqaddams* or the peasants gradually established itself in place of farming out of lands to the *kardars*.[54] In 1873, Maharaja Ranbir Singh got the village contracts divided into *assamiwar khewats*. The *khewat* or village cash assessment, was made and the state share was taken either in cash or in kind from each man. R.K. Parmu without any evidence states that in 1870 Maharaja Ranbir Singh introduced a settlement department on the Punjab pattern. But this fact is not borne out by any of the Persian or English records of the time. Even Wingate who presented the preliminary report for carrying out elaborate land settlement does not corroborate this statement of Parmu.[55] In 1876 fresh contracts were made either with the *muqaddams* or *kardars* or peasants and two *traks* per *kharwar* were added to the previous assessment.[56] In 1877, due to famine, new contracts could not be carried out and the state share was collected in kind only. This system lasted up to 1880, when a new *assamiwar khewat,* or village cash assessment, was made, which was based upon the previous years' collections.[57] These were estimated in cash but the amount was payable in cash or in kind as it suited the peasants.[58] This method of *assamiwar khewat* was arrived at by taking the collections of two years, i.e. AD 1877 and 1878, and an average was worked out. Then gross produce was recorded and one half was taken as the government share; to this, 25 per cent was added as *trakee.* The collection was made on the *kharwar* of 16 *traks* and after that the whole quantity was converted into 15 *trak kharwars*. The 15 *trak kharwar* was called *kachha kharwar* and was used for all crops which included cotton, oilseeds, saffron and other crops, if any.[59] The quantity obtained thus in these *kharwars* was commuted into money at standard prices which were used for commutation.[60]

In 1882 another method of assessment known as *izadboli* or

auctioning of the villages was introduced.[61] Under this system, the *mustajir*, or bidder, paid a lumpsum money to the state and then exacted as much as he could from a village without taking into consideration the condition of the crop. Sometimes the *mustajir* absconded without making payment to the state. As a result, it was immediately discontinued after registering huge losses to the state revenues and the *khewat* system was resumed.[62]

Table 3.2 shows how the *assamiwar khewat* was arrived at by taking one village as a sample.[63]

TABLE 3.2: GROSS PRODUCED AND THE STATE SHARE OF EXTRACTION

Crop	*Gross produce 16 trak kharwars*			*State share after adding trakee*			*Govt. share calculated in rupees*		
	kh.	*tr*	*ch.*	*kh.*	*tr.*	*ch.*	*Rs.*	*a.*	*pies*
Serson	0	6	0	0	3	0	1	8	0
Oilseed	4	13	0	2	6	2	21	11	6
Cotton	3	0	1½	1	8	2	21	3	3
Mong	1	5	1	0	12	1½	6	1	9
Paddy	1,438	0	0	897	1	0	1,844	2	0

Source: A. Ningate, *Preliminary Report of Land Settlement in Kashmir*, Lahore, 1889, p. 54, Jammu Archives.

From Table 3.2 it becomes clear that the rates of assessment varied from crop to crop. For sarson the rate, including *trakee*, is one-half; while for paddy it is more than one-half.

Under the *khewat* system, each *tahsildar* was informed of the amount he was expected to contribute to the total. He converted this quantity into cash on the basis of Rs. 2 per *kharwar*, and out of every one rupee, 10 annas were fixed as his share.[64] Then he would give instructions for the collection of so many *kharwars* from each village, and the total collections would come to the amount that was fixed at the headquarters or sometimes more than that. However, the *khewat* system of assessment was no more oppressive than the *batai* system. In the *khewat* system, the peasant was certain to retain at least a small portion of the produce. But there was constant opposition to the *khewat* system of assessment from revenue officials who preferred the collection of revenue in kind. The influential *lambardars* and other revenue officials who stood between the state and the peasants tried their best to prevent any permanent settlement because it went against their interest. Even the officials like Dewan Lachman Dass, the Dewan of Kashmir Province, himself a big landlord, wanted the crop settlement to continue, because the *khewat* system reduced their share in produce,[65] while as in *batai* they were able to collect in prerequisites more than what they had been getting under *khewat*.[66] The *batai* system also provided them with the opportunity to appoint subordinate staff, i.e. the watchman, the weigh man, etc.,[67] who could help them in all their fraudulent practices.

Soon after the accession of Maharaja Pratap Singh, a land settlement was commenced. Since 1869, Maharaja Ranbir Singh had been negotiating with the British government for the services of two ICS land experts. It was on 15 January 1887, that A. Wingate joined as the Settlement Officer of Kashmir to carry out a detailed land settlement.[68] Wingate made preliminary arrangements for the land settlement in 1887, but it was not until 1889 that a regular land settlement commenced. The work which had been entrusted to Wingate was taken over by W.R. Lawrence. A settlement department was established. A code of rules and forms (*athavatri*) were given to the peasants for settlement purposes. A system for accounts was arranged and details of the subordinate staff to be locally entertained were decided upon with the help of Colonel Wace, then Financial Commissioner of the Punjab, and later Narsing Dass, who was appointed as the Assistant Settlement Officer.[69]

Laurence, after careful examination of the situation and after looking into the previous methods of assessment, was in favour of assessing the land revenue demand in cash only, but under various pulls and pressures, he had to agree to a settlement whereby the land revenue was made payable both in cash and in kind.[70]

In the initial stages, Lawrence also had to surmount many difficulties in introducing this kind of land settlement. In one of the assessment reports, he says, 'It is my duty to purpose such an assessment as can be paid and, as a rule, in fixing the assessment I take into consideration the amount which has been paid by the village on account of *girftani*, i.e. arrears.' If *tahsildars* are allowed to collect the *girftani* in addition to the proposed revenue, then they will again get opportunities of peculation, the work done by the settlement will become useless, and the state revenue will again fall into hopeless confusion. 'I should remark here that several villages were not ready to accept the new assessment. They preferred the old fictitious system so that they might be regarded as broken villages, i.e. *Skim-ul-Hal,* because, with the consultations of tahsil officials, a large suspension of revenue was made annually. As a result, the officials pocketed half the amount thus suspended. So I had to face much difficulty in getting the HEW assessment accepted.'[71]

Lawrence took pains to convince the peasants that the new assessment was fair, and nothing beyond the amount assessed was to be taken from them. Lawrence states in his settlement records that the revenue of these areas, which had been assigned by the state to individuals as *jagirs*, was not subject to the settlement establishment for the new methods of assessment. So far as the *muafi* lands were concerned they were looked after by the *dharmarth* Department. The records do not mention whether it was the state or the *jagirdars* who denied access to these records of *jagir* holdings and did not permit Lawrence to impose the new assessment on them. Second, since the *muafi* lands were dealt with by the *Dharmarth* Department they should have dealt with those *muafis* only which had been granted to the Hindus and their religious institutions. It is not clear who looked after the Muslim *muafi* lands. However, *muafi* lands continued in possession of *muafidars* even up to present and there is a good number of *pattas* in some of the Brahmin and Sayyid families substantiating this fact.[72]

According to the new land settlement, the assessment was fixed for 14 years, and due thought was given to all the problems that the peasants had to face in carrying out cultivation. The basis of the assessment was that the net produce of each village was estimated, taking into account the crops grown in different villages. The main features of the settlement introduced by Lawrence were:

1. The state demand was fixed for 14 years.
2. Payment in cash was substituted for payment in kind. (But records show that payment in kind continued for some time.)
3. Use of force to collect revenue was abolished.
4. Begar system was to be abolished gradually.

5. Occupancy rights were conferred on cultivators in undisputed lands.
6. Permanent but non-hereditary rights were granted to those who accepted the first assessment.
7. All land was valued on the basis of produce previous collection and irrigation.
8. *Rasum* and other exactions were abolished.
9. Rents and liabilities of cultivators were defined.

The state share of the revenue was fixed at 30 per cent of the gross produce.[73]

Land Revenue Demand

From the time of the Mughals 1586 until 1887, when regular land settlement began, the demand for land revenue was erratic and arbitrary. During the Mughal period, after the conquest of Kashmir, Akbar ordered that one-half land revenue should be demanded, but the revenue collectors charged at times as much as two-thirds.[74]

Under the Afghans, the state demand for the chief cereal was very high. They charged five-eighths for rice, though all vegetables and other minor cereals remained untaxed. The state demand worked to 60-65 per cent. [75]

The Sikh rulers of Kashmir fixed the state's share of produce generally at one-half, but over and above this demand, the state also levied certain cesses such as *mandri*, *tambul*, *rasum-i-daftar*, and *nazrana*. *Mandri* meant a share from temples and other religious endowments; *tambul* was marriage levy; *rasum-i-daftar* was a share from the peasants for clerical staff of the revenue department. It is not certain whether or not the *numbardar* or village headman actually distributed the whole amount among the clerks; *nazrana* was levied four times a year on festive occasions.[76] In addition to these, the *trakee* system of the Afghans was continued by the Sikhs. The Sikhs charged four *traks* per *kharwar* of paddy from the peasants.[77] Only *pirs* and urban *pandits* paid this cess at the rate of two *traks* per *kharwar*. Here it appears that the Sikhs did not dispense with the system they had inherited from the Afghans.[78] An addition of Rs. 1-9-0 per cent was charged by the state. Besides this half a *trak* was charged per *kharwar*, which was shared by the *patwari* and the *qanongo*.[79]

Cesses were also levied on cash and *kimiti* crop as well as on sheep and goats. The cash crops included cotton, tobacco, saffron, while the *kimti* (commercial) crops included oilseeds, honey, and fruits like almonds and walnuts.[80] These cesses charged over and above the land revenue to such an extent as to leave very little with the peasant. The total burden of taxes levied on the peasant amounted to 60 per cent of their gross produce.[81]

Under Governor Mian Singh, who was considerate enough to abolish many cesses, the state share of produce was fixed at half of the produce. However, the same rate was demanded on pulses, tobacco, cotton, and red pepper. He also levied *trakee* at the rate of five *traks* though he later reduced it to four *traks* per *kharwar*.[82]

The last Sikh Governor of Kashmir maintained the same system, except that he granted a remission of two *traks* to peasants on *sirkasht* lands in exchange for increasing the area under cultivation.[83]

The magnitude of land revenue demand was little less severe under Maharaja Gulab Singh than it was under the Afghans and the Sikhs. Though the Sikh procedure was followed in general but some slight relaxation was made in favour of lands newly cultivated. A few large areas of land were lying waste. It seems that under Maharaja Gulab Singh much of the waste lands was reclaimed.[84] The state under Gulab Singh realized the land revenue in kind, theoretically at the rate of one-half of the produce. Maharaja Gulab Singh reduced the rate of *trakee* on *sirkasht* lands of the whole country to three *traks*. However, no concession was made on *paikasht* lands and *trakee* was levied at the rate of two *traks* as before.[85] Besides Maharaja Gulab Singh reduced the rate on cotton from Rs. 10 to 7.[86]

But this was hardly the end of the exactions. Under Maharaja Gulab Singh the state collected levies such as *kharch* and *abwab*, like *rasudat* (it was a tax on fruit trees, willows and vegetables according to the quantity produced. Generally it varied from Rs. 10 to 100 per village).[87] *Tilsiah chahar magz* (it was a separate tax on walnut trees. One rupee was charged for 2,500 walnuts),[88] *rusud-i-khah* (this cess was levied on straw at the rate of one anna per hundred *kharwars*),[89] *sur-i-dehee* (it was charged at the rate of one rupee for all small and big villages),[90] *dawga-i-daftar* (this cess amounted to Rs. 150 on the whole country),[91] *rusud shumag-khulbul* (it was levied at the rate of Rs. 2 per hundred *kharwars* of rice),[92] *sur-i-sudhee-jinsi* (this was charged at one *kharwar* per 100 *kharwars*),[93] *chungee* (it was deducted on account of toll at the rate of 4 *traks* per 100 *kharwars*),[94] *thandari* (the state used to levy 41/2 *seers* in every *kharwar* to meet the expenses of *hanjis* [boatmen] as a hire for transporting the collected revenue from villages to the city),[95] *musad-ah* (this cess was levied on account of seeds provided by the state to the peasants. The state did not advance the seeds to the peasants regularly but taxed them regularly. This cess was shared by the state with the *kardar* who would get one *seer* out of two *traks* levied per *kharwa*),[96] *khuskraza* (it was known as a tax of one's own choice for keeping revenue officials obliged and kind, which they never were, and was charged at the rate of Rs. 2 per head),[97] *boodkee* (the purpose of this cess is not known but it was charged at the rate of two *traks* per *kharwar*),[98] *sur-sudhee-nukdee* (it was levied at the rate of Rs. 1-9-0 per hundred *kharwars*),[99] *munwatee* (it was levied at the rate of 1.5 *seers* per *kharwar*),[100] *neem manwattee harkaree* (this cess was realized, for meeting the expenses of *harkar,* the state spy appointed for looking after the crops and amounted to one *seer* per *kharwar*),[101] *shiqdaree* (on account of *shiqdars* expenses [the watchman of crops]; 2 *seers* were deducted per *kharwar* of paddy),[102] *sazowuli* (this tax was collected at the rate of about 2 *seers* per *kharwar* of paddy for the *sazawul,* another revenue official),[103] *tehvildaree* (a tax levied for the *tehvildar* who was kept in-charge of the collected share and under whose guidance and supervision it was transported to the city; this tax was realized at the rate of 1.5 *seers* per *kharwar* for the expenses of the said official),[104] *khidmatgaree* (this cess was levied for meeting the expenses of the palace attendants and the subordinate staff of the revenue officials; this cess was demanded at the rate of 3 *seers* per *kharwar*),[105] *kardaree* (4 *seers* were deducted from every *kharwar* for the *kardar*),[106] *rusud-i-deodi* (this was a tax demanded from the revenue officials for the maintenance of the palace at the rate of Rs. 200 to 300; but these officials like the *kardars* and *thanedars,* expectedly charged this cess from the peasants),[107] *terazudari* (1.5 *seers* was levied per *kharwar* for the weignman),[108] *quanongoi* (one *trak* per *kharwar* was deducted for the *qanongo*),[109] *dolljinsi* (from 1846 another cess was levied on the Kashmir peasantry for maintenance of the sepoy regiments),[110] *bhat fund* (for improving the condition of the Bhat community of Jammu, a cess known as *bhat fund* was demanded from every Kashmiri),[111] *zaffran* (it was a tax on saffron for which the valley was famous; it was levied in addition to the usual state share),[112] *zari-chopan* (even the cattle wealth of the peasant was not spared; 2½ annas were collected for heads for sheep and goats), Wazir Ratnu, Governor of Kashmir during Gulab Singh's time, collected 80,000 heads of sheep and 16 *kharwars* of wool, although the total revenue fixed under this head was Rs. 70,000 only. (In 1863 the amount collected under this head was Rs. 80,000.)[113] *Sakh-shomari,*[114] *zari-i-murakab* (Mirza Saif-ud-Din, mentions it as *zar-i-nakhas.* He says that even horse keepers had to supply horses or ponnies as a tax. Here he refers to Shunga Kotwal who was extremely oppressive. When he entered the stables he could take away any number of horses he laid his hands on),[115] *zar-i-nikh,*[116] and *rasum-i-sabsi.* Though the vegetable growers were not charged for their produce but during Gulab Singh's time there is evidence to prove that even the vegetable growers and kitchen gardeners were not exempted from the network of taxation. Sultan Pahalwan, to whom the revenues of the vegetable lands were farmed out, paid the revenue of Rs. 1,200 annually.[117] Inspite of all these cesses and taxes, there was a large room for graft.

When Maharaja Ranbir Singh (1857-85) took over the administration, he decreed that peasants, traders, and all men of various professions who were under financial stress would be granted remission in arrears if they resumed their professions. But the magnitude of land revenue demand remained more or less the same.[118]

The state took three quarters of the cash crops and pulses.[119] With regard to the system of *trakee*, a slight relaxation was made. Instead of four only two *traks* were charged and this system lasted up to 1960. Urban *pandits* and *pirs* who had their *chaks* in different places in rural areas were charged only one *trak.*[120] After 1860 attempts were made to introduce cash assessment but in vain. The assessment became heavier and resulted in further depressing the position of the peasant. In 1870 *trakee* was reduced two *traks* but in 1872-3 it was again levied at the rate of five *traks* in some villages and in sortie at the rate of three *traks.*[121] In 1869 there was a slight reduction and again only two extra *traks* were levied instead of four.[122] But the whole system was so full of abuses that no significant improvement was registered in the state's finances or in the condition of the peasantry.

In 1875 the harvest was a poor one but the state still took two shares of the produce and left only one share for the peasant.[123] Next year in 1876 two *traks* per *kharwar* were again added to the assessment besides an aggregate cess which amounted to a *kharwar* and twelve *traks* per hundred *kharwars*.[124]

In 1877, bad weather added to excessive taxation. Assessment was delayed, and the peasants preferred to leave their crops to rot in their fields. As a result, trade also came to a standstill. Villages were deserted and people died of starvation.[125] This situation appears to have continued up to 1880. In 1880 under the *assamiwar khewat* the state share was made payable both in kind and cash.[126]

The state demand during Maharaja Pratap Singh's reign was made payable partly in cash and partly in kind as a result of the cash crop settlement introduced by W.R. Lawrence. The state reduced the land, revenue demand to 30 per cent of the gross produce.[127] However, in addition to it the *patwari* and *lambardari* cesses of 2 and 5 per cent respectively were levied on each individual assessment.[128] In 1890-1 the custom of exempting villages from land revenue belonging to influential persons was abolished.[129] Attempts were made to assess the newly broken up waste lands.[130] However, the heavy receipts from these lands continued to fill the pockets of *patwaris* and tahsil officials.[131]

Table 3.3 shows the land revenue demand and collection for some of the years. These figures have been collected from the administrative reports of the given years available in Srinagar, Jammu and National Archives of India.[132]

From Table 3.4 it becomes clear that during 1880-1 the gap between the amount demanded and actual collection was as usual; in 1882, for some strange reason which we cannot locate, the collection actually far exceeds the demand. From 1883, however, this gap grew significantly. It can possibly be attributed to the fraudulent revenue machinery, which collected the revenue in full but did not deposit it.

In 1891-2, it was laid down that collection should be made in cash on an extensive scale in the newly assessed tehsils. The unassessed

TABLE 3.3: AMOUNT OF LAND REVENUE DEMAND AND ACTUAL AMOUNT COLLECTED

(in Rs.)

Year	*Demand*	*Amount collected*
1888-9	29,56,222	n.a.
1889-90	31,72,977	n.a.
1890-1	31,78,731	n.a.
1891-2	31,87,812	n.a.
1892-3	35,78,000	15,08,946
1893-4	32,96,187	14,54,352
1894-5	35,72,413	15,32,262
1895-6	15,36,324	14,92,070

Source: Administrative Reports from 1888-1896 Collected from Jammu & Kashmir, National Archives of India.

tehsils continued to make payments in kind as before, according to an estimate made by *kardars* and provincial governors.[133] Attempts were made to check the mismanagement of grains received in land revenue. Steps were taken to recognize the grain department by placing it under the charge of the head treasurer Wazir Ratnu.[134] The rules were laid down regulating the receipt of the quality of food grains paid by *tehvildars* and putting a stop to thefts and illegal exactions.[135] But all these measures failed to meet the desired success due to the apathy of the governor and the dishonesty of his subordinate staff.[136]

Hence, in spite of all these measures, it was not until the second half of the twentieth century that a genuine effort was made to avoid confusion, secure confidence and attach peasants permanently to their holdings when a fair distribution of the produce between the state and the peasants took place. It was in 1950 that the Big Landed Estates Abolition Act was passed besides some other measures to provide relief to the peasants.[137]

Revenue Functionaries

The valley of Kashmir was divided into various *parganas* and *wazarats* from time to time for purposes of revenue administration. Maharaja

Gulab Singh in the beginning did not introduce any new system but allowed the valley to remain divided into different *parganas*, 36 in all.[138] After some time when he roughly estimated the fiscal condition of the valley he divided it into three main divisions and entrusted the administration of these three divisions to wazirs—Wazir Ratnu, Wazir Narayan Bhan, Wazir Kanhaya Singh and Pandit Raja Kak Dhar. The civil administration was handed over to Kanhaya Singh and the military administration to Wazir Ratnu.[139] However, they not only neglected to undertake steps to improve agricultural production and thereby ameliorate the condition of the peasantry but equally ignored the increasing corruption in the State's revenue department. *Kotwal* Kanhaya without looking into the conduct of some of the *kardars*, dismissed them and gave birth to serious difficulties. As a result he was supplanted by Shunga *kotwal* in early 1847.[140] Their effort to obtain the Maharaja's favour adversely effected even the existing revenue collection machinery. To quote Maharaja Gulab Singh, 'Owing to the activities of Wazir Ratnu, the administration of the valley became defective and the revenue was not collected satisfactorily with the result the entire administration was in a shambles.'[141]

This division of valley into three main units continued up to 1852 when again the valley was divided into seven main divisions. This time the administration was entrusted to:

1. Pandit Raja Kak Dhar,
2. Wazir Punoo,
3. Wazir Zorawroo,
4. Mian Amir Singh,
5. Munshi Trilok Chand,
6. Colonel Beji Singh, and
7. Janki Dass.[142]

All these above mentioned officials made the chief *jagirdars* of the valley responsible for the parent of revenue. The *jagirdars,* on their part, appointed *kardars* for the collection of revenue. However, the whole system of revenue became more complicated and workable only in the interest of corrupt revenue officials.[143]

Though there are scattered references in the records that Gulab

Singh appointed adequate revenue staff and established the department of *Dobjinsi* (department of revenue collection in kind), nothing appears to have been done which can be termed as definite. The other departments established by Maharaja Gulab Singh were those of *Daftar-i-Diwani* (the audit accounts department) and the *Daftar-i-Nizamat* (the land record office). [144]

During Maharaja Ranbir Singh's time the entire valley was divided into *wazarats* of *Shar-i-Khas*, Kamraj, Anantnag, Shopian and Pattan.[145] In 1880 this number of *wazarats* was further reduced to four by merging the *wazarat* of Shopian together with Anantnag *wazarat.*[146] Each *wazarat* contained a number of *tahsils* and was kept under the control of the *wazir wazarat.*[147] This division continued down to Maharaja Pratap Singh's time. The head of the revenue department was *Hakim-i-Ala,* or the governor of the Province. Under him, the executive control of the revenue department rested with *Diwam-i-Jins,* or the Revenue Commissioner. Maharaja Gulab Singh always appointed his relatives and friends to this post. During his regime, Mian Hattu Singh, Mian Ranbir Singh and Moti Singh of Poonch were appointed one after the other to this post.[148] Besides, the overall supervision of the revenue department his duties included transportation of grain to the public storehouses, its distribution at fixed rates, and the maintenance of its account, with the help of subordinate staff.[149]

Then there were the *wazirs* of the *wazarats.* The principal business of the *wazirs* was the realization of revenue. According to Charles Girdlestone, 'Wazir is the deputy commissioner of British territory, his charge being small, his authority more restricted and his duties less multifarious.'[150] He dealt with the revenue cases, the superintendence of roads, dispensaries, police and postal communication.[151]

For the purpose of administration, these *wazarats* were further divided into *tahsils* which were kept under the supervision and control of the *tahsildars.*[152]

Tahsildar: He generally fixed the yearly assessment of crops. It was upto the *tahsildar* and the establishment attached to him to take the final decision regarding the total produce of the village crop.[153] Evidently the avenues of graft open to him were enormous. He had under him a number of officials like the *naib-i-tahsildar*, the *thanedar*, the *kardar*, the *sazawul*, the *patwari*, the *muqaddam*, the *shiqdar*, the *lambardar*, the *harkar* and the *tarazudar*.[154]

Naib Tahsildar or *Naib-i-Zilla Sahib:* He was put in-charge of the *nayabat* (group of villages) where he exercised his revenue and administrative functions and maintaining the revenue records at the *Nayabat* level. In this work he was assisted by the *sadr daftri*, the *daftri* and the *khazanchi*.[155]

Thanedar: He was the chief official of the *pargana* who combined in himself both revenue and judicial authority. His duty was to look after the condition of the people in his jurisdiction and to report to the *tahsildar* from time to time.[156] Besides, he had the authority to decide the disputes that occurred among the peasants. He had under him 40 to 50 sepoys called *Nizamat Paltan* who assisted the revenue officials at the time of assessment and collection. He possessed the power to give minor punishments in cases of fraud and deceit.[157]

Kardar: In the revenue machinery of the Dogras, the *kardar* held a very important position. He had full authority for assessment and collection of the revenue. He used to superintend the crops before fixing the assessment. His establishment comprised the *parchanavis* (the record writer), the *tarazudar*, etc.[158] It was in fact the duty of the *kardar* to maintain the record of peasants holdings and to submit them for inspection yearly, but he appears to have done this job very rarely during the period of our study. Though their pay was included in the *trakee*, they used to charge an extra share for themselves at the time of harvesting.[159] These *kardars* used to demand *salamana* from the peasants individually on festive occasions like Dussehra and Nouroz (new years day).[160] In 1860 these were replaced by the *chakladars*.[161]

Sazawul: He was usually in-charge of ten villages and his duty was to supervise the work of the *shiqdar* (the watchmen of crops) and to report to the *kardar*.[162] To quote R. Thorp, 'It is said that he (*Sazawul*) commonly extorted money from the villagers.'[163]

Patwari: His duty was to keep a separate register wherein the entries of all *jagirdars* and the tenants under them were being entered; in every village there was a *patwari* or the village accountant.[164] There is reference in records to *mir patwari* also who was the head of seven *patwaris* and used to inspect their work.[165]

Tahildar: He was the official incharge of the storage of the paddy which was collected from the peasants as the state share. Second, it was his duty to make arrangement for the transportation of the procured paddy to the city.[166]

Muqaddam: He was the village headman. His duty was to keep an eye on thefts in the village. He also used to provide assistance to revenue officials during the period of collection.[167]

Shiqdar: A village could have anywhere between one and four *shiqdars*, depending upon its size. His duty was to watch the crops until the state collected her share. It is said that *shiqdars* extorted money from peasants by threatening to accuse them of stealing grain. According to Lawrence, the *shiqdar* received eight *kharwars* of *shali* (paddy) from village and took twelve *kharwars* from the state.[168]

Lambardar: He was the hereditary tax collector of villages and was responsible to *tahsildar* for the revenues of villages from which he collected. Besides the usual pay he retained 2 per cent of the revenue from the collected sum as reward for his labour. He was also responsible for making necessary arrangements for such officials and visitors as entered the village.[169] E.F. Knight says, 'it is he who too often receives the pay of these (coolies working under him), and how much he retains as his *dastur* and how much he hands over to them is difficult to say. In some villages he is not much below the position of a village scapegoat and a powerful lambardar would never render the state its due.'[170]

Harkar: He was a police constable. In every twenty villages there used to be a *harkar's* house. All the male members of his family were *harkars*. His duty was to secretly report the transactions going on in the village. He also gave directions to the other revenue officials and to the *doom* community (the watchmen of the villages). This *doom* community was generally fed by peasants of the villages. It may be noted that after many land reforms the *doom* community is still landless and works as agricultural labourers and watchmen in villages.[171]

Tarazudar: He was simply a weigh man and was always in attendance upon the *kardar* and *tehildar* when the state commenced collection of revenue. He was the chief, though lowly, instrument of exploiting the peasants on behalf of the state, for it was he who overweighed the produce to extract a large revenue. There is evidence that sometimes instead of a *kharwar* of sixteen *traks* he took from the peasants a *kharwar* of 18 *traks*.[172]

Illustration 3.1 shows how even at the time of threshing paddy all the officials and moneylenders landed there to extract arbitrarily their share of peasants' produce leaving very little or nothing for his own sustenance.

All these officials appear to have been paid by the state meagerly in kind and that too irregularly. This may have justified, in their eyes, their resort to corruption, though they were not the only ones steeped in corruption.

Working of the Land Revenue Administration

The land revenue demand and the taxes and cesses actually realized were far in excess of those that finally went into the treasury. The whole work of realization was in the hands of a machinery that was corrupt from top to bottom. It was very rarely that the incidence of *trakee* was actually reduced to two *traks* per *kharwar*. As though this was not enough, there were revenue payments and other *abwabs* to be paid to the state officials. Lawrence wrongly remarks that only air and water were exempt from taxation.[173]

As a result of the heavy demand of the revenue officials, the peasants were often forced to give up their cultivation and, consequently, payments fell into arrears. In 1851, Rs. 30 lakh were in arrears because most of the peasants had left their lands due to extortionate demands of the state and its officials. There was a deficit of Rs. 5 lakh, Maharaja Gulab Singh advised Dewan Jowala Sahai and Mian Ranbir Singh, his son, to whom the revenue administration had been entrusted to make the remission of Rs. 3,000 to 4,000 so that this concession could ensure the collection of some more amount of revenue.[174]

In 1852 the revenue which was in arrears was assigned to the army as their salary but the condition of the country was so bad that they could not collect more than Rs. 8,000.[175] The financial statements of Munshi Trilok Chand indicate that in 1852 the arrears amounted to Rs. 15,00,000 with a revenue deficit of Rs. 23,00,000.[176]

Illustration 3.1: Painting shows the presence of moneylender in thrashing floor even before the paddy was fully thrashed. *Source:* Harbans Mukhia's Collection of Pictures from India Office Library, London.

In 1857, when Ranbir Singh became Maharaja of Kashmir, an order was issued that all arrears if not paid by Nouroz (the new year's day) may be charged interest at the rate of Rs. 2 in cash and two *kharwars* of rice for every hundred per month. On 1 August 1857, this entry was published.[177]

In some villages the *chakladar* applied and got land which he afterwards abandoned. The village in which the land was situated was held responsible for payment of the revenue assessed on *chak*.[178] The peasants of the village neither took possession nor paid the land revenue but the amount was entered against them as arrears. There are various such instances in records both Persian and English.[179] Often the *mustajirs* made a bid for a village and offered a large increase on fixed revenue. In these circumstances both the peasant and the state had to suffer losses but between the two the peasant appears to have suffered more than the State. He was left with as little as was perhaps sufficient to keep his body and soul together.

Table 3.4 shows how the collections had fallen during Maharaja Ranbir Singh's time in 252 villages for which information is available owing to the contraction of the arable.[180]

TABLE 3.4: DECREASE IN COLLECTION OF REVENUE UNDER RANBIR SINGH

Year	*Actual demand for 252 villages*	*Actual collection from 252 villages*
1880	3,88,613	3,45,031
1881	3,96,274	3,51,547
1882	4,23,440	6,53,673
1883	4,64,200	2,44,389
1884	4,69,701	4,09,562
1885	4,36,872	1,97,841
1886	4,41,357	2,31,550
1887	4,41,403	2,48,369
TOTAL	34,61,904	23,81,962

Source: A. Wingate, Preliminary Report of Land Settlement in Jammu and Kashmir, 1888-1889, Jammu Archives [unpublished report].

They remained in a village for three or four years of good harvest, embezzled large sums of money out of the amount the villagers had paid as revenue and subsequently these were entered as arrears against the village.[181]

The *mustajir* collected half the crops and sometimes even more, as his share. In some villages arrears of revenue outstanding against the peasants were added to the fraudulent accounts of the *patwaris* and *lambardars* whose records were seldom straight and reliable. Wingate states on the basis of his information that the *patwari* carried three editions of his records and all on scraps of paper. One of them was meant for himself, one for the *tahsildar* and the third one for the villagers.[182]

In Pargana Dansu the peasants had paid the revenue in full for the period 1880-8; still Rs. 31,747 was shown as outstanding against them.[183] The *mustajir* had paid the state demand in full but at the same time succeeded in taking from the treasury an equivalent sum in the form of an agricultural loan on behalf of the peasants. In practice, however, it was never advanced to the peasants, but was only entered against each name on paper, sold in the market, or sold at a high rate to their relatives. Even if a peasant did not take loan for agricultural operations the state officials demanded one *trak* as an item of *kharch* for the agricultural loan. Generally, 2 *seers* were demanded as tax for agricultural loan by the state from each *kharwar* of produce.[184]

The system of management of water chestnuts (*singhara*) called *Mahal-i-Singhara* was no less oppressive. The peasants could hardly afford bare subsistence. It was customary to lease out surfaces covered by water chestnuts called Mahal through public action. The highest bidder got the lease and entered into a contract with the government. He employed labourers from the surrounding areas where the picking, extraction, and collection of *singharas* had become a profession through generations. The labourers, after spending weeks together in water, handed over the *singharas* to the contractor and, in return, got very little wages, or sometimes nothing at all.[185]

No less oppressive was the system practiced for the collection of saffron. Saffron fields were not assessed like the other cash crops, where the state share was collected straightaway in cash. Instead, the share due to the State amounting to more than half the produce was auctioned to a contractor who himself arranged to collect the share at harvest time. The peasant who worked for the contractor got a handful of salt in return. The state share was nominally half the crop but the villagers asserted that after satisfying the corrupt officials only a quarter of the crop remained with them.[186]

It is clear from this that the revenue system in Kashmir had continued to corrode the entire agrarian economy in the region; perhaps payment in fixed cash assessments had mitigated the impact of corruption to some extent. In fact Lachman Dass is an extreme example of what must have been a type among the high officials. Payment of land revenue in cash was the one form that could have benefited the peasant; but then the officials such as Lachman Dass were dead against such assessment.[187]

Last came the taxes on handicrafts. These too were exacted with severity and oppression. But the burden of these taxes most likely fell on those peasants who tried to supplement their income from land with income from wool manufacturing, wood work, and embroidery. Mostly the peasants of small holdings engaged themselves in handicrafts during winter months.[188] Very likely some of the revenues collected from this source must have stuck of official's fingers. There was, of course, hardly any person who could escape the network of the taxation system. Men of all professions were taxed. In 1847 the sum of Rs. 120 was fixed as a professional tax on shoe makers. Though they made a representation to Sahaz Rain Trisal, the Assistant of Raja Kak Dharbut, nothing was done to relieve them from this burden. Instead each of them was handed over a chit showing the amount that he had to pay.

According to the revenue schedule of 1848, Rs. 8,500 was collected from butchers as professional tax. The boatmen were charged Rs. 6 to 8 per adult and Rs. 4 to 6 per minor. All non-agriculturists had to pay *baj* and *kharaj*.[189] To quote Vigne, 'Even the grave digger and the dancing girls were, not exempted from taxation.'[190]

Hence, until the commencement of the land settlement and fixed cash assessment of revenue in the year 1889, Kashmir was never subject to a regular fixed assessment. These peasants regained uncertainty about their future liabilities. From the time of Maharaja Gulab Singh, the crude system of fluctuating assessments, not regulated by any recognized theory of principle but mainly depending on the will of the *kardars*, the provincial governors and their subordinate staff, was in vogue to the great detriment of the cultivating class. Every year, the provincial governors enhanced their demand, irrespective of the paying capacity of the peasants, simply to show a thriving budget estimate.[191] As a result of this, large balances accrued against the peasants and the state officials pocketed heavy illegal exactions.

The arbitrariness of the entire administrative machinery was exemplified by Gulab Singh's own conduct, who could be approached irrespective of time and place. All one had to do was to hold a rupee in his hand and cry, 'Maharaja, arzhai', tender the rupee, and obtain the Maharaja's decision spontaneously.[192] No method was allowed to establish itself whereby default or fraud in the revenue machinery could be prevented.[193]

Needless to say, such arbitrariness of the revenue collection machinery combined with the ruthlessness of revenue officials kept the peasants at the lowest scale of existence and often drove many of them out of it into the dismal hands of death. Even this tragic circumstance could have been mitigated if the revenue thus collected had been invested for technological or economic advancement of state leading to a brighter future. However, given the character of ruling class and state officials, conspicuous consumption, more than economic betterment of the region, were their chief concern. As such, even during the second half of the nineteenth-century Kashmir still remained locked up in medieval economy and polity when the rest of India was making the first hesitant advances towards modernity.

NOTES

1. Lawrence, *Valley of Kashmir*, p. 196. P.N.K. Bamzai, *Political and Cultural History of Kashmir*, pp. 473-8. H.M. Lawrence, *Transfer of Govt. to Maharaja Gulub Singh*, Section C, 28th January 1848, file nos. 33-44, Jammu Archives. Dewan Kripa Ram, *Gulab-nama*, English tr. by S.S. Chark, Delhi, 1977, pp. 290-315. A.P. Nicholson, *Scraps of Paper, India's Broken Treaties, Her Princes and Her Problems*, The Whitefriars Press Ltd., London 1930, pp. 88-90. See also S.M. Latif, *History of Punjab*, Delhi, 1964, pp. 440-54. K.M. Panikkar, *Gulab Singh, The founder of Jammu & Kashmir State*, Martin Hopkinson, London, 1930, pp. 104-5.

2. Irfan Habib, *Agrarian System of Mughal India*, Oxford University Press, Bombay, 1963, pp. 215-16. Kripa Ram, *Majmu-i-Report (1872-73)* (Urdu), pp. 17-18.
3. Ramju Dhar, *Kaifiyat Intizam-i-mulk-i-Kashmir* (Per. Ms.), Research Department Library, Srinagar, ff. 2-3. It was compiled around 1883. One of its chapters is exclusively devoted to the description of the Afghan rule in Kashmir. A detailed account is available particularly on a variety of subjects such as taxes and cesses collected, magnitude of the state-share, method of assessment, mode of revenue collection, land revenue functionaries and their relations with the peasantry, *ijaradari* system, etc. A reference to the total revenue of Kashmir during the reign of Muhammad Azim Khan, is not far to seek. See also Dewan Kripa Ram, *Gulzar-i-Kashmir*, pp. 256-7. Dewan Kripa Ram, *Majmu-i-Report* (1872-73), Urdu, pp. 17-18. Dewan Anant Ram, *Report Majmu-i-Jammu-va-Kashmir and Tibet (1873-75)* (Urdu), Jammu Archives, pp. 32-3.
4. H.M. Lawrence, *Transfer of Govt. to Maharaja Gulab Singh*, Section C, 28th January 1848, file nos. 33-44, Jammu Archives. *Diary of P.S. Melvill, Punjab Government Records*, Lahore, 1911-15, vol. VI, pp. 191-7, 217. Maharaja Ranjit Singh's rise to prominence had been at the expense of the declining Afghan Empire (As already discussed at length in Chapter 1). In 1799, while Zaman Shah was king of Afghanistan, Ranjit Singh acquired Lahore and the title of Raja from him. In 1802, he conquered Amritsar and chaos and confusion in the royal circles of Kashmir motivated him to strategize its conquest. After six years of famine, the Kashmiri treasury was empty and Afghan ruler Azim Khan believed that one of his revenue collectors, namely, Pandit Birbal Dhar was guilty of embezzlement and placed him under arrest while the accounts were audited. When he was released on bail, Birbal Dhar fled from the valley with the help of two Muslim landowners, Malik Kamdar and Malik Namdar. Birbal left for Jammu where he was received by one of Ranjit Singh's favourite vassals, Gulab Singh. Birbal Dhar's message to Ranjit Singh was of support against Afghans but Ranjit Singh now was more cautious about giving help and kept Pandit Birbal's son Raja Kak as a hostage until his mission was completed. Ranjit Singh also sought the support of other local rulers on the way from Bhimber to Shopian to ensure a safe passage to his army. An advanced column left Lahore on 26 February 1819 under the command of Ranjit Singh's heir, Prince Kharrak Singh. Ranjit himself left two months later and set up a base camp at Wazirabad. D.C. Sharma, *Kashmir Agriculture and Land Revenue*

System Under the Sikh Rule 1819-49, Rima Publishing House, Jammu, 1986, p. 54. Dewan Krishan Lal, *Account of Kashmir Foreign and Secret Correspondence*, 31 March 1848, No. 68, NAI. Ramju Dhar, op. cit., ff. 4-6. Indu Banga, *Agrarian System of the Sikhs*, Delhi, 1978, p. 88, n.2.

5. Amarnath, *Zafarnama-i-Ranjit Singh*, Punjabi trans. by Janak Singh, (ed. Kirpal Singh), Patiala, 1983, p. 163; Giani Gian Singh, *Tawarikh Guru Khalsa*, Vol. II, p. 360.
6. Amarnath, *Zafarnama-i-Ranjit Singh*, p. 176.
7. Munshi Hukam Chand, *Tarikh-i-Multan*, Lahore, 1884, p. 47, cited in Fauja Singh, *Some Aspects of State and Society Under Maharaja Ranjit Singh*, New Delhi, 1982, p. 181.
8. E.B. Steedman, *Report on the Revised Settlement of the Jhang District of the Punjab 1874-1880*, Lahore, 1882, p. 39; *District Gazetteer of Jhang, 1883-4*, p. 36. Ali-ud-Din Mufti, *Ibratnama*, vol. II, Lahore, 1961 (Punjabi trans.), p. 516; According to Giani Gian Singh, *Tawarikh Guru Khalsa*, vol. II, p. 341; Sukhdyal was got the *ijara* of Jhang in Rs. 1,60,000.
9. Steedman, *Report on the Revised Settlement of the Jhang District of the Punjab 1874-80*, p. 39; *District Gazetter of Jhang, 1883-4*, p. 36.
10. Sohan Lal Suri, *Umdat-ut-Tawarikh*, Daftar II, English trans. by V.S. Suri, Amritsar, 2002, p. 228.
11. Ibid., p. 264.
12. Hari Ram, *History of Sikhs*, p. 350.
13. Amarnath, *Zafarnama-i-Ranjit Singh*, p. 80.
14. Sohan Lal Suri, *Umdat-ut-Tawarikh*, Daftar II, p. 308.
15. Ibid., Daftar III, pt. I, p. 23; pt. II, p. 233, Diary of L. Browning, Punjab Government Records (1847-9), Vol. IV, Allahabad, 1911, pp. 406, 408-9; Diary of A. Cocks, Punjab Government Records (1847-9), vol. IV, Allahabad, 1911, p. 44.
16. Sohan Lal Suri, *Umdat-ut-Tawarikh*, Daftar III, pt. II, p. 138.
17. Murray, *History of the Punjab*, vol. II, Patiala, 1989 (2nd edn.), p. 151.
18. Shahamat Ali, *The Sikhs and the Afghans*, p. 19.
19. Cunningham, *A History of the Sikhs from the Origin of the Nation to the Battles of the Sutlej*, New Delhi: Low Price Publications, 1977, p. 387.
20. Shahamat Ali, *The Sikhs and Afghans*, p. 22.
21. Cunningham, *A History of the Sikhs*, p. 384.
22. Ibid.
23. Ibid. Appendix XXXVIII.
24. Moorcroft William and Trebeck George, *Travels in the Himalayan Provinces of Hindustan and the Punjab: In Ladakh and Kashmir, in*

Peshawar, Kabul, Kunduz and Bokhara from 1819 to 1825, New Delhi: Asian Educational Servives, 1989, pp. 123-4.

25. Dhar Ramjo, *Keefat-i-Intizam-i -Mulki Kashmir* (Persian Ms., Sri Pratap Singh Library, Srinagar, Jammu and Kashmir), ff.43.
مالیات در دوران حکومت سکھ ها در مقابل خاندان افغانان خیلی اندک بود.در حقیقت عصر سکهان یک دوره امنیت در کشور محسوب می شد.مردم تحت این حکومت آسائش خاطر به دست آوردند و مردم به راحتی و امنیت زندگی می کردند.
'The taxation under the Sikh rule as compared to the Afghans was very light. Sikh rule was a rule of justice. People heaved a sigh of relief. They lived their lives in peace and harmony.'
26. Lepel Griffin, *Ranjit Singh*, New Delhi, 2002 (rpt.), p. 145.
27. Hari Ram Gupta, *History of Sikhs,* p. 505. During Maharaja Ranjit Singh's reign no regular budget was prepared. The money received from different sources was ear-marked for specific purposes and Government roughly knew the expected income and expenditure. The main heads of the expenditure were the royal household, the administration, the army, the pious and charitable organizations, works for the improvement of agriculture, public works and rewards, gifts and presents bestowed by the Maharaja. The expenses of administration comprised salaries of public servants including Ministers, Governors and other officers and personnel of the Government. Despite various changes, financial administration remained in an unsatisfactory condition till the last years of Ranjit Singh's reign. He was personally responsible to a large extent for this state of affairs because he trusted his memory for remembering complicated accounts of his expenditure and for many years periodically allowed the rough memoranda of those who were responsible to him to be destroyed. In the absence of records, embezzlement became quite easy, not to speak of lower-grade officials, men at the top took advantage of the situation. Diwan Sawan Mal surpassed everyone in trade or in any speculation in which rapid fortune could be made. A.C. Banerjee, *The Khalsa Raj*, New Delhi: Abhinav Publications, 1985, p. 136.
28. Mirza Saif-ud-Din, *Akhbarat,* vol. I, ff. 1-4. Lawrence, op. cit., Section C, 28 January 1848, file nos. 33-44, Jammu Archives. John Lawrence, *Condition of Kashmir Secret Committee*, 31 March 1848, nos. 66-77, NAI. Kripa Ram, *Majmu-i-Report* (*1872-73*), p. 18. Wingate, op. cit., p. 54.
29. H.M. Lawrence, op. cit., Section C, 28 January 1848, file nos. 33-44, Jammu Archives. Nicholson's letter containing information of Kashmir Foreign and Sec. C. December 1846, No. 1266, NAI. See also R.K.

Parmu, *History of Dogra Rule in Kashmir*, typed Ms. pp. 29-31. Dr. Parmu (Director, History Unit, Jammu and Kashmir) was kind enough to permit me to go through his manuscript of Dogra history before sending it to press.

30. Badan Powell, *Land System of British India*, Delhi 1967, 3 vols., vol. I, pp. 274-5. But the system of *batai* applied to Kashmir apears dissimilar from these systems of *batai*.
31. Lawrence, op. cit., Section C, 28 January 1848, file nos. 33-4, Jammu Archives.
32. Kripa Ram, *Gulzar-i- Kashmir*, pp. 256-7. Ramju Dhar, op. cit., ff. 2-3. See also *Diary of R.G. Taylor*, Punjab Government Records (1847-9), vol. VI, p. 80.
33. Lawrence, op. cit., Capt. Cunnigham's Memo, *Foreign Deptt.* Sec. C, 31 March 1848, nos. 66-77.
34. Lawrence, op. cit., Section C, 28 January 1848, file nos. 33-44, Jammu Archives.
35. Lawrence, op. cit.
36. Ibid. The market rates were determined by the state.
37. Ibid.
38. Ibid. See also R.K. Parmu, *History of Dogra Rule in Kashmir*, Ms. p. 31.
39. Ibid.
40. Mirza Saif-ud-Din, *Akhbarat*, vol. I, f. 45.
41. Ibid., vol. II, f. 87.
42. Ibid., vol. II, ff. 87-8.
43. Ibid., vol. II, ff. 3 and 46.
44. Ibid.
45. Ibid., vol. V, ff. 60-2.
46. Ibid., ff. 60-2. Baden Powell, *Land Systems of British India*, pp. 532-4.
47. F. Younghusband, *Kashmir*, pp. 173-4.
48. See Mirza, op. cit., vol. IV, f. 114, also vol. VIII, ff. 8, 62.
49. A. Wingate, op. cit., pp. 54-5. *Diary of G.R. Taylor*, Punjab Govt. Records (1847-49), pp. 24-5.
50. *Diary of G.R. Taylor*, Punjab Govt. Records (1847-49), Vol. VI, pp. 24-5.
51. Wingate, op. cit., pp. 54-60. Ramju Dhar, op. cit., ff. 8-9.
52. Lawrence, *Valley*, p. 402. See Dewan Anant Ram, *Majmu-i-Report of Jammu Kashmir and Tibet (1873-75)*, pp. 30-4. P.N.K. Bamzai, *History of Kashmir, Political, Social and Cultural*, Delhi, 1962, p. 688.
53. H.L.P. Wynne, *Report on Kashmir*, 1872, For Pol. A, file nos. 343-9. January 1873, NAI.

54. Wingate, op. cit., pp. 54-5.
55. Ibid., R.K. Parmu, *History of Dogra Rule in Kashmir*, Ms., p. 85.
56. Ibid.
57. Dewan Kripa Ram, *Majum-i-Report*, pp. 21-3. Lawrence, *Valley*, pp. 402-5.
58. Wingate, op. cit., pp. 54-5.
59. Ibid.
60. Ibid.
61. W.R. Lawrence, *Report on the Position of Cultivating Classes, in Kashmir*, Foreign Deptt. Sec. E., Feb. 1890. NAI. See also Lawrence, *Valley*, p. 408. Bamzai, op. cit., p. 689.
62. Ibid. See Dewan Kripa Ram, *Majmu-i-Report of Jammu-va-Kashmir and Tibet*, pp. 21-3.
63. Wingate, op. cit., pp. 54-5.
64. Lawrence, *Report on the Position of Cultivating Classes in Kashmir*, Foreign Deptt. Sec. E, February 1890, NAI.
65. See *Petition of Dewan Lachman Dass against the Cash Settlement, Chief Secretariate Pol. and Gen. Deptt.*, file no. 2 of 1896, Jammu Archives.
66. Ibid. See also a Wingate, op. cit., pp. 55-6.
67. *Petition of Dewan Gachman Dass against the Cash Settlement, Chief Sec.* op. cit., for details see Lawrence, *Valley*, pp. 404-80.
68. *Foreign Deptt. See. E. October 1886,* file no. 235-300 NAI. S.R. Temple, *India in 1880*, London, 1881, pp. 213-15, Lawrence, *Valley*, p. 407. A.P. Nicholson, *Scrapes of Paper, India's Broken Treaties Her Princes Her Problem*, pp. 96-109. Younghusband, op. cit., pp. 190-3.
69. Pandit Bhag Ram, *Administration Report of Jammu and Kashmir State* (*1889-90*), Jammu, 1891, pp. 22-3.
70. Ibid., Lawrence, *Valley*, p. 407. See *Petition of Dewan Lachman Dass against the Cash Settlement 1896*, op. cit.
71. W.R. Lawrence, *Assessment Report of Ich-Nagam Tehsil of Kashmir*, Jammu, 1891, pp. 7-9.
72. Ibid.
73. D.K. Palit, *Jammu and Kashmir Arms*, p. 91.
74. Irfan Habib, *Agrarian System*, pp. 192-3.
75. Kripa Ram, *Majmu-i-Report* (1872-73), pp. 17-18. Kripa Ram, *Gulzar-i-Kashmir*, pp. 256-7. See also *Gazetteer of Kashmir and Ladakh*, p. 105.
76. Lawrence, op, cit., *Diary of R.G. Taylor*, Punjab Govt. Records (1847-49), Vol. VII, pp. 24-5, see also *Gazetteer of Kashmir and Ladakh*, p. 105.

77. Wingate, op. cit., p. 54. Lawrence, op. cit., *Gazetteer of Kashmir and Ladakh*, p. 105.
78. Hassan, op. cit., vol. II, p. 657. *Gazetteer of Kashmir and Ladakh*, p. 105.
79. Mir Ahmad, *Dastural-Amal-i-Kashmir*, Ms. M. 829, Punjab State Archives, Patiala, pt. II, f. 59.
80. Ganeshi Lal, *Sayahatnama*, pp. 37-8. *Diary of R.G. Taylor* (1847-49), *Punjab Govt. Records*, Vol. VI, pp. 24-6.
81. *Gazetteer of Kashmir and Ladakh*, p. 105.
82. H.M. Lawrence, op. cit., Kripa Ram, *Gulzar-i-Kashmir*, pp. 256-7. See also Dewan Amamath, *Zafarnama-i-Ranjit Singh* (Persian Ms.), ed. by Sita Ram Kohli, Lahore, 1928, pp. 226-7. Lawrence, *Valley*, p. 200. *Tarikh-i-Kalan*, ff. 204-6.
83. S.N. Koul, *Kashmir Economics*, p. 58.
84. Wingate, op. cit., p. 54.
85. Mirza, op. cit., vol. I, f. 26. Lawrence, op. cit.
86. H.M. Lawrence, op. cit. See also S.K. Koul, *Kashmir Economics*, pp. 58-9.
87. H.M. Lawrence, *Transfer of Government to Maharaja Gulab Singh*, 28 January 1848, Section C, file nos. 33-44, Jammu Archives.
88. Ibid.
89. Ibid.
90. Ibid.
91. Ibid.
92. Ibid.
93. Ibid.
94. Ibid.
95. Ibid.
96. Ibid.
97. Mirza Saif-ud-Din, *Akhbarat*, vol. I, ff. 22-23.
98. Lawrence, op. cit.
99. Ibid., (purpose unknown).
100. Ibid.
101. Ibid. See also Ramju Dhar, op. cit., f. 3b. (Persian Ms.)
102. Ibid.
103. Ibid.
104. Ibid.
105. Ibid. Mirza, op. cit., vol. II, ff. 3-5.
106. Ibid.

107. See also Mirza, op. cit., vol. II, ff. 3, 5-7, 9, 11.
108. Ibid. Vol. II, f. 5.
109. Ibid. See Mirza, op. cit., vol. I. See also Ramju Dhar, op. cit., f. 3.
110. Mirza, op. cit., vol. II, ff. 6, 7-9.
111. Ibid.
112. *Foreign and Political A. July*, 1863, nos. 73-5, NAI.
113. Ibid.
114. It was a tax on buffaloes. Ibid.
115. It was a tax on ponies. Ibid. Mirza, op. cit., vol. I, f. 3.
116. It was a tax on marriage. Ibid.
117. Ibid., vol. II, f. 7.
118. Mirza, op. cit., vol. X, f. 316.
119. Lawrence, *Valley*, pp. 303-4.
120. Wingate, op. cit., pp. 54-7. *Majmu-i-Report of Jammu-va-Kashmir and Tibet* (1873-5), pp. 33-5, *Gazetteer of Kashmir and Ladakh*, pp. 105-6.
121. Dewan Kripa Ram, *Majmu-i-Report* (1872-73), pp. 18-20. Wingate, op. cit., p. 55. S.N. Koul, op. cit., p. 59.
122. *Majmu-i-Report of Jammu-va-Kashmir and Tibet*, pp. 30-3.
123. *Majmu-i-Report Jammu-va-Kashmir and Tibet* (1873-5), pp. 32-4. Wingate, op. cit., p. 55. Lawrence, *Valley*, p. 403. *Gazetteer of Kashmir and Ladakh*, p. 108.
124. Wingate, op. cit., p. 55.
125. Ibid., pp. 54-6. Lawrence, *Valley*, pp. 446-7.
126. Dhar, op. cit., ff. 8-10, Koul, op. cit., pp. 58-9.
127. Palit, op. cit., p. 91.
128. Lawrence, *Report on Position of Cultivating Classes in Kashmir*, op. cit., Younghusband, op. cit., p. 197. R.G. Wreford, *Census*, 1941, vol. XXII, p. 15. Koul, op. cit., p. 59.
129. Pandit Bhag Ram, *Annual Administration Report of Jammu and Kashmir*, (1890-91), Jammu, 1892, p. 42.
130. Ibid.
131. Ibid.
132. These figures have been collected from the administrative reports of the given years available in Srinagar, Jammu and National Archives of India.
133. Pandit Bhag Ram, *Annual Administration Report of Jammu and Kashmir* (1891-92), pp. 34-9.
134. Ibid., pp. 34-40.
135. Ibid.
136. Ibid.

137. See *Big Landed Estates Abolition Act*, 1950.
138. Mirza, op. cit., vol. I, f. 27.
139. Ibid., vol. I, ff. 26, 29.
140. Ibid., f. 29.
141. Ibid., f. 26.
142. Ibid., f. 5.
143. Mirza, op. cit., vol. I, f. 3; vol. II, f. 175. See also Ibid., vol. VII, ff. 130-3.
144. S.N. Koul, *Kashmir Economics*, p. 228.
145. Charles Girdlestone, *Memorandum on Kashmir*, pp. 7-8. C.E. Bates, *Gazetteer*, pp. 95-7. M.D. Fauq, *Rahnumai-Kashmir*, pp. 72-3.
146. Fauq, ibid., pp. 72-3.
147. Girdlestone, op. cit., pp. 8-9.
148. Mirza, op. cit., vol. VII, ff. 120, 123 and 126.
149. Ibid.
150. Girdlestone, op. cit., pp. 8-10.
151. Ibid., pp. 8-10.
152. R.G. Wreford, *Census*, 1941, vol. p. 14; Bamzai, op. cit., pp. 687-9.
153. Girdlestone, op, cit., pp. 8-10.
154. Ibid., Banzai, op, cit., pp. 687-9.
155. Girdlestone, op. cit., pp. 8-10.
156. Bamzai, op. cit., pp. 687-9; R.K. Parmu, *History of Dogra Rule*, Ms. p. 72.
157. Lawrence, *Valley*.
158. R. Thorp, *Kashmir Misgovernment*, p. 2.
159. Ibid., F. Henry, op. cit., 1882; C.E. Bates, *Gazetteer*, pp. 95-7; Bamzai, op. cit., p. 689.
160. Lawrence, op. cit., Section C, 28 January 1848, file nos. 33-44.
161. Mirza, op. cit., vol. I. f. 106. H.L.P. Wynne, *Report on Kashmir*, For Pol. A. file nos. 343-9, Jan. 1873, NAI.
162. Bates, *Gazetteer*, pp. 95-7; Girdlestone, op. cit., pp. 8-10.
163. Girdlestone, op. cit., pp. 8-10. Thorp, op. cit., p. 4.
164. Ibid., p. 3. *Gazetteer of Kashmir and Ladakh*, p. 110, Bamzai, op. cit., vol. I, f. 27.
165. Mirza, op. cit., vol. I, f. 27.
166. Lawrence, op. cit., Section C, 28 January 1848, file nos. 33-44, Jammu Archives.
167. *Gazetteer of Kashmir and Ladakh*, p. 110. Bates, *Gazetteer*, op. cit., p. 97, R. Thorp, op. cit., p. 3.
168. *Lawrence, Valley*, p. 402.

169. Maharaja Pratap Singh, *Diary of an Inspection Tour to Gilgit*, p. 22, Jammu Archives.
170. E.F. Knight, *Where Three Empires Meet*, London, 1905, pp. 64-5.
171. Lawrence, op. cit., Section C, 28 January 1848, file nos. 33-44.
172. Ibid., Thorp, op. cit., p. 4.
173. Lawrence, *Valley*, p. 417.
174. Mirza, op. cit., vol. IV, f. 114. See also ibid., vol. V, f. 8.
175. Ibid., vol. V, f. 8.
176. Ibid., f. 62.
177. Ibid., vol. VI, f. 6.
178. W.R. Lawrence, *Assessment Report of Ich-Nagam Tehsil*, 1891, Jammu Archives, pp. 2-6.
179. Ibid., *Karvai-jalsa Council Aliya Jammu-va-Kashmir, 1898-1908*, State Archives, Srinagar.
180. Wingate, op. cit., pp. 60-7.
181. Ibid.
182. Wingate, op. cit., p. 49.
183. Lawrence, *Assessment Report of Ich-Nagam Tehsil*, op. cit., pp. 5-6.
184. Lawrence, *Transfer of Government to Maharaja Gulab Singh of Kashmir*, Secton D, 28 January 1848, Section C, file nos. 33-4, Jammu Archives. *Majmu-i-Report Jammu-va-Kashmir and Tibet* (*1877-78*), pp. 21-2. Lawrence, op. cit.
185. Ibid. Mirza, op. cit., vol. I, ff. 7-9. See also M.M.A. Beg, *Zara-i-lslahat*, pp. 45-7.
186. Ramju Dhar, *Kaifaiyat-Intizam Mulk-i-Kashmir*, f. 3. Dewan Anant Ram, op. cit., pp. 105-6. *A Note on Jammu and Kashmir State*, p. 29.
187. Dewan Lachman Dass, *Petition Against Cash Assessment*, 1896, op. cit., Jammu Archives.
188. Girdlestone, op. cit., pp. 30-2.
189. Mirza, op. cit., vol. I, ff. 62-4. See also vol. II, f. 7, 27 and vol. VII, f. 64 of the same.
190. Vigne, *Travels*, vol. I, p. 119. This statement is supported by Mirza Saif-ud-Din also. See Mirza, op. cit., vol. II, ff. 40-4.
191. Pandit Bhag Ram, *Annual Administration Report of Jammu and Kashmir*, 1889-90.
192. Mirza, op. cit., vol. VII, ff. 55, 57, 175-6. See K.M. Panikkar, *Maharaja Gulub Singh; The Founder of Jammu and Kashmir State*, p. 149.
193. Girdlestone, op. cit., pp. 3-8. *Imperial Gazetteer of India*, vol. XV, pp. 136-7. Wreford, *Census*, 1941, vol. p. 14. See also O.N. Dhar, 'Land Reforms in Kashmir', *Indian Affairs Record*, vol. III, no. 4, Delhi, 1954, p. 475. Lawrence, *Valley*, pp. 418-21.

CHAPTER 4

Land Revenue Assignees and Other Grantees

The system of assigning large and small tracts of land and its revenue to members of various social classes appears to have been in vogue in ancient Kashmir. This fact of giving land assignments for various services is also mentioned in connection with the office of *Akspatala*. According to one view, the *Akspatala* is mentioned as a court of justice but the more authentic version would make us believe that *Akspatala* was the office of the accountant general where the land grants or *Pathopadhyaya* were executed by the recorder of official documents. Such large assignments were made in Kashmir during the reign of Suganda (AD 904-6), Chakravarman (AD 936-7) and Ananta (AD 1028-62).[1]

During the Sultanate period (1320-1586) there are frequent references to show that land was assigned to *ummra* and *ulema* who assisted the king in carrying out the administration.[2] *Nayakas* are referred to as the military chiefs who held lands for maintaining retainers to safeguard against foreign invasions.[3]

In the wake of its conquest by Emperor Akbar in AD 1586, Kashmir was made a Sarkar of the Province of Kabul. The lands of Kashmir were assessed for higher rates than had hitherto been charged and the whole land was declared to be Crown land. Soon after the conquest of Kashmir, Akbar found that the inquiry into the sources and the amount of revenues of Kashmir caused deep discontent to Mirza Yusuf Khan, the first Governor of Kashmir. He made it dear to the Emperor that there was every possibility of revolt. Yusuf Khan considered himself incapable of resolving this question and resigned.[4]

The Afghan rulers of Kashmir (1753-1818) followed the Mughal system and no material change seems to have been effected except for the fact that they replaced the Mughal governors and officials of administration with counterparts appointed by them. It is stated that every governor used to appoint his own secretarial staff, which is explained from the Kashmiri proverb '*Yelih Yamsund Subahdar Telih Tamsundpeshkar*', i.e. Every Subahdar had his own secretarial staff.[5]

From 1819 to 1846, Kashmir remained part of the Sikh Empire. Ranjit Singh is said to have resumed all assignments of land granted by his predecessors and reduced the landed aristocracy to a low ebb. Here this resumption should not be taken to mean that Ranjit Singh wanted to invent a new device of payment for rendering of military or non-military service; he merely wanted to plant his own landed aristocracy there. He was assisted by his own Dewans to whom he gave *jagirs* in return of civil or military assistance. One *jagir* assignment worth Rs. 6,000 was assigned to Dewan Dinanath in the Kashmir Province.[6] To quote Moorcraft, 'When the country came into the hands of Sikhs, Ranjit Singh made a general resumption and ousted the possessors of grantees of land of every class, thus summarily reducing thousands, who had long lived in comfort to a state of absolute destitution.'[7]

During the period of our study the revenue assignees and grantees of Kashmir were the *jagirdars*, the *muafidars* and the *chakdars*. Under the Mughals when the reorganization of administration took place, this system of land assignments to nobles and courtiers became a regular part of Mughal administration and thereby came to be organized into a well developed system. The *muafidars* were such grantees as received rent-free lands from the state. Such grants were made even in ancient times mainly to religious personages and charitable institutions. The *chakdari* system is of very recent origin. The state in a bid to restore waste lands assigned sizeable tracts of lands to the state officials for their services.[8] These officials extracted illegal fee on each valuation they made, where the bribe decided the genuineness of peasant claim and where inefficient supervision would allow the crop to rot in the fields. One can't deny that there might have been occasions when both the parties wilfully shared the loss of crop but some instances are there which are proof of the state's inefficient administration resulting in the miseries of the peasants. In 1877, a good quantity of crop was destroyed by the heavy rainfall, the peasants by hook or crook managed to save a part which they harvested and stacked. The appraising party delayed the task of distribution and in the meanwhile there was a heavy snowfall which destroyed the heaped crop resulting in scarcity and ultimately paved the way for the great famine of 1878-80.[9] The state also suffered in the crop sharing due to the dependence on a number of officials for carrying out this method and the more officials connected with the revenue collection more were the chances of misappropriation. Although it proved to be irksome for both the parties yet it continued to be the chief method of assessment during Gulab Singh's time. If his biographer is to be believed, 'Ghulab Singh was very well aware that the *batia* is irrelevant, immune to fraud and expensive and collection in cash is easy and beneficial. Still, this procedure was not abandoned due to the smooth functioning of grain procurement policy.'

The existing procedure of revenue collection witnessed change during Ranbir Singh's time (the successor of Gulab Singh). In 1859 villages were formed out to contractors called as *kardars*. There was a shift in the position of *kardars* from mere revenue collectors to revenue farmers. These *kardars* divided the land into three belts. Rice was allowed to be grown only in the lower and middle belts because on high altitudes rice cultivation was not profitable.[10] Thus the *kardar* not only dictated the method of assessment to the peasant but also thrust upon him the crop to be sown.[11] While collecting revenue, the *kardars* adopted coercive measures and arranged the cultivation of estates on the bases of the *nafre* system. To the *nafre* (each unit consisting of three adult members of a family) were given 4 acres of irrigated land, to *nim nafre* (man and his wife) were given 2 acres of land and the *pau nafre* (a bachelor) were given 1½ acres of land. This system was put under the supervision of a *shikdar,* one for each threshing-floor. Over the *shakdar* was an official known as *sazawal.* During the harvesting season a regiment consisting of 7,429 soldiers known as *nizamat paltan* was sent in to the villages for the collection of revenue. This system lasted till 1860 and peasants had not only to pay the government share but also to fill the pockets of the *nizamat paltan* and other corrupt revenue officials. The peasant continued to live a miserable life as before. In 1860, with the assistance of Diwan Kripa Ram, the *chakladari* system was introduced by creating new circles called *chaklas*. Its important feature was that instead of division of actual produce, the base taken was the average *hasil* of previous five years.[12] The system failed because the *chakladars* acted as a sort of speculating contractors and robbed the state as well as the cultivators.[13] On the other hand, cash settlement was introduced by Dewan Kripa Ram in Jammu and the duty of revenue collection was entrusted on the *tahsildars* in place of the *kardar*. The whole agreement between the villages and State was carried out only after the ratification of the concerned village headman.

Jagirdars: The contemporary estimates do not figure out the exact number of *jagirdars* nor the actual amount of land that they held. After taking charge of Kashmir, Gulab Singh made investigations into the *jagirs* which had been granted by his predecessors.[14] In order to have effective control over the civil and military administration of Kashmir Maharaja Gulab Singh resumed some of the *jagirs*.[15] However, serious opposition came from various quarters, like Hazara and Muzaffarabad, and from other hill chiefs. Finally, Maharaja Gulab Singh came to the conclusion, after negotiating with the British authorities at Lahore, that the resumed *jagirs* and *muafis* should all be released to restore peace in Kashmir.[16] Hence a policy of reconciliation was followed and *jagirs* were released and granted to *jagirdars* for rendering military and civil services. The military service was rendered by the three Bomba Rajas belonging to Kathai, Dupatta and Muzaffarabad. They were asked to pay a revenue of Rs. 9,000 annually and had to maintain 5,000 armed retainers.[17] The Khakha chief of Buniar, Chikar, Kotli, Dhana, and Uri had to maintain 7,000 armed troops and pay Rs. 4,14,000 as annual revenue. For supplementing the military requirements of the Maharaja of Kashmir, there were seven regiments of artillery. The total number of regiments was 600 of all ranks, three regiments of infantry with 1,000 *sawars*. Besides this regular and irregular army, an army of 2,500 persons armed with firelocks and swords was provided by tributary chiefs.[18]

The leading *jagirdars* rendering civil service to Maharaja Gulab Singh were:[19]

1. Pandit Kamal Bhan (Chief Record Keeper)
2. Munshi Trilok Chand (Chief Treasurer)
3. Hakim Azim (Chief Physician)
4. Lachman Pandit Dhar (Governor of Kashmir)
5. Wazir Ratnu (Kotwal)
6. Ganesha (Chief Tosh Khana)

Besides these the *jagirdars* of Maharaja included Wazir Punoo, Wazir Zorawroo and Raja Kak Dhar.[20]

Every *jagirdar* had certain villages wholly or partially assigned to him as *jagir*. Besides the people who were in active service of the Maharaja there were a few who were considered to be loyal to the Maharaja and enjoyed *jagir* holdings, as a sign of loyalty. These people used to maintain retainers. These loyal *jagirdars* were given *mukararee* or cash grants also for the maintenance of the retainers. These loyal *jagirdars* of Dogra rulers were known as *double tazimi sardars*. Though these *double tazimi sardars* were not bound to maintain retainers for the king but being the confidants of the Maharaja, maintained these retainers out of courtesy. No decision could be taken without seeking their opinion on administrative matters. None of the *patta* or records state the number of retainers which were maintained by the *jagirdars* and *double tazimi sardars*.[21] They used to get the revenue of these *jagir* villages directly. Usually the *jagirdar* took away 75 per cent of the produce and left the remaining 25 per cent to the *zamindar*. Significantly, the term *zamindar* in Kashmir has invariably been used to denote the tiller of the soil whether he had his own land or was absolutely landless. The *zamindar* has a special connotation in medieval Indian parlance where he held superior rights in land. There is always a possibility of this term being misconstrued in the context of Kashmir.

We came across a number of references both in Persian and English records where it has been used to refer to the tiller of soil and him alone.[22] The *jagir* assignments included not only land taxes but also customs and market, duties, forest revenues and judicial fines. The *farman* is in possession of Pt. S.L. Dhar, Dalgate Boulevard Road, Srinagar. Shri Dhar has a huge collection of more than 25 documents which are mostly in the form of *bia-namas*, letters, *farmans* and orders dealing mostly with the grant and release of *jagirs*. I am extremely grateful to him for letting me consult this *farman* and some other documents.[23] These *jagirdars* exacted the payment not in the form of agricultural commodities alone but also of forest, cottage industry products, animals, etc. Here it is of interest to note that if a small river passed through the *jagir* lands, the peasants cultivating these lands had to provide fish to the *jagirdar* irrespective of whether the river bred fish or not.[24] The absence of a well developed administrative and judicial system gave an ample opportunity to *jagirdars* for tapping non-agricultural sources of revenue.[25]

Legislative and judicial remedies were provided only in the last quarter of the nineteenth century. In *jagir* lands, a *jagirdar* could exact a grazing fee on the cattle in the same manner in which he recovered the land revenue. Within his *jagir*, the right of the landholder dying heirless, instead of escheating to the state, devolved on the *jagirdar*. Some of the *jagirs* were assigned on a hereditary basis. [26] Apart from this, the state lands given on rent entitled him to receive the rent. Besides the income from water mills within his *jagir* also accrued to him.[27] He also had the power to exercise his choice in appointing the village headman.[28] Generally speaking, the *jagirdar* enjoyed higher prospects than were indicated in the *patta* granted to him. Even in the event of crop failure *jagirdars* appear never to have allowed appropriate remissions to the peasants. Ordinarily, a *jagirdar* could appropriate an income which was several times higher than the salary pertaining to his position. They preferred land assignments to cash salaries because the land assignments were subject to various arbitrary exactions unlike the fixed cash salaries. No doubt the agricultural rents were paid only once but there were other customary payments made to the *jagirdar* on different festivals, etc.[29] The chief *jagirdars* responsible for revenue appointed their own *kardars* in their *jagirs* to collect the revenue and to administer the *pargana*. The *Dastur-al Amal* of Miya Singh states that in the year AD 1847, all *jagirs* were in the grip of *kardars*, the assessors of revenue and sepoys were despatched to villages for the security of revenue. This was an ancient practice. We have evidence to prove that the military force of *Ekangas* was attached to the *Akspatala* (office where *pattas* or documents regarding the grant of land *Pattapodhyaya* were executed). Likewise, during the Dogra period, the *Daftar-i-Nizamat* (office dealing with land revenue and its administration) had under its control the military force called *nizamat paltan* which closely corresponds to that of *Ekangas.*[30] These *jagirdars* were allowed considerable latitude in their treatment of the peasantry. In 1873 Ryotwari Settlement was introduced in order to check the influence of the *chakladars* and other revenue functionaries. The State used the *patwari* papers which contained the records of each man's *abi* and *dry* land approximately. The state fixed the taxes wholly in cash and calculated after ascertaining the amount of grain that a *zamindar* had paid to the state.[31] If Hassan Khoyhami is to be believed, the *ryatwari* settlement was introduced to provide a sort of relief to the cultivators from the earlier lease system.[32] The settlement of revenue in cash for three years opened many advantageous doors for the peasant as he now became aware regarding the future tax liabilities. The direct dealing with cultivators eliminated the role of revenue officials which in turn decreased the chances of misappropriation. These officials who lived on perquisites throughout ages halted the efforts of this system.[33] However, the system too suffered from the ambiguities as the earlier ones. The rates fixed on the villages varied greatly. Further, the rates imposed on the villages were three times more than the demand imposed by the Punjab Government. Further, the headman emerged as an authoritative figure making the cultivators to move on his orders.[34] However, the efforts of the *ryotwari* settlement were nullified by the great famine of 1877-8 which put the whole state into confusion and new contracts could not carried out.[35]

In 1880 an assessment on the villages was made, known as *assamivar khewat* on the basis of average collections of past three years.[36] It was a revised form of the earlier one but different. Under this system the village was fixed as the unit of assessment instead of cultivator's holding.[37] *Hakim-i-Ala* had the authority to determine how much he would take in cash and how much in kind. This settlement of demand in cash and kind was known as *mujwaza* system.[38] This system was full of drawbacks as peasants deposited the state share in both cash and kind. In this regard, the revenue officials manipulated the system by depositing cash with the state treasury and kept the kind for themselves which was shown as *baqi* (arrears) against the cultivators.[39] These *baqi* got accumulated year after year and were entered in the revenue register. Wingate also talked about this system in disparaging terms.[40] Although the system was abandoned by 1882, yet it was followed in some areas until the Land Revenue Settlement was introduced by the British. In 1882, the state introduced *izzad boli*, which means the system of auctioning villages.[41] The bid for the villages in auction was given by the speculating bidders called as the *mustajirs* who used to speculate about the year's crop. When the year's produce was not good, the speculative bidders extracted maximum from the cultivators and absconded without depositing even a single rupee to the Government treasury. Thus the entire burden of arrears came on the cultivators. These *mustajirs* defrauded the state and robbed the peasants. The state registered huge loss of revenues and therefore was immediately discontinued.[42]

Thus it is clear that the revenue system under the Dogra rulers was ill-organized and there was a total absence of a regular fixed assessment. One system followed another but each one was faulty and oppressive in nature. The peasants were always uncertain of their future liabilities. The existence of crude system of assessment which was not regulated by any recognized theory but dependent upon the will of the *kardars* proved to be a source of great torment for the cultivating class. According to Wingate, the system of assessment and collection was haphazard and complicated. Francis Younghusband described that the system of assessment in Kashmir was exceedingly complicated and fulfilled the interests of corrupt officials as the demand of revenue was twice that of British India. The provincial governors used to enhance the demand every year without seeing the paying capacity of the peasant.

During the Dogra period, the peasants of the *jagir* lands appear to have lost all interest in cultivation. At times, they were forced by the sepoys to carry on cultivation because their negligence must have resulted in the fall of state revenue. In 1852, 300 sepoys were despatched to the *jagir* of Pandit Raja Kak Dhar, 400 to the *jagir* of Wazir Punoo, 30 to that of Wazir Zorawroo, 12 to the *jagir* of Munshi Trilok Chand and 40 to the *jagir* of Mian Amir Singh to make the peasants work on their lands from morning till evening.[43]

During Maharaja Pratap Singh's rule, a committee was appointed to look into *jagirs* and *muafi* lands. The committee, instead of giving relief to the peasants from the burden of land aristocracy, strengthened the exploitative structure by introducing a new class of landholders who also held *pattas* and therefore came to be known as *pattadars*.[44] These *pattadars* were persons who enjoyed *jagirs* below Rs. 3,000.[45]

This type of *pattadar*, who was only an assignee of revenue and had no proprietary rights, used to recover the rent in kind as a result of some special privileges granted to him.[46] Besides these privileges the *pattadars* were given the right to recover all arrears of *jagir* money from the peasants as arrears of land revenue. The *pattadars* mostly rendered civil services.

However, under this *jagir* system the peasant was not only exposed to the land revenue demand but was subjected to innumerable legal and illegal exactions. Besides, the ususal land revenue demand these *jagirdars* levied a number of cesses like *nehri*. This cess was realized at the rate of one *pai* for every *kharwar*, i.e. 2 maunds and was realized to defrag expenses of feeding the *jagirdar* during his stay in the village for the purpose of collection. Levy of cesses in and reassessment of *jagirs* in the state and validity of *pattas* granted[47] *maswarichamyar* (this was levied at the rate of 3 *pais* for each holding for the payment of men who supplied firewood and fodder to the *jagirdar* and performed other services for him),[48] *maswaridom* (this was levied for Doom for keeping strict watch on the harvest of the *jagirdars*),[49] *nazar-sayeer* (was levied during the *kharif* harvest from 4 annas to Rs. 4 for the horses maintained by the *jagirdar*, if any),[50] *banor* (was realized at the rate of 4 annas to Re. 1 during the *rabi* season),[51] *kama* (the rate of the realization of this cess varied from place to place. It was realized from 4 annas to Rs. 28).[52] *Hari-nazrana* (was levied from 4 annas to Rs. 6 during *kharif* season),[53] *thakur* (was levied at the rate of one *topa* for each *gumao* as an indication of *haq-i-milkiat*, which practically they never possessed,[54] *khalna* (purpose of this cess is not clear from the documents but it was realized at the rate of two *topas* for each *gumao*),[55] *malba* (was realized with the intention of defraying miscellaneous expenses of the village at the rate of one *topa* for each *gumao*, however, this cess did not benefit the *jagirdar* in any way),[56] *nanwan* (was levied at the rate of two *topas* for each *gumao*),[57] *muqadami* (was realized for *muqaddams* to whom the *jagirdar* paid only one *topa* though he realized three *topas* for each *gumao*),[58] *jhuwar* (was levied on account of wages for the carriers engaged by the *jagirdar* for carrying the produce to his own place at the rate of one-fourth of a *topa*),[59] *sunhar* (was levied for meeting the expenses of the goldsmith, the *jagirdar* levied a separate cess at the rate of one-fourth of a *topa*),[60] *begaree* (the *jagirdar* paid nothing to *begarees* (the forced labourers) though he ostensibly realized two *topas* for each *gumao*),[61] *batwal* (one *topa* on each *gumao* was realized for the maintenance of the *batwal* who was the personal *chowkidar* of the *jagirdar*),[62] *jogi* (*jagirdar* realized half a *topa* from each *gumao* for persons who were supposed to have power of preventing hailstorms).[63] *Chowkidari* (was levied for the payment to *chowkidars*, whom *jagirdars*, however, paid nothing. It was realized half a *topa* for each *gumao*),[64] *zohar* (was levied on account of payment made by *jagirdar* to ironsmiths and carpenters in the service of the *jagirdar* irrespective of whether he paid them anything or not),[65] and *tarkhan* (in addition to all these cesses, 4 annas were annually deducted from the peasants as *nazarsayer*, etc.).[66] These cesses were recovered by the *jagirdar* before the distribution of crop.

Hence though the *jagirdari* system rendered military and non-military assistance in several capacities to the state under the Dograss, it generally tended towards accentuating social injustices in course of time. Few and far between were the occasions when *jagirs* were bestowed for military services. The fact is that the impact of the British necessitated the reorganization of armed forces of the state. The proximity of the British power in the neighbouring Punjab after 1846 made it very necessary for the state and its ruler to reorganize the entire army.[67] The system of maintenance of retainers was progressively abandoned in favour of regular and well-trained armies by the state. Army personnel were now paid salaries from the state exchequer.

Some of the *jagirs* were still in existence until recently. These were those of Thakur Kartar Singh of Jammu, Pandit Premnath Dhar of Karan Nagar, Raja Sahib Pandit Sham Sunder Lal Dhar, Raja Rajwali Khan of Zachaldar and Khawaja (Peer) Salam Shah of Jamia Masjid, Srinagar.[68] Since the *jagirdari* system was loosing its importance and the number of *jagirs* was on the wane, little care was taken to maintain regular records of *jagirs* and *jagirdars* and their doings in the *jagirs*. Even during the last years of Dogra rule, it was reported that *jagirdari mujawaza* was extracted from 56 villages of the Kulgam *tahsil*. The collection in kind at a limited scale also continued in the Khalsa tracts through the scheme of food control.

Table 4.1 exhibits the land revenue generated by the state from 1885 to 1947.[69]

TABLE 4.1: LAND REVENUE FOR THE YEARS 1890 TO 1941

Year	*Revenue in Rupees*
1890-1	34,69,631
1895-6	35,73,259
1900-1	38,77,960
1905-6	38,90,717
1910-11	45,40,725
1915-16	43,77,712
1920-1	40,39,367
1925-6	49,72,762
1930-1	45,60,016
1935-6	52,60,434
1940-1	52,77,867

Source: Annual Administrative Reports for the Years from 1890-1941, Jammu & Kashmir Archives.

During the reign of Maharaja Pratap Singh (1885-1925), the state army came to be reorganized on modern lines. The British Government of India loaned senior army officers to train and discipline the state armed forces, and the British top brass were frequently appointed to lead the state forces.

Since British interest and influence in the northern reaches of India had grown to such large proportions in the later part of nineteenth century, British officers and men had involved in undertakings which would otherwise have been solely the officers of Jammu and Kashmir State and reciprocally J&K forces more and more frequently framed a part of British endeavours....[70]

Obviously the practice of basing the better disciplined and modernized army on an outdated exploitative institution of *jagirdari* must have looked absurd. Moreover, the rulers of the State themselves would scarcely want the army officials retain *jagirs* lest they strengthen their position and become a danger to the rulers.

Besides *jagir* grants, which were connected with the military or non-military services, there were the *muafi* grants, which involved the remission of revenue. The practise of granting large tracts of land, both irrigated and unirrigated, as revenue-free continued from ancient times down to the Dogra period. The term *muafi* implies exemption from land revenue. This institution of *muafi* grants is also of an ancient standing in Kashmir. We have evidence to show that ancient rulers of Kashmir endowed revenue-free land grants (*agraharas*) to the charitable or religious institutions or personages. *Agrahara* as used by Kalhana meant a piece of land, the revenue of which was assigned to an individual or an institution for maintenance of sacred shrines. Among others M.A. Stein also mentions the fact that the custom of bestowing rent-free lands continued during Muslim and Sikh period.[71]

During the Muslim rule in India, it was customary to grant land to Sayyids, Sheikhs and other non-Muslim subjects by way of *Madad-i-Maash* grants. *Madad-i-Maash* was land granted for subsistence to charitable institutions and religious persons. Another such revenue free grant came to be known as *Altamgha*, a grant by the royal stamp (*Tamgha*). The term *Altamgha* denoted a grant which was permanent and could not be resumed 'except in case of misconduct'.[72] Even the Sikh rulers continued this practice of granting lands as *Madad-i-Maash* to Muslims and Hindus. In fact, Mir Ahmad has referred to thousands of muslim grantees of all categories.[73]

During the Dogra period, as usual, the *muafi* grants to Kashmiri Brahmans and Sayyid families remained intact. These families held this property under the pretext of institutional (temples, mosques, mathas, etc.) ownership. The religious and charitable aspects of this phenomenon, at times, gave rise to quite a few problems in land relations. During the study period, many of these temple pandits and Sayyids joined the state services; however, they continued to receive the produce of these lands as absentee landlords, and the rights of the peasants who cultivated these lands were not determined. In course of time, the practise of granting rent-free lands to people in institutions was abused even by ministers and provincial governors, who in order to avoid payment of revenue due to the state from them got their lands enlisted in the *dharmarth* allotment. One such example is of Dewan Badrinath who gradually got his *chak* enlisted as *muafi* and made huge sums of money.[74]

However, during the Dogra period, *muafis* were of two kinds: one was religious and the other non-religious. In religious *muafi*, one-third of the amount of land revenue assigned was received by the *muafidar* in cash and two-thirds in kind. Non-religious *muafis* were granted to people for the construction of public works such as bridges and wells. In case of non-religious *muafis*, the whole of assigned land revenue was received either in cash or partly in cash and partly in kind.[75] In AD 1848 Vansagnew wrote to John Lawrence that the land revenue of Rs. 84,375 was assigned to the free grants held by religious personages and other learned men in the Persian, Arabic and Sanskrit language.[76] The *muafi* grants were frequently hereditary in nature,[77] indeed some of the *muafi* lands still remain attached to temples and *mathas*.

Chakdars: Next in the hierarchy of the revenue assignees of Kashmir were the *chakdars*. Although they were also a privileged class, they stood quite low in comparison to the *jagirdars*. It was in 1862, when the state felt the need to get more and more waste lands under cultivation, that it decided to grant pieces of land called *chaks* out of such waste lands. In fact these *chaks* were mostly allotted to the revenue officials and other favourites of the ruling family.[78] In the first instance grants called *chaks* were made for some ten years on condition that the wastelands should be brought under cultivation and only those should be employed to carry out cultivation who were not already cultivators in the lands of *jagirdars* or some other revenue assignee.[79] Some terms and conditions were laid down for these *chakdars* (holders of *chaks*), i.e.

(i) all state rules were to be followed;
(ii) the specific sanction did not cover all rules;
(iii) the lands would not be abandoned once the concessional rate period had expired without payment for the period of possession at full rates;
(iv) the holder must be loyal to the state as well as true to the caste;
(v) if the state authorized the sale, the purchasers would be similarly obligated; and
(vi) the assessment would be levied whether the land was cultivated or not.[80]

These *chaks* were granted to the state employees in lieu of their services. They were entitled to hold possession of *chak* and to take away its agricultural produce so long as they paid state dues onland in due time.[81]

The *chakdars* were entitled, free of charge, to use all the ordinary brushes and brushwood removed by them in cleaning the land for cultivation. But they were not entitled to trees on the land allotted to them without any payment.[82] Every *chakdar* was given a concession, i.e. a fixed price that he had to pay for the purchase of any tree; it was to be paid by him in instalments, not exceeding five years from the date of the lease.[83] These *chakdars* were liable for payment, through the *lambardar* of all state dues, according to the instalments fixed for the payment of land revenue in tracts in which the *chak* was situated.[84] If at all any *chakdar* failed to pay the instalment by due date, he was liable to be treated as a defaulter under the law in force for realizing land revenue. However, this law came into force after the commencement of land settlements made by W.R. Lawrence.[85] In case of the *chakdars* who cultivated no part of land with their own hands, the state demand was subject to reduction of 12½ per cent of revenue but not of the cesses assessed thereon. This indeed was the ususal case. No *chakdar* cultivated the land with his own hands because mostly they lived in cities and used to visit their *chak* generally at the time of harvest. As a result they came to be known as absentee landlords.[86]

The other obligations imposed upon these *chakdars* after the land settlement of 1889 were that they were asked to use due diligence in bringing the land under cultivation of not less than 80 per cent of the total area granted, within a period of 10 years from the date on which they received possession. The land allotted to a *chakdar* could not be leased out for grazing or grass cutting instead of cultivating it.[87] He was entitled to transfer his right as such by sale, mortgage, gift or otherwise. He was also permitted, on application to the *wazir-wazarat,* to have the name of any person closely related to him added on as co-sharer with himself, provided that the person was a subject of the state.[88] The *chakdar,* after receiving possession of land and on fulfilment of the conditions of the grant, received permanent right as an *assami* or occupancy tenant. He had thereafter the same rights and was subjected to the same liabilities as the other *assami* or occupancy tenants had in that area.[89] No *chakdar* could be elected by the state within a period of twenty years from the date of his lease otherwise than for failure to comply with the condition of his lease. Besides *mukarraree* and *ishtiharee chaks*, the other kinds of *chaks* were those of *zar-niasi*, *ahalikaree* and *hanudee*. Information regarding them is extremely scant. The *pattas* concerning the grant of *mukarraree chaks* generally date from AD 1870 but no one paid any special attention to them because what the landlords desired was the means of occupying or obtaining land, and they knew how to manipulate it. For instance during the famine of 1877, when most of the peasants, had left their lands and had gone to the Punjab, the landlords got the opportunity of entering upon new lands temporarily left uncultivated and when the peasants returned from the Punjab, they found themselves ousted. Generally, land grants were made under the general order of the *dewan* and *wazir-wazarat* under their own signatures.[90] In the event of eviction, he was entitled to payment by the state of compensation for improvement, to be fixed by the Governor in accordance with the law regulating compensation payable by landlords to tenants on ejectment. It was further laid down in the obligations imposed on these *chakdars* that if a *chakdar* to whom an *assami* right or permanent status had been granted, refused or with sufficient reason, neglected to take up an area which was granted to him or if he withdrew his application at any stage after the measurement had commenced, he was liable under the order of the Governor for *harjana* (cash penalty) at the rate of 2 annas per *kanal* to cover the cost of measurement.[91]

These *chaks* were of different kinds but the obligations or terms and conditions laid down were the same for all. From AD 1879 another class of landlords was created by granting *mukarraree chaks* and *ishtiharee chaks*.[92] The terms and conditions for all these *chaks* were the same but the assessment for *ishtiharee chaks* was usually lighter than those of *mukarraree chaks*. *Mukarrarees* were a class of land holders, who were in receipt of fixed cash grants from the state either as a reward for their services to the state or as a charity.[93]

Table 4.2 gives the rate of assessment on both.[94]

Those in possession of *ahalikaree chaks* got land in lieu of wages and on lump sum as will be clear from Table 4.3.[95]

But the holders of all these *chaks* never observed the rules and regulations. They treated the orders of the Durbar as mere formalities and exploited the peasants through rack renting and arbitrary and

TABLE 4.2: THE ASSESSMENT ON DRY AND WET LANDS

Year	*Rate of assessment for dry land*			*Rate of assessment for wet land*		
	Rs.	*annas*	*pies*	*Rs.*	*annas*	*pies*
1st	3	-	-	6	-	-
2nd	6	-	-	12	-	-
3rd	6	-	-	12	-	-
For *Ishtiharee chak* the assessment was as follows:						
1st		Free			Free	
2nd	0	10	-	1	-	-
3rd	1	-	-	2	-	-
4th	2	-	-	3	-	-
5th	2	-	-	4	-	-
6th	3	-	-	5	-	-
7th	4	-	-	6	-	-
8th	5	-	-	7	-	-
9th	6	-	-	8	-	-
Rate of assessment: per 2 acres						

Source: A. Wingate, Preliminary Land Settlement Report 1888-1889, Jammu and Kashmir, Jammu Archives [unpublished report].

often forcible ejectment of tenants. They appropriated the major portion of the produce and hardly spent any money to improve the land. To quote Lawrence, 'This was a common incident in Kashmir village.' A pandit obtained a grant of waste land in a village but neglected to cultivate it. The state then insisted on the village paying the assessment fixed by the state. The *chakdar* did not cultivate it; the village was called upon to do so. 'In fact after the end of nineteenth century, these *chakdars* who were mostly urban Hindu families, became an important force to reckon with.'[96]

The *chakdars* occupied much of the uncultivated land and included cultivable lands in their *chaks*. They evaded the payment of revenue and even held lands in excess.[97] We can cite a number of cases in which the *chakdars* held lands in excess of the grant by illegal means.

He got a grant of a deserted government garden and with it some

TABLE 4.3: AMOUNT OF ASSESSMENT ON AHALI KARI *CHAKS*

Year	*Amount in Rs.*
1st	Free of assessment
2nd	25
3rd	50
4th	75
5th	100
6th	125
7th	175
8th	250
9th	350
10th	500
11th	550

Source: A. Wingate, Preliminary Land Settlement Report 1888-1889, Jammu and Kashmir, Jammu Archives [unpublished report].

land he had bought from a woman who appears to have been resourceless. For this land, Dewan Badrinath was to pay Rs. 48 per annum. A few years later, he bought some more land for Rs. 100, which he included in his *chak* and then, being Governor of Kashmir, he never paid even the usual revenue of Rs. 48 on the whole land, which measured nearly 8 *kharwars* and 32 acres. As if it were not enough, the Dewan gradually tried to convert it into *muafi* lands, which were assessment-free.[98]

In another case, a Pandit got a *chak* for ten *kharwars* of land, but he modestly took possession of 9½ *kharwars* and held it for Re. 1 for wet land and Rs. 8 for dry land per *kharwar* for 10 years. In 1873, Wazir Punoo doubled the assessment and after an enquiry in 1877, it was found that the Pandit held six *kharwars* and eight *traks* more than he ought to have, but he successfully resisted any increase in his assessment.[99]

These *chakdars* invented new devices of adding to their estates. Soon after taking possession of *chaks*, they immediately ousted and expelled all the old cultivators in order to destroy any proof of land having been cultivated when they entered upon it.[100] This would enable them to claim exemption from assessment for some time. Second, they would extend their possession to every bit of land in the neighbourhood they could lay hands on.[101] A *tahsildar* cast his eye upon a fine village within his charge, close to Srinagar. There were six or seven *kharwars* of land fallow and waste, which supplied a pretext for developing the country and improving the revenue by applying for *chak*. He had good influence at the headquarters, and his friend the Dewan about five years earlier gave him a *mukarraree patta* for twenty *kharwars* of land at the rate of Rs. 12 for wet land and Rs. 6 for dry land. But the *tahsildar* took care to get it inserted that all lands were dry. He paid Rs. 150 only and was in possession of 29 *kharwars* of land, of which 20¾ were irrigated and could produce a good *shali* crop. Here it becomes clear that to be in state service and particularly in the Revenue Department was a good fortune where the officials had ample chances of making wealth by resorting to fraudulent practices.[102]

If a peasant died, leaving his wife and children behind, the neighbouring *chakdar* was very alert in taking possession of his land under an agreement which would make him answerable for the revenue on the condition that the land would be restored to the family when the children grew up. Inevitably, though not in all cases, the land was thus restored. Sometimes these *chakdars* picked up a quarrel about their boundary and made an addition of a few *kharwars* of land to their estate. When, during the last years of Maharaja Ranbir Singh's reign and the early years of Maharaja Pratap Singh's reigns, it became known to all the revenue assignees and grantees that the land settlement was to commence very soon and it had become less difficult for all the *chakdars* to obtain land, they resorted to other means of occupying *chaks*. They used to extract a pledge from the villagers that such and such a village, in which they were interested, had been the property of such and such pandit, and pretended that somehow the possession had been lost, and then the villagers recognized him as proprietor and agreed that he should pay the assessment. Wingate states that in one *tahsil* villages were made over to influential officials like the *wazir-wazarat*, secretaries and the governor and none of them used to pay the revenue. Consequently a great loss was registered in state finances.[103] At times deeds of sale were executed for a very meagre amount which was never paid.[104]

Illustration 4.1: Land Settlement Commissioner on tour accompanied by *vakil* (advocate) using river transport. *Source:* Harbans Mukhia's Collection of Pictures from India Office Library, London.

With the commencement of regular land settlement in 1889, the state attempted an enquiry and laid down that the authority granting the land should first be examined. With regard to the land held in excess by the *chakdars,* possession was to be recognized unless on report of the settlement the excess was resumed.[105]

As to the tenure of land, with regard to the peasants under *chakdars,* it was laid down that the settlement officer should be entrusted with full powers to decide which cultivators should have the right of occupancy under *chakdars,* and they were usually given such a right of occupancy in respect of lands reasonably believed to have been cultivated land, whether temporarily followed or not.[106]

With regard to the assessment of *chakdars chak,* the Durbar decided with the advice of Wingate that the grant of possession to cultivate waste lands at reduced rates for a specific period did not confer upon any grantee any privileges in respect of assessment after the term of years specified elapsed, and the settlement was therefore free to impose the same assessment upon any *chakdar* as upon any peasant and *patta* since the commencement was declared useless.[107]

After a consideration of how and why the land was obtained, the expenditure attendant on bringing it under cultivation, the treatment of peasants, the amount hitherto paid as compared with the land taken possession of, and other such points, the settlement officer was asked to seek the sanction of the Durbar. For this, he was asked to make such a reduction on full assessment that seemed fair to him, and this reduced assessment was to be demanded during the term or period of settlement.The reasons for this reduction were that almost all revenue officials were in receipt of *chaks,* so the Durbar did not deem it just, not politics, on their part to force out all *chakdars*; and second if the full assessment was to be levied there was no room for middlemen.[108]

NOTES

1. Kalhana, *Rajatarangini* (Eng. tr. M.A. Stein), vol. I, London, 1900 (Book seventh), pp. 218-87. See also nn. 161-2, 249, 301. Ibid., vol. I, p. 223, n. 301. See also S.C. Ray, *History and Culture of Kashmir*, Delhi, pp. 143-4.
2. R.K. Parmu, *History of Muslim Rule in Kashmir*, Peoples Publishing House, Delhi, 1969, pp. 399-400.
3. Jonaraja, *Rajatarangini*, Vol. III, Eng. tr. J.C. Dutt, Calcutta, 1889,

p. 66. See also *Tuhfat-ul-Abwab* (Per. Ms.), Anonymous, Research Department Library, Srinagar, p. 64.

4. Abul Fazil, *Akbar-nama*, English tr. by Hentry Beveridge, 3 vols., Calcutta, 1897, vol. III, pp. 827-30. Sir W. Haig, *The Cambridge History of India*, ed. Sir R. Burn, Delhi 1957, vol. IV, pp. 136-40.
5. Moorcraft G. Trebeck, *Travels*, vol. II, p. 125. See Parmu, *History of Muslim Rule in Kashmir*, op. cit., p. 402.
6. See *Khalsa Durbar Records*, Punjab State Archives, Patiala, Bundle no. 5, vol. XIII, pp. 323-7.
7. Moorcraft, op. cit., vol. I, p. 125. See Shamat Ali, *Sikhsand Afghans*, Patiala 1848, p. 36. See also Indu Banga, *Agrarian System of Sikhs*, Delhi, 1978, p. 124.
8. Kalhana, op. cit., vol. I, p. 354. See also Baden Powell, *The Land Systems of British India*, London, 1892, Indian reprint, Delhi, 1967, vol. I, pp. 528-9. Kalhana, op. cit., vol. I, pp. 15-20. D.D. Kosambi, 'Origins of Feudalism in Kashmir', *Journal of Bombay Royal Asiatic Society*, 15th Anniversary, Bombay, 1957, p. 120.
9. For details, see 'Note by Fanshawe,' 3; 'Henvey's Revised Note, 1883,' p. 17.
10. Lawrence, *Valley of Kashmir*, p. 402.
11. Ratan Lal Hangloo, *Agrarian System of Kashmir*, p. 51.
12. Wayne to Secretary, p. 7.
13. Wingate, *Preliminary Report*, p. 7.
14. Major-General D.K. Palit, *Jammu and Kashmir Arms*, Dehradun, 1972, p. 49.
15. Foreign Deptt. Sec. December 1846, file no. 1266, NAI.
16. *Lahore Political Diaries*, III, pp. 66, 143-8.
17. *Arzi* submitted by Hill Chiefs to Henry Lawrence, For. Sec. Cons., file no. 1125, 26 December 1846, NAI.
18. *Jagirdars* and hill chiefs of Kaghan, Uttarmachipora and Kama. H.M. Lawrence's *Report from Kashmir* dated 15 November 1847, For. Sec. Cons., file no. 1243-7, NAI. See also *Taylor's Report*, dated 27 September 1847. For Pol. Cons., nos. 452-3, dated 30 December 1848, NAI.
19. Mirza Saif-ud-Din, *Akhbarat*, vol. I, ff. 2-6. See also vol. V of *Akhbarat*, ff. 21-3.
20. Ibid.
21. *List of Ruling Princes, Chiefs and Leading Personages in Jammu and Kashmir State and digit agency* (Government Publication), Delhi, 1939, pp. 10-12 (available in NAI).
22. Ibid.

23. *Forman, regarding jagir with cash and kind in Martand and Devasar in favour of Raja Kak Dhar*, vs 1905.
24. Chief Secretariat Pol. and Genl. Deptt., file no. 76 of 1876, JK. See *Karvai-Jalsa-Council-Aliya Riyasat Jammu-va-Kashmir*, January 1898, JK.
25. Mirza Saif-ud-Din, *Akhbarat*, vol. I, f. 166.
26. See *Patta regarding grant of jagir of Kava Chak illaqa on hereditary basis in the name of Pandit Raja Kak Dhar*, 1863. In fact, there are various such instances in record. The photocopy of the *patta* was consulted from Mr. Sham Sundar Lal Dhar's collections and also from Shree Shiv Ji Bhat the former land reforms commissioner and a great knowledgeable person about agrarian system of Kashmir. He singlehandedly consolidated revenue records for present government with meticulousness and truthfully. He has been a great source for providing information on critical issues. See also *List of Ruling princes chiefs and leading personages in Jammu & Kashmir State and Gilgit Agency*, pp. 7-15.
27. *Patta regarding grant of jagir in Nunar illaqa in favour of Pandit Raja Kak Dhar*, January 1857.
28. Chief Sec. Pol. and Genl. Dept., file no. 76, 1896.
29. Saif-ud-Din, op. cit., vol. I, f. 27.
30. See Kalhana, op. cit., vol. III, pp. 223-4, n. 301. Ibid., Lawrence, *Valley*, p. 305.
31. Ibid.
32. Khoyhami, *Tarikh-i-Hassan*, vol. 2, p. 648.
33. Ibid. 'Wayne to Secretary', p. 9; J.L.K. Jalali, *Economics of Food Grains in Kashmir*, Lahore: Mercantile Press, 1931, p. 39.
34. Lawrence observes that generally the revenues were fixed so high that the villagers would refuse to enter into a settlement. The powerful headmen and the assessors would lure the villagers into believing that the assessment was a nominal one and would never be collected. That way, on the one hand, the assessors, in cahoots with the village headmen would be able to show very high jama figures and, on the other hand, the peasants were never able to pay the assessment in full, leaving them in arrears. Lawrence, *Valley*, p. 404.
35. Hangloo, *Agrarian System of Kashmir*, op. cit., p. 53.
36. Lawrence, *Valley*, p. 403.
37. Khoyhami, *Tarikh*, vol. 2, p. 657; Lawrence, *Valley*, p. 403.
38. *Annual Administrative Report of Jammu and Kashmir State, 1889-1890*, p. 45.

39. Sukhdev Charakh, *Life and Times of Maharaja Ranbir Singh*, Jammu: Jay Kay Book House, 1985, p. 122.
40. Wingate, *Preliminary Report,* p. 23.
41. Ibid., p. 6.
42. Hangloo, *Agrarian System of Kashmir*, p. 54.
43. Mirza, op. cit, vol. IV, ff. 114-115.
44. M.M.A. Beg, *Zarai-Islahat*, pp. 8-9..
45. Karvai-Jalsa Council, *Aliya Riyasat Jammu-va-Kashmir*, January 1898-1900, pp. 62-5.
46. Ibid.
47. Chief Sec. Pol. and Genl. Dept, file no. 76 of 1896, Jammu Archives, pp. 20-1.
48. Ibid.
49. Ibid.
50. Ibid.
51. Ibid.
52. Ibid.
53. Ibid.
54. Ibid.
55. Ibid.
56. Ibid.
57. Ibid.
58. Ibid.
59. Ibid.
60. Ibid.
61. Ibid.
62. Ibid.
63. Ibid.
64. Ibid.
65. Ibid.
66. Ibid.
67. D.K. Palit, *Jammu and Kashmir Arms*, pp. 50-5.
68. Ibid.
69. The table has been prepared after consulting annual administrative reports and settlement reports from 1885 to 1947.
70. Palit, op. cit., pp. 73-4, 86.
71. Kalhana's *Rajatarangini*, Eng. tr., vol. I, pp. 87-100, 121-75, 307, 340–1 and 355. Ibid., pp. 15-16, also n. 87.
72. Mir Ahmad, *Dastural Amal-i-Kashmir*, Per. Ms. ff. 215. Indu Banga,

Agrarian System of Sikhs, pp. 148-53. For details see B.N. Goswamy and J.S. Grewal, *Mughals and the Jogis of Jakhabar* pp. 17-46, 47-188, see also Athar Ali, *Mughal Nobility under Aurangzeb*, pp. 98-9. Powell, op. cit., pp. 530-1.

73. Mir Ahmad, op. cit., ff. 184a, 206b, 207b, 208-9, 283a, also see ff. 326a-341b.
74. Wingate, op. cit., p. 64.
75. *Karvai-Jalsa Council Aliya Jammu-va-Kashmir*, for the year 1898-1900. See R.C. Raina, *Land Reforms' Kashmir*, vol. 2, nos. 25-6, 16 December 1952.
76. For. Dept. Sec., 31 March 1848, file nos. 60-77, NAI.
77. *Jammu and Kashmir State Council Proceedings*, 26 October 1904, p. 14, Jammu Archives.
78. A. Wingate, op. cit., pp. 60-2. In fact, these *chaks* were mostly allotted to the revenue officials and other favourites of the ruling family.
79. Ibid.
80. Ibid., pp. 60-4.
81. Ibid. See also *Rules Regarding Grant of Waste Land for Cultivation as Sanctioned by His Highness the Maharaja Sahib Bahadur*, Jammu 1917, Jammu Archives.
82. Ibid.
83. Ibid.
84. Ibid.
85. Wingate, op. cit., pp. 62-8. See also *Rules Regarding the Waste Land*, op. cit., Jammu Archives.
86. *A Review of the Working of Land Reforms with Special Reference to Big Landed Estates Abolition Act in Jammu and Kashmir*, Jammu 1952.
87. *Rules Regarding Grant of Waste Land for Cultivation as Sanctioned by His Highness the Maharaja Gulab Bahadur*, Jammu, 1917, Jammu Archives.
88. Ibid.
89. Ibid.
90. Ibid.
91. Ibid.
92. Wingate, op. cit., pp. 64-7.
93. M.M.A. Beg, 'Land Reforms in Jammu and Kashmir', *Mainstream*, New Delhi, 14th Annual Number, 1976, pp. 27-9.
94. Wingate, op. cit., pp. 60-3.
95. Ibid., p. 63.
96. See Report by W.R. Lawrence, Position of Cultivating Classes in Kashmir, NAI, Foreign Department, Secret, February 1890.

97. Ibid.
98. Wingate, op. cit., pp. 63-4.
99. Ibid., see *Report of W.R. Lawrence Regarding the Position of Cultivating Classes in Kashmir*, February 1890, NAI. See also Foreign Deptt. Secretariate, E. file nos. 295-326.
100. Wingate, op. cit., pp. 63-4.
101. Ibid.
102. Ibid., p. 64.
103. Ibid.
104. *Rules Regarding Grant of State Wasteland for Cultivation.*
105. Ibid.
106. Ibid. See also Wingate, op. cit., pp. 68-9.
107. *Ain Pratap Code Part II. Ain* no. 5, Jammu Archives. See also *Rules Regarding Grant of State Waste Land for Cultivation.* See also Pandit Bhag Ram, *Report on Administration of Jammu-va-Kashmir*, 1889-90, pp. 37-43; *Big Landed Estates Abolition Act*, XVII, Jammu, 1953.
108. *Karvai Jalsa Council Aliya for the Year 1889-90* (see portion on *Mahkama-Mal*).

CHAPTER 5

Condition of the Peasantry

To analyse the condition of the peasantry of a particular region, ideally very many aspects should be examined in detail, viz., the size of land holding per household, the nature and extent of production, the technology and social organization of labour use, stratification within the peasantry and the relationship among various social classes. In studying the rural society of Kashmir, one of the most persistent weaknesses is the difficulty to distinguish between various social classes in the agrarian class structure in which they arise and the different strata to which, they belong. This difficulty is rooted in the lack of sources, relevant to rural property and class structure. As a result, the peasantry of Kashmir has often been treated as an undifferentiated group. In the case of Kashmir, the sources provide us with very little information on many of these aspects. On the basis of such information as is available, only broad distinctions amongst different ranks of the peasantry can be attempted, such as the landless agricultural labourer, the tenant, and the peasant proprietor.

The condition of the peasantry, taken as a whole, had already reached a low ebb when Maharaja Gulab Singh took over the administration in AD 1846. Until the annexation of the Punjab by the British, Kashmir had been a part of that state. But with the conclusion of the treaty of Amritsar between Maharaja Gulab Singh and the British in AD 1846, Jammu and Kashmir with certain adjustment of frontiers were constituted into the state of Jammu and Kashmir and handed over to Maharaja Gulab Singh. Though the political future of Jammu, Kashmir and the Frontier Territories was settled, their economic conditions remained more or less the same. Whereas Punjab began to register some progress as a result of ameliorative measures of the British Government, the state of Jammu and Kashmir did not receive any settled advantage. Hence the condition of the newly founded state was deplorable.[1]

Lawrence in a letter to Currie wrote, 'The people seem in a wretched state of poverty. It will be years and years before this country can recover its prosperity. It will be pleasant land for a man to dwell in.'[2]

As far as the material life of the peasantry was concerned coarse rice and knolkhol or khol Rabi (*hak/sag*) constituted their usual food.[3] In many areas where a little paddy was grown, people depended on maize.[4] Even though very little wheat was grown here, the cakes of bread prepared out of wheat flour were taken with tea and not for the chief meals. The poor peasants subsisted on fruits and vegetables. Vegetables and fruits did not comprise the staple food of Kashmiri peasants and the sense that fruit was a constituent of a rich diet was not present. Its supply being abundant, there was practically no commercial demand for fruit. In the absence of quick and inadequate means of communication and transport with the outside world, a perishable commodity like fruit could not be carried over long distances. Therefore, it commanded no price.[5] Although milk was abundant but the peasants consumed very small part of it. Out of the major share *ghee* was made and handed over to the moneylender.[6] Frederick Drew rightly remarked, 'The country people are poorly off.' I think indeed that they get a fair meal, but they can afford little beyond their simple daily food, and are unable to provide for a rainy day. When a bad year comes, and though it does not often happen, it does sometimes happen, they are put in great straits and will perhaps leave the country in number for the isolation of the place, such that it is exceedingly difficult for any great importation of corn to be made to redress the failure of the harvest.[7]

The vegetables in regular consumption were knolkhol, turnips, pumpkins, radish and brinjal.[8] The poor peasants living near the Wular Lake or on its banks subsisted on *singharas*. Hasan says, in *Tarikh-i-Hassan*:

"مغز سنگارا مردم بخیر بادر علاقه باندی پوره و حاجن ولولپور
فلله در تمام علاقه پایین آرش کرده می خورند"

'The poor people of Bandipore, Hajan and Sopore rather the entire poor population of lower region below these subsisted on boiled *singharas* (water chestnuts).'[9]

Though salt and tea were costly items, the consumption of salt was higher because the Kashmiri peasants preferred salty vegetables and took salty tea twice or thrice a day. Mutton was beyond the reach of this section of the population even on festive occasions.

The peasants of Kashmir could hardly afford utensils other than those of clay. They lived in simple huts, the roofs of which were covered with straw and rice husk; straw was considered the best for it.[10] Moorcraft says, 'The houses were unplastered and badly constructed with broken doors. Near the forests the roofs were made of wooden singhals and the houses were real log huts, the wall being made of whole logs laid one upon the other, like the cottages of Russian peasantry.'[11] There was no furniture and no bedsteads in their homes; instead, at night, a cloth was spread on the ground for each person and a blanket was used to cover him. In some areas, the peasants used to sleep on mats only.[12]

Oil was used for lighting purposes and in higher villages, use was made of torches of pine wood. Fire was used in winter. Lawrence says, '*Kangar* (firepot) forms an important part of the Kashmiris life…', *Kangri* (portable brazier) is an interesting feature of the life of Kashmiris. Every Kashmiri makes use of it during winter. They cannot afford to part with it at least for four to five months in a year. It becomes a constant companion of Kashmiris. It is only recently that in most urban areas the dependence on it has diminished because of the electric heaters, etc.[13]

At the lowest rung of the peasantry was the agricultural wage labourer. His condition was truly dismal. He was given one meal and 6 *seers* of unhusked rice a day. After feeding this family, he could save one anna a day or Rs. 2 a month on disposing of his surplus rice. Among the agricultural labourers there were two categories—one of those who knew cultivation and the other was those of unskilled labourers in general.[14] It is to be noted that this agricultural wage labourer was engaged in agricultural pursuits only for a specific period not exceeding five months a year. Therefore, this section of labourers migrated to the plains during the winter months to earn their sustenance. Many of them used to carry loads to the Punjab and also worked as potters in Lahore to earn their living during winter months.[15] Very few, if any among this section, supplemented their income at home by taking to weaving of woollen blankets and baskets while staying at home. Since the basket makers job was not a regular opening, the agricultural workers had to move out of his village and find for himself the job of preparing the *kangris* (fire-pots, etc.).[16]

Another section of the peasants comprised the tenants who worked on the lands of the *jagirdars*, *chakdars* and *muafidars*. This class of landed aristocracy rented out their lands to the tenants and shared the crops annually with them.[17] The tenancy system was very widespread in Kashmir.

Partly, the administrative system of the period compelled large sections of the peasants to give up cultivation and work as tenants, as we shall discuss below. Besides, the widespread existence of parasitic landlordism also encouraged the tenancy system.[18] These rented holdings varied greatly in size.[19] Though these tenants had to pay half the produce in rent, they were never free from other obligations in the form of produce and labour.

In Kashmir, this tenancy appears to have served a useful function when the land-owning class had no interest in maximizing agricultural production but merely wanted to maximize their own surplus. Leasing out land enables a landlord to collect any effort on the peasant's part, frees him from the tedious choice of supervising a hired labour force, and allows him to reap the surplus produce quietly and unostentatiously. In the wake of heavy pressure of land, the practice landlord could take advantage of the competition for land by extracting onerous rents from the tenant and it was also a means of hiring labour at below subsistence wages.[20] Hence, the position of these tenants was deplorable. The landowner shifted much of the risk of the crop failure to the tenant. As a result, the income of the tenant became variable. The landowners never provided any input to the tenants. These tenants usually did not possess heritable rights, and landowners could reoccupy the property at will. Due to poverty, the tenant was forced to lease land on whatever terms were available to him to feed his family. They had to carry or bear the charge of transporting the share of produce to their lords' place and to enable them to live as absentee landlords.[21]

In some cases, these tenants were of long-standing on the estate but in many cases they were migratory persons who could move freely and change their masters. They were, however, entirely unprotected by the law. Their share of rent could be enhanced without adequate notice. They could be evicted at any time for defaulting on the payment of rent or any other obligatory service. Their eviction too was not regulated by any procedure framed for their protection.[22]

Next comes the peasant proprietors about whose rights in land a lot of confusion has been created by the then corrupt officials.The question of ownership of land is a legal question with very little socio-economic content in the medieval context, as has been argued by Harbans Mukhia. Irfan Habib on the basis of thoroughgoing examination of the evidence has very rightly disputed the assertion of foreign travellers and some scholars that land belonged to the king. The tradition of agrarian system or landholdings was quite contrary to the statement made out by these travellers and scholars. Payment of land tax should not be taken to mean that land belonged to the ruler. In case of Kashmir, during the period of our study, officials supported the view that the ownership vested with the king and not the peasant. But in actual practice ownership in Kashmir rested with the peasant proprietor.[23] The revenue officials deprived the peasants of their proprietory rights through fraudulent practices, some of which have been described graphically by Wingate: 'To please the Durbar and allay apprehension, every official glibly agrees that land belongs to His Highness.' Accordingly, deeds of sale and agreements generally refer to the rights possessed by the *zamindars*, with a judicious mixture of words denoting ownership and property. These documents are duly registered by the courts. Petition are based on them, and much correspondence is ensured; finally, the Durbar passes orders and thus endorses the whole. For instance, the son of an influential official took a contract in the old days for two villages. In 1880, the *khewat* (cash assessment) was made with him. Next year, he petitioned to the *wazir-wazarat* that he was being hindered from paying the revenue of the village, which was his property. Then *wazir-wazarat* submits the case for orders and an endorsement is written across a corner that the petitioner was allowed to pay the revenue of the villages which are his *milkiat* and *zamindari.*[24] It is as a result of this confusion that both the travellers and the native writers stated that the ruler was the owner of land and not the peasant.

Generally, the sale and mortgage of the land was not disallowed. Besides, *karvais* provide us with frequent references to the sale and mortgage of land. The disappearance of the proprietorship in land took place because of some economic problems like *begar* (corvee) and the heavy tax burden.When peasants were taken away from their lands to render corvee, on their return they often found themselves landless. Besides, when the maximum produce of the peasant proprietors was snatched away by the revenue officials under various heads he left the field and recruited himself as wage labourer but at times when he came back after some time he found himself ousted and his holding was entered by officials against their own names.[25] It was as a result of such practices that the holdings of the peasant proprietors were transferred to revenue officials.[26]

Though the peasant proprietors paid land revenue, they were not free from interference on the part of the state at the time of reaping and storing of the grains.[27] This left them with little incentive to improve productivity of their land.

The other allied pursuit, apart from cultivation, which the peasant practised, was bee-keeping. Honey was produced not only for consumption but also for sale. However, the earnings from this were negligible and too meagre to substantially add to the low returns from their holdings. James Korbel who visited Kashmir in the first half of the twentieth century says that about 60 per cent of the peasants had the holdings of about 16 *kanals* (2 acres) each. Their net annual income was Rs. 10-10-3, per head. The rest of the peasantry was without land. Even as late as 1944-5, the per capita income of the peasant did not exceed Rs. 11.[28] It was this class of peasants who took to weaving of blankets and baskets during the off season.Since the basket making, was not a regular opening during the off season the peasants of Kashmir used to weave home spun cotton and wool for their domestic use but their methods were primitive and looms were also of an indent type.[29] The migration of this class of peasants was not a taboo and a few of these, particularly those oppressed by the moneylenders' exacting demands left their homes during winter months to earn their livelihood.[30] In undertaking these subsidiary crafts, the peasants usually suffered from the greedy and rapacious middlemen. Wazir Ganganath very rightly remarks, 'Substantial gains could accrue to the cultivator only where these crafts were organized on a cooperative basis, thus eliminating the middlemen and being sufficiently accessible to marketing centres.' These subsidiary crafts included manufacturing of *pattu* (woollen cloth), cloth weaving, needlework, oil pressing, pottery, epiculture, poultry keeping, and silkworm rearing. There were, besides, the occupations of horticulture and collection of medicinal herbs.[31]

Nature too occasionally takes its toll on peasant lives. In 1848, owing to heavy rainfall, the peasants of Kashmir suffered from various diseases in large numbers, so much so that every family lost a few of their members to it. The same year saw a famine, which destroyed the peasant's vast cattle wealth due to a lack of grass and fodder.[32] Mirza Saif-ud-Din says that as a result of excessive heat in the preceding seasons and the drought, the soil became so hard that it became difficult for the peasant to plough and to lay seeds; then suddenly it rained so heavily that fields were lost in flood.[33]

In 1852 there prevailed general scarcity of food grains and the peasants had to depend on barley and many of them left the country.[34] In 1856, the peasants' distress was intensified by the terrible earthquake coupled with the failure of the season's rains, so that all lands were sown with maize or other coarse cereals to avoid loss in revenue and something to fall back upon. In 1877 as well, the peasants had to face a very harsh situation. The crops were destroyed by unusual rains and more than half of the crops was lost. Consequently, a large section of the population died.[35] This calamity dislocated the peasantry; charity houses were opened at different places.

This was followed by the terrible femine of 1879 which caused a further loss of men and material. Even during this period the state did not relax its control over the peasantry. Instead the state continued to leave no surplus grain with peasants. Everything was taken from them and stored in the state stores at Srinagar. [36]

Table 5.1 gives detail of charity houses and the expenditure incurred therein for feeding the people who were tormented with famine in 1877.[37]

TABLE 5.1: NUMBER OF CHARITY HOMES AND AMOUNT INCURRED FOR FEEDING PEOPLE

S.No.	*Name of Wazarat*	*No. of charity houses established*	*No. of people*	*Quantity of grains distributed*		*Expenses incurred*		*Miscellaneous expenses*	
				Maunds	*Seers*	*Rs.*	*Annas*	*Rs.*	*Annas*
1.	Shahar-i-Khas	5	58,896	1,178	-	2,945	-	312	8
2.	Kamraj	3	60,261	1,324	20	2,948	12	155	13
3.	Patan	5	33,150	813	-	1,657	8	85	10
4.	Shopian	5	31,787	1,038	-	1,095	-	123	5
5.	Anantnag	5	62,595	2,032	10	3,102	8	235	5
6.	Muzaffarabad	4	13,485	285	37	1,181	8	929	9
	GRAND TOTAL	27	2,60,174	6,671	27	12,930	4	1,842	2

Source: Majmni Report, Jammu Kashmir and Tibet 1877-1878, Jammu Archives.

In 1885, the earthquake made its appearance and increased the suffering of the people by causing distress and starvation. The suffering has been described by Hasan in these words: 'During Maharaja Ranbir Singh's time, Kashmir was visited by an earthquake which took a heavy toll of men and material, accounting to 35,000, which included 20,000 horses, 10,200 cows, and 1,500 human lives.'[38]

Again, in 1893, Kashmir was visited by flood which cost the state Rs. 64,804 in land revenue alone, 35,426 acres under crops were submerged, 2,225 houses were wrecked and 329 cattle killed.[39]

Hence, the peasantry of Kashmir appears to have been in a constant state of agony. The frequency of these natural calamities gravely undermined the position of the peasant, and he had no alternative but to rush to the moneylender. The moneylending system was known as *wadhadari* (system under which the *khoja* traders [village shopkeepers] and *galladars* who by charging interest multiplied their profits and called it *wadh*). The usual time for moneylending in Kashmir was winter and summer season.[40]

In favourable seasons too the peasant was hardly in a position to improve his lot. The state had a monopoly over grain trade and it was not possible for the peasant to sell or obtain grains at reasonable prices. During Maharaja Gulab Singh's reign in 1856, the state procured *shali* (unhusked rice) from the peasants at the rate of Rs. 1-14-0 per *kharwar* and sold the same quantity for Rs. 2-12-0.[41]

Due to the lack of credit facilities on the part of the state necessary for productive operations, the peasant was at the mercy of the *wadhadar* (moneylender). Whenever the peasant required a loan for cattle, the moneylender advanced it to him against the security of the crop, whose value was assessed at lower rates than those prevailing in the market.[42] Table 5.2 is a clear example of the moneylenders device.[43]

If the crops failed due to a natural calamity and the peasant could not meet the quantity of crop contracted, the moneylender charged the residue of the crop at enhanced rates and a new contract took place. In this way, a loan once contracted was seldom liquidated, even for generations.[44]

It is a notorious fact that year after year more difficulty was experienced in obtaining *shali* for the population of Srinagar, and the tendency was for the cultivators to pay more of their land revenue in

TABLE 5.2: GRAINS AND THE RATES OF MONEYLENDERS

Name of grain	*Fixed rates of moneylender*			*Rates in the market*		
	Rs.	*Anna*	*Paise*	*Rs.*	*Anna*	*Paise*
Shali	1	8	0	1	12	0
Maize	1	8	0	1	12	0
Wheat	3	0	0	4	0	0
Til-gogulo (oilseed)	4	0	0	5	0	0

Source: Assessment Report of Partap Singh, Pora *Tahsil*, Jammu Archives.

cash and less in kind than heretofore, as mentioned earlier. There is no good ground for supposing that the revenue in kind, chiefly coarse red unhusked rice, thus retained by the cultivators was exported. The only reasonable conclusion is that it was consumed in the state. Eurther, it is, I think, very doubtful whether the rice which is chiefly grown in Kashmir at present would, even if available, pay to export except in times of scarcity in India. I am not well acquainted with the different varieties of rice, but it is a well-known fact that natives of Kashmir who are able to afford Panjab rice will not touch the ordinary rice grown in the country, and that it is only eaten by persons who cannot obtain a better sort. The wheat also is said to be much inferior in quality to good Indian varieties. There can he no doubt that better rice and wheat could be grown, and in much larger quantities, than at present. It will, however, take some time to introduce better varieties and to improve the present slovenly methods of the Kashmir cultivator.[45]

On the other hand, social customs dictated spending beyond one's means on occasions like weddings, births, deaths, etc., and the *wadhadar* was at hand to offer a loan. Once the peasant fell into the hands of the moneylender, he remained for generations in the vicious cycle of repayment of interest and debt with little hope of redemption.[46] Yet, the moneylender was seldom looked upon with bitterness, for he was the only source on which the peasant could fall back upon whatever his need.

Even as late as 1906, 60 per cent of the peasants were affected by this moneylending system. The average annual rate of interest was

81 per cent. The average landholding in the valley was about 4 acres. With an average debt rate at Rs. 9-6-4 per acre, it amounted to Rs. 37-9-4 per holding and the annual interest on it came to Rs. 13-2-5 at the minimum and Rs. 48-7-9 at the maximum exacted by the moneylender.[47]

H.W. Brailsford, a prominent English journalist who visited Kashmir in the first half of the twentieth century, observed, 'The peasants of Kashmir are sunk in unimaginable poverty. Their mud huts contain hardly any trace of visible property, save a pot or a jar. When I put my question in a typical village, every household was in debt and the usual rates of interest were 45 per cent.'[48]

For Kashmiri peasants, forced labour (*begar* or corvee), was another despised institution. The system had been developed in Kashmir by former rulers, but it touched new heights under the Dogra rulers. Kalhana states in *Rajatarangini* that Samkarvarman, who ruled Kashmir during AD 833-902, is well known for his fiscal oppression. He levied fines on those villagers who did not carry loads voluntarily. The fines levied amounted to the value of the load. Stein observed that suffering arising out of *begar* continued till the construction of Gilgit Road. During the medieval times, this oppressive practice remained intact. Mughal emperors turned it into a regular institution and the peasants were made use of for carrying the baggage of the visitors and army men to Kashmir.[49] Maharaja Gulab Singh introduced reforms regarding *begar* but did not abolish it.

The peasants of Kashmir were often pressed into *begar* at the time of sowing and reaping and were made to work for several other purposes. For instance, they were asked to carry the loads of the British visitors to Kashmir, to construct *bandhs* and bridges, to cultivate the lands of revenue officers and also to carry rations to different army quarters. In 1848, Wazir Ratnu collected a good number of peasants; 1,000 from *pargana* Lal, 500 from *pargana* Pakh, 20 from *mouza* Pain (lower portion of the same *pargana*), and 1,000 peasants from *pargana* Ich Nagam for raising *bandhs*.[50] In 1847 the peasants of Kashmir were forcibly collected for cleaning the wool which had been collected by the revenue officials without any payment. The custom of *begar* appears to have been not only forcible but at times unpaid also.[51]

P. Grevis observes, 'The dreaded *begar* system of unpaid labour, which was nothing less than slave hunting, was reintroduced in the country.' The state armed forces rounded up all the able-bodied men, sending them away for long periods to distant places to labour as coolies [and] often never returned. The fields were tended by the old men and old women as best as they could. The young women hide themselves under long wide *burqas* which cover them from the crown of their heads to their feet, whilst the boys suffer the same fate as their brothers had done hundreds of years before in Corinth. Again, thousands fled the country; this time they were Muslims.[52] As a result of this custom, the peasants of Kashmir had lost all attraction for [their] home and started fleeing to other parts of the country leaving behind their family and children. During the *chilas* campaign in 1851, Dewan Jowala Sahai ordered that one man from each peasant family should be collected for carrying ration, army equipment and other necessaries of life for soldiers deputed to the campaign.[53] Thus an army of 30,000 *begarees* was collected which included peasants, non-agriculturists, boatmen and common people.[54]

Every year, thousands of peasants are driven off from their lands to toil as carriers of burdens on the Gilgit Road. In 1856, the recruitment of 2,000 coolies was made from among the peasants of Kashmir to carry grains, etc., to the Gilgit campaign.[55] An enormous transport service was needed to supply the garrisons on the northern frontier with grain. The Kashmiri authorities were very careless about the lives of their unfortunate peasants, who were dragged from their homes and families for months together to starve on the Gilgit Road.[56] 'Gilgit is the name of terror throughout the state. Hasan says, 'In samvat 1937, i.e. 1880, the inhabitants of Gilgit demanded their usual rights … revolted and a few soldiers raided the fort of Sher-Qilla.' And when Maharaja Ranbir Singh heard this news, he sent 3,000 soldiers. To transport their luggage and food up to Hasura, peasants were brought to render forced labour. In this operation, many of the peasants lost their lives, and thousands of rupees were given as bribes by the peasants to escape the forced labour.[57]

The system was highly discriminatory. The government officials and the peasants who worked on *khalsa* lands, *jagirs* and *chaks* of the influential officials and lands allotted to temples and *mathas* were exempted from *begar*. The silk rearers were also free from this forced labour.[58] Pandits, pirs and the urban people were also exempted from this dreaded custom.[59]

The peasants could hardly escape the clutches of the revenue officials. The system also encouraged large-scale corruption by obtaining wood, grass, milch cows and sheep free of any cost. Besides, the revenue officials cultivated their lands and built houses for their use with the unpaid labour of the peasants.[60] It also led to the destruction of proprietary rights of the peasants and reduced them to a state close to serfdom. It is not be wondered, therefore, that the peasants started fleeing to the Punjab. The villages of Kajliban and Bhagtur which were reduced from 15 to 6 and 150 to 30 respectively are clear examples of depopulation of villages.[61] Most of the *begar* was carried on in summer when the peasants were needed in their fields; thus the crops largely suffered in their absence. They were given only as much food as could sustain them. As a result of this their families too suffered in the absence of their bread-winner.[62] Sometimes these peasants would lose their lives during the course of their service in *begar* and it was then that their families would permanently become victims of hunger and starvation.[63]

These were the defining features of the agrarian economy of Dogra rule and naturally had an adverse effect on the agrarian economy of the country. The oppressive system led to the depopulation of the peasants and, in a way, led to the growing migration of peasants. In order to avoid the brunt of *beg,* the peasants sought refuge elsewhere, so they had to flee from one village to another. This consequently led to the transference of the land from the actual owners of the soil to the powerful bureaucracy of Dogra rulers, for there are reports of some villages being sold by the peasants for a petty sum in order to earn exemption from *begar.* In one case three villages were sold to the *Hakim-i-Ala* (Governor of Kashmir) for miserly amounts giving an average of about Rs. 40 per village. Because once a peasant rendered himself landless he could easily escape from *begar* after making a move from his habitation to any other part of country.[64]

Begar, however, was not unique to Kashmir. It was resorted to in the Punjab where it continued for good many years.[65] But in Kashmir, the abuse rather than the use of *begar* was the real evil. As Lawrence very rightly remarks, 'A man could sometimes hide his grain in secret pits (*zusu*) and could save enough food to keep him and his children alive till the fruits and vegetables came, but it was more difficult to hide himself when the officials were on the look-out for human carriage, and the Kashmir pressgang would watch and wait if a reluctant villager was fleeing to the mountains.' *Begar* means to the Kashmiris far more than imprisonment of labour, for under its comprehensive name, every kind of demand for labour or property taken but not paid for by the officials was included.[66]

The position of the peasants was also undermined by numerous religious and social factors. The peasants of Kashmir, like their counterparts in other parts of the country, were deeply steeped in conservatism and tradition. The fatal hold that was exercised by Sayyids, Rishis, Babas and the Brahmans did not permit the peasant to make efforts for improving their lot. Indeed, remedy for the prevalent deficiency of irrigation was sought by the peasants in the 'Supernatural' powers of the Sayyids and Saints. This is understandable, in the absence of any institutional support to cultivation.[67] They attributed all natural and man-made calamities to the curse of God. The droughts, earthquakes, cholera, famines and the cruality of rulers were all attributed to God. In order to get relief from these calamities, though temporarily, the peasants were made to part with their cattle-wealth and the surplus amount of produce, in the shape of offerings by these Sayyids and Saints.[68]

This entire structure of backward, agriculture, a highly exploitative ruling class and the cultural primitiveness pushed the peasant constantly below poverty, but helped to maintain the other sections in relative affluence.

Besides, the Kashmiri peasant was ruled by customs (*rewaj*) and traditions. It was very difficult for the peasant to maintain a subsistence level when he had to spend lavishly on occasions of marriage, birth, death and other religious and social ceremonies.[69] The peasantry comprised different groups that belonged to various religions and castes. In a study of the peasantry of Kashmir, one comes across a peculiar feature, namely, the absence of rigidity in the caste system, which among other things, distinguishes it from other regions of India. The caste system has become quite flexible except for Pandits and Peers. The *nongars* (non-agriculturists) could take to agriculture easily.

Illustration 5.1: Painting of *nouful* (procession) depicts people depended on shrines of local saints for mitigating their problems during natural catastrophies. *Source:* Harbans Mukhia's Collection of Pictures from India Office Library, London.

Even village menials could indulge in agriculture and rank themselves with agricultural classes in society. Because land was the determining factor in society, there was no caste barrier.[70] Perhaps the utter poverty at the lower ends of society, which compelled the poor of all castes to supplement their income from land by various other means, introduced an element of flexibility in the caste-system.

Hence, from the foregoing account, the peasantry of Kashmir appears to have been constantly dipped in poverty and starvation. It was all as a result of the combined effects of natural and man-made calamities. On the one hand, there prevailed a low level of production due to backward agricultural technology and inadequate irrigation. On the other hand, the increasing tax burden went on casting darker shadows over the prospects of the peasantry.

The only means of escape from all these problems faced by the peasantry was to move to other parts of the country, but that was no real escape.

NOTES

1. S.M. Rai, *Partition of Punjab*, New York, 1965, p. 22. See also Elizabeth Whitecombe, *Agrarian Conditions in Northern India*, Delhi, 1971, vol. I, pp. 64-75.
2. The letter from H.M. Lawrence to Gurrie. See nos. 1240-1, 8 December 1846, Jammu Archives.
3. The term *sag* implies green vegetable leaves and is cooked in every Kashmiri house almost everyday. W. Wakefield, *History of Kashmir and Kashmiris*, The Happy Valley, London, 1879, Indian edition, Seema Publications, New Delhi, 1975, p. 136.
4. Hargopal Koul Khasta, *Guldasta-i-Kashmir*, p. 75. M.D. Fauq, *Rahnuma-i-Kashmir*, pp. 63-4.
5. Ganeshi Lal, *Sayahatnama*, p. 34. *Statement of Moral and Material Progress* (1888-89), Jammu Archives, p. 168.
6. Wreford, *Census*, 1941, XXII, p. 19.
7. F. Drew, *Jammu & Kashmir Territories*, London, 1875, p. 176.
8. Fauq, op. cit., pp. 61-6.
9. Hassan, *Tarikh-i-Hassan*, vol. I, p. 186.
10. David Ross, *Land of Five Rivers and Sind*, p. 105. T. Biscoe, *Kashmir in Sunlight and Shade*, London, p. 87. W. Wakefield, op. cit., p. 265. E.F.

Knight, *Where the Empires Meet*, London, 1915, pp. 76-7, Wreford, Census of India 1941, vol. XXII, Jammu 1943, p. 37.

11. Moorcraft, as cited in Lawrence, *Valley*, p. 249.
12. E.F. Knight, op. cit., pp. 76-7. Charles Girdlestone, *Memorandum on Kashmir*, Calcutta, 1873, , pp. 155-62.
13. Ibid.
14. Vigne, *Travels*, vol. II, p. 120.
15. Lawrence, *Valley*, p. 253.
16. Charles Girdlestone, *Memorandum of Kashmir*, p. 30.
17. A. Wingate, op. cit., pp. 60-71.
18. Ibid., see also *Karvai-Jalsa-Council Aliya*, for the year AD 1898-1900, Srinagar Archives.
19. A. Wingate, op. cit., pp. 60-71.
20. *Karvai-Jalsa-Council-Aliya*, 1898-1900, Srinagar Archives.
21. *The Big Landed Estates Abolition Act No. XVII*, Jammu, 1953.
22. *Patta Granted to Pandit Raja Kak Dhar Regarding Grant of Jagir-in Hamal Ilaqa*, 1866, Srinagar Archives. See for details. A. Wingate, op. cit., pp. 60-7 and M.M.A. Beg, *Zara-i-Islahat*, pp. 8-9.
23. Harbans Mukhia, 'Was there Feudalism in Indian History?', Presidential Address, Medieval India Section, India History Congress, Fortieth Session, Waltair, 1979; Irfan Habib, *Agrarian System of Mughal India*, pp. 111-13. Other eminent historians like B.R. Grover have also argued in favour of peasant, ownership of land, see his 'Nature of Land-Rights in Mughal India', *IESHR*, vol. I, no. 1, 1963, pp. 2-5 and 'Nature of Dehat-i-Taaluqa (Zamindari villages) and the evolution of the Taaluqdari system during the Mughal Age', *IESHR*, Vol. II, No. 2 & 3, 1965, pp. 261-2. In case of Kashmir during the period of our study officials supported the view that the ownership vested with the king and not the peasant.
24. Wingate, op. cit., p. 65..
25. Ibid., pp. 60-4.
26. *For Dept. Sec., C. March* 31, 1848, files nos. 66-70, NAI.
27. Mirza Saif-ud-Din, *Akhbarat*, op. cit., vol. I, f. 44. See also H.M. Lawrence, *Transfer of Govt. to Maharaja Gulah Singh*, Section C, January 1848, File Nos. 33-44, J.A.
28. J. Korbel, *Danger in Kashmir*, Princeton University Press, 1954, reprint 1966, p. 16.
29. Lawrence, *Valley*, op. cit., pp. 310-11. *A Note on Jammu and Kashmir State*, p. 36. See also Charles Girdlestone, op. cit., p. 30.

30. A.L. Admas, *Wanderings of a Naturalist in India*, Edinburg, 1867. See also Wreford, *Census of India*, 1941, op. cit., vol. XXII, p. 8.
31. Wazir Ganganath, *Report on Jammu & Kashmir State*, 1943 (typed script), Jammu Archives, p. 69.
32. Mifza, op. cit., vol. I, ff. 52-3.
33. Ibid.
34. Ibid., vol. V, ff. 71-2.
35. Younghusband, *Kashmir*, op. cit., pp. 180-1, G.C. Bruce, op. cit., p. 39. See for details Lawrence, *Valley*, p. 213. Please see the table at p. 111.
36. Lawrence, *Valley*, op. cit., p. 217.
37. *Majmu-i-Report Jammu, Kashmir and Tibet*, 1877-78, op. cit., pp. 18-19.
38. Hassan, *Tarikh-i-Hasan*, op. cit., vol. I, pp. 471-2. The number of 35,000 is obviously a rough computation, for the details, given by Hassan add upto only 31,700.
39. Lawrence, *Valley*, op. cit., p. 205.
40. Ibid., p. 5. See also *Assessment Report of Pratap Singh Pora Tehsil*, Rambir Government Press, Jammu, 1917 p. 45.
41. Mir Saifullah, *Tarikhnama-Kashmir* (*1806-66*) (unpublished Persian Manuscript). Late Prof. Z.L. Jalla of Kashmir University has been kind enough to lend me this manuscript for consultation.
42. *Assessment Report of Pratap Singh Pora Tehsil*, op. cit., p. 45.
43. Ibid.
44. Dewan Krishan Lal, op. cit., pp. 20-2, Lawrence, *Valley*, p. 5.
45. *Report on the Financial Condition of the Kashmir State,* 10 August 1891. In accordance with instructions received from the Government of India.
46. *Karvai-Jalsa-Council Aliya for the year 1898-1900*, Jammu Archives.
47. *Note on the Review of Six Tehsils of the Valley* (published by Jammu & Kashmir Government), Jammu, p. 11.
48. H.W. Brailsford, 'Kashmir Today through Foreign Eyes', Bombay, 1948.
49. Kalhana, *Rajatarangini* op. cit., p. 209, ibid., vol. II, pp. 172-4.
50. Mirza, op. cit., vol. I, f. 74.
51. Ibid., vol. I, ff. 29, 62..
52. Grevis, ,op. cit., pp. 57-8.
53. Mirza, op. cit., vol. IV, ff. 61, 78 and 84. For details see A.P. Nicholson, *Scraps of Paper, India's Broken Treaties, Her Princes and Her Problems*, London, 1930, pp. 100-2.
54. Mirza, op. cit., vol. IV, f. 84.
55. Ibid., vol. IX, ff. 43-50.

56. Hasan, *Tarikh-i-Hasan*, op. cit., vol. II, pp. 869-70. *Imperial Gazetteer of India*, op. cit., vol. IX, p. 78.
57. Hasan, op. cit., pp. 869-70.
58. Lawrence, *Valley*, p. 412. Grevis, op. cit., p. 154.
59. Knight, op. cit., p. 70. Wingate, op. cit., p. 70. See also N.D. Nargis, *Tarikh-i-Dogra Desh,* p. 425.
60. Lawrence, *Valley,* p. 414. Knight, op. cit., p. 69.
61. Ibid., pp. 12-22. Maharaja Pratap Singh, *Diary*, op. cit., pp. 20-2.
62. Knight, op. cit., pp. 69-70. Pol. Dept. S.A.R., 1906, file no. 77, JA. See also Pol. Dept., S.A.R., 1913, file no. 213, JA.
63. Foreign Dept. Sec. E., December 1890, file nos. 196-211, NAI, Foreign Dept. Sec. E., February 1891, file nos. 295-306, NAI. Knight, op. cit., p. 70.
64. Lawrence, *Valley*, p. 414.
65. Foreign Dept. file no. 15, 29 January 1890, R.P. Nisbets, *Letter to the Secretary to Govt. of India,* NAI.
66. Lawrence, *Valley*, p. 411.
67. Ibid., pp. 215-17. G.T. Vigne, *Travels*, vol. II, p. 171.
68. Charles Baron Hugel, *The Punjab and Kashmir*, John Petheram, London, 1845, rpt. Asian Educational Services, Jammu and Kashmir, Jammu, 1972, 1995, p. 90. Victor Jacqoue-Mont, *Letters from India*, op. cit., p. 328.
69. Lawrence, *Valley*, pp. 256-61. See also *Administrative Report of Jammu and Kashmir State, 1921-22*, Government Rambir Press, Jammu, 1923, p. 28.
70. Lawrence, *Valley*, pp. 305-6.

CHAPTER 6

Pattern of Trade

Besides agriculture, trade and industrial activity, though on a very limited scale, constituted another means of livelihood for Kashmir's population. But until the end of the nineteenth century, the internal and external trade of Kashmir was not based on any sophisticated network of local markets. Bad roads, inadequate communication, a variety of weights and measures, and a poor administrative and financial system all impeded trade in and outside the country. During Maharaja Gulab Singh's period there were two kinds of weights and measures. The weights of stone were introduced. One kind among these was used for official dealings the other was used to defraud the people.[1]

So far as trade in agricultural products was concerned, the limited nature of production and technical backwardness did not aid its expansion. It was the state alone which played the role of the grain trader in Kashmir.[2] To that end, the state annually collected a good number of *kharwars* of grain in the form of land revenue and various other cesses and stored the grain in the state stores. Until the government stock from these state stores was sold, the grain merchants throughout the valley were not allowed to engage in trade. If at all they intended to do so, they had to purchase their stock from the government, which they could market.[3] To prevent any infringement of this order, grain was sold in small quantities not only to the grain dealers but even to the needy. The state feared that if the people, particularly in towns, were left with surplus grain, they might sell it at high rates and encourage the grain trade at the hands of grain dealers.[4] In view of this, rice sufficient only for fifteen days' consumption was sold at a time. Capt. Cunnigham, who visited Kashmir during Maharaja Gulab Singh's reign, observed, 'It is impossible to obtain so much as one rupee's worth of wheat in the city of Kashmir.' Not more than 5 or 6 *seers* could be purchased at one time, and this was considered to be a great hardship by the middle class, who had been accustomed to buying wheat sufficiently.[5]

On the other hand, since the state demand was collected in kind for most of the time, the state had arbitrarily reserved the right to fix the market rates. Under this system, the peasants were not left with enough food for the whole year and, consequently, they had to purchase it from the market like all other non-cultivating sections of the population.[6] This system made peasant families dependent on money.[7] The state virtually enjoyed monopoly of trade in food grains. There was no open market for food grains and as such open market operations were absent. It was, therefore, a question of people purchasing whatever the state had to sell at a rate arbitrarily fixed by it. The movement of food grains inside the village and town was associated with long established modes of economic domination and exploitation. The state itself was the dominating party in food procurement and trade. The regulation of the whole operation was arbitrary and as such it provided extensive scope for exploitation of various sections of society, particularly the landless peasants. The main aim of the peasants was, naturally, to grow food crops and to feed themselves. But their fortune was linked with the urban areas where they had to feed the lords, the state functionaries, and other non-cultivating sections of the population, among whom the majority were shawl weavers.[8] Hence, in one way or the other, they had to part with most of their food crops and obtained, in return a bit of iron, salt, and cloth. Some of the peasant proprietors who possessed grains in addition to their subsistence requirements, used to carry them to the Punjab, Rawalpindi and other areas in northern India, in exchange for salt and clothes. In fact, this development in transport should have easily exposed Kashmir to the world at that time when rapid industrial development was taking place almost in every part of the world. Europe was making great strides in science and technology. Industry was superseding agriculture as the main source of livelihood for a majority of people. But Kashmir remained primitive in its self-imposed isolation.[9] It was not just the state's monopolistic policy that prevented grain merchants from standing between the actual producer and the market. Kashmir lacked modern means of communication and transport. Even as late as 1890, W.R. Lawrence wrote, 'One of the points which at once strikes a visitor to Kashmir is the absence of roads fit for wheeled carriage.... The roads as understood in other countries do not exist.'[10] Some of the agricultural and pastoral products such as wool, barley, hides, drugs, oil seeds, wood, and other cereals which should have served a variety of useful purposes could not be transported to urban areas in handsome quantities. Aside from it, there was a lack of capital and a lack of initiative on the part of grain merchants. There were other constraints too which hampered the development of trade beyond a certain limit during the period of our study.[11]

TABLE 6.1: CHIEF ITEMS OF EXPORT AND IMPORT

Imports	*Exports*
Raw cotton, piece goods, brass, iron, salt, sugar tobacco and snuff.	Drugs, raw fibres, manufactured fibres, fruits, skins and hides, oil seeds, wool, shawls and woollen piece goods.[12]

Source: W.R. lawrence, *Valley of Kashmir*, London, 1895, pp. 390-4.

Among the articles of export, drugs, fibres, fruits and woolen piece goods were of chief importance not only to the traders but also to the peasants in general. The lack of statistical figures in our sources presents great difficulty in determining the actual volume of trade in agricultural products.[13]

TABLE 6.2: RUPEE VALUE OF ARTICLES OF EXPORT FROM 1886 TO 1893

Article	*1886-7*	*1887-8*	*1888-9*	*1889-90*	*1890-1*	*1891-2*	*1892-3*
Drugs	1,78,843	2,47,016	2,61,016	2,09,571	3,40,672	4,07,969	1,60,625
Fibres	6,279	14,861	13,466	10,245	10,435	11,570	8,919
Fruits	1,41,485	2,57,542	2,43,501	3,01,068	2,27,782	2,22,645	2,36,683
Woolen piece goods	5,93,257	5,49,463	6,00,729	7,17,721	6,37,522	5,11,235	5,91,439

Source: W.R. lawrence, *Valley of Kashmir, London*, 1895, pp. 390-4.

Table 6.2 suggests the meagreness of the volume of exports even though there was a marginal increase in the export volume. The drugs included *chob-i-kuth*, lac, leaves of *kah-i-zaban* (Macrolomiabarithrui) and the leaves and seeds of Hyonrcyanuis, Niger, Henbane, and other medicinal plants and flowers. Among these medicinal plants and flowers, roses were very important because they were made into jam (*khimbeer*) and then exported to the Punjab. It was as a result of this that Maharaja Gulab Singh got some of the places converted into rose gardens like the western bank of Kut-Kul Canal where mainly roses were grown.[14] They were collected by the peasants from forests, which they handed over to local shopkeepers in return for tea and salt.[15]

Kashmir also appears to have exported a great quantity of woollen goods to other regions like the Punjab and other parts of Central Asia.[16]

Utilization of fruits for commercial purposes appears to have increased during the period of our study. Due to it being a perishable commodity and due to a lack of quick means of transport, the fruits could not be exported to far-off markets. Among fruits, walnuts, apples, and grapes had some demand in the market. Walnuts were used for extracting oil by wanies and grapes were used for making wine.

The given figures in Table 6.3 have been collected from the Administrative Reports of the period from 1882 to 1900 which are available in State Archives at Jammu and Srinagar.[17]

Merchants and *bakals* provided the agricultural population or the sellers of fruits with snuff, iron implements, tobacco, cotton piece goods and some amount of sugar.[18]

The trade of Kashmir was almost entirely with the Punjab and Ladakh.

Trade

The exports to Punjab consisted of rice, fruits, *ghee*, hides, oil seeds, timber, wool and sheep; the imports were wheat, gram, sugar, salt, hardware, piece-goods, tea, snuff, tobacco, kerosene oil, and metals. The value of Kashmir trade with Panjab in 1890-1 was nearly Rs. 113 lakh, and with Ladakh upwards Rs. 6 lakh. These figures do not, however, include the rail-borne traffic between Jammu and

TABLE 6.3: TOTAL SALES OF WINE FROM 1882 TO 1900 IN BOTTLES

Year	*White Wine*	*Red Wine*	*No.1 Brandy*	*No. 2 Brandy*	*Apple Brandy*	*Vinejar*	*Spirits of Wine*	*Cider Absinthe pagne and Cinchona*		*Chem-Cheery Brandy*		*Total*
1882-3	-	841	-	113	3,996	36	-	-	-	-	-	4,976
1883-4	750	1,778	-	13	5,894	44	-	-	-	-	-	8,479
1884-5	880	1,448	6	194	5,736	70	-	-	-	-	-	8,342
1885-6	194	98	2	98	7,144	52	48	-	-	-	-	7,336
1886-7	639	1,024	1	4	4,708	109	-	-	-	-	-	6,485
1887-8	1,455	4,803	-	166	11,722	109	-	-	-	-	-	18,257
1888-9	880	2,091	60	26	10,055	98	-	-	-	-	-	13,210
1889-90	1,208	2,832	122	209	16,448	27	-	-	-	-	-	20,846
1890-1	1,218	4,663	81	129	14,197	1	-	-	-	-	-	20,294
1891-2	723	3,307	69	157	14,764	57	-	-	-	-	-	19,077
1892-3	903	3,814	49	417	17,298	61	28	-	-	-	-	22,579
1893-4	1,347	3,082	109	417	16,322	175	67	59	-	15	-	21,578
1894-5	879	5,271	185	436	18,462	363	57	799	-	-	-	26,467
1895-6	1,162	3,578	77	394	16,482	158	122	351	-	-	-	22,324
1896-7	1,126	3,671	190	259	22,576	85	626	160	-	-	-	28,193
1897-8	1,650	4,666	166	229	19,864	200	199	419	-	-	26	27,516
1898-9	2,190	7,078	141	288	23,323	126	222	659	-	6	70	34,103
1899-1900	1,720	6,870	139	317	25,760	105	233	1,077	194	7	225	36,547

Source: Annual Administrative Reports, Jammu Archives.

TABLE 6.4: TOTAL CASH REALIZED FROM THE YEAR 1882-1900 FROM WINE SALES

Year	*White Wine*	*Red Wine*	*No. 1 Brandy*	*No. 2 Brandy*	*Apple Brandy*	*Spirits of Wine*	*Wine jar*	*Cider*	*Anisette & Absinthe*	*Champagne & Cinchona*	*Cheery Brandy*	*Miscell-aneous*	*Total receipt*
1882-3	-	853	-	158	2,293	-	13	-	-	-	-	-	3,317
1883-4	756	1,848	-	22	4,681	-	25	-	-	-	-	-	7,332
1884-5	948	1,810	18	366	4,072	72	38	-	-	-	-	-	7,252
1885-6	328	196	6	183	5,043	-	22	-	-	-	-	-	5,860
1886-7	643	1,373	3	10	2,742	-	18	-	-	-	-	-	4,789
1887-8	1,422	4,000	-	200	9,000	-	90	-	-	-	-	-	14,712
1888-9	1,001	2,370	176	52	5,972	-	57	-	-	-	-	-	9,628
1889-90	1,400	4,000	334	353	9,850	-	25	-	-	-	-	-	15,140
1890-1	1,362	2,370	235	245	11,353	-	1	-	-	-	-	-	18,432
1891-2	792	3,178	199	296	11,990	-	35	-	-	-	-	-	16,787
1892-3	996	5,236	146	815	13,445	42	53	-	-	-	-	-	19,872
1893-4	1,286	3,475	309	789	14,776	85	106	18	-	-	-	462	20,772
1894-5	827	4,375	494	804	14,263	72	218	250	-	30	-	378	22,396
1895-6	1,106	2,940	214	745	14,005	152	98	110	-	-	-	136	20,400
1896-7	1,098	5,062	527	489	17,458	158	53	50	-	-	-	156	23,927
1897-8	1,447	3,834	458	624	17,281	294	125	131	-	-	52	558	25,689
1898-9	1,866	3,938	388	550	19,278	277	79	220	-	18	139	301	30,746
1899-1900	1,613	4,766	383	612	22,446	291	66	340	77	21	450	501	34,603

Source: Annual Administrative Reports, Jammu Archives

TABLE 6.5: BOTTLES DEPARTMENTALLY USED AND THE DRYAGE

Year	*Departmentally used no. of bottles*	*White Wine*	*Dryage*		*Total Dryage*	*Total*
			Red Wine	*Brandy*		
1882-3	1,172	-	-	25	25	1,197
1883-4	450	-	-	4	4	454
1884-5	335	-	-	-	-	335
1885-6	462	1,500	-	541	2,041	2,503
1886-7	1,909	547	243	126	915	2,824
1887-8	470	685	352	3	1,040	1,510
1888-9	434	784	593	1,308	2,685	3,199
1889-90	1,674	1,727	1,681	2	3,410	5,084
1890-1	634	1,666	1,286	3	2,955	3,589
1891-2	806	1,455	929	8,608	10,992	11,798
1892-3	640	2,741	1,707	6,555	11,003	11,643
1893-4	1,841	1,829	3,671	938	6,438	8,279
1894-5	7,416	2,492	387	1,122	4,001	11,447
1895-6	7,304	3,242	1,531	1,245	6,018	13,322
1896-7	1,822	3,089	1,421	1,065	5,575	7,307
1897-8	27,530	696	372	2,940	4,008	31,338
1898-9	278	1,677	1,577	1,715	4,969	5,247
1899-1900	635	1,539	1,901	1,712	5,152	5,787

Source: Annual Administrative Reports, Jammu Archives.

TABLE 6.6: DETAILS OF EXPENDITURE ON THE WINE INDUSTRY FROM 1882-1900

Year	Building		Machinery etc.	Establishment	Cropes	Apples	Miscellaneous & Fuel	Total
	PWD	Civil Department						
1882-3	-	-	2,544	866	1,000	2,996	1,103	8,509
1883-4	-	-	3,396	1,439	1,635	1,893	954	9,317
1884-5	-	-	2,435	1,804	2,750	2,450	1,264	10,703
1885-6	-	-	354	259	2,053	190	283	3,179
1886-7	-	-	2,499	7,605	2,975	-	19	13,098
1887-8	19,480	-	7,794	7,488	4,187	-	22	38,971
1888-9	1,367	24	6,834	7,917	-	-	-	16,142
1889-90	5,561	-	2,326	7,297	1,534	-	2,333	19,951
1890-1	912	10	919	6,731	1,296	67	1,587	11,522
1891-2	228	150	2,856	5,427	3,760	-	3,039	15,460
1892-3	1,185	-	-	6,435	627	-	7,259	15,516
1893-4	-	-	-	7,072	2,574	-	4,537	14,177
1894-5	5,547	-	-	7,831	2,300	2,310	2,802	23,790
1895-6	520	-	1,530	7,975	44	371	5,713	16,153
1896-7	-	-	-	9,701	4,271	2,246	5,885	22,103
1897-8	509	-	3,830	10,483	1,351	120	3,738	20,031
1898-9	22	-	160	10,275	199	1,236	2,566	15,458
1899-1900	437	-	200	10,386	1,474	2,952	2,921	15,370

Source: Annual Administrative Reports, Jammu Archives.

Sialkot, which is not registered, and cannot in consequence adequately represent the entire trade of the state. The chief means of communication with the Panjab are by (1) the Banihal route from the railway station near Jammu to Srinagár through the Ohenab valley, 163 miles; (2) the Punch route from the town of Jhelum to Srinagar by the Punch valley, 198 miles; (3) the Panjar route from Rawalpindi to Srinagar by Punch and the Jhelum valley, 180 miles; (4) the Abbottabad route from Kala ke Serai to Srinagar through Hazara and the upper Jhelum valley, 210 miles; and (5) the Jhelum valley route from Rawalpindi to Srinagar via Murree, Kohala and Baramulla, 195 miles. This last route, the Jhelum valley route, is destined to be by far the most important route for all purposes. By means of it tongas and carts one can travel from Rawalpindi to Baramulla on the Jhelum, a distance of 165 miles, over a good road with easy gradients. An extension of the road from Baramulla to Srinagar, 34 miles, would be quite easy to construct, if money were available. Towards Central Asia, a road 230 miles long, which will, it is hoped, be passable for light carts, is being constructed to Gilgit on the northern frontier of the state. There is also a fairly good road, 259 miles long, from Srinagar to Leh in Ladakh. At present the most important trade route is probably the Banihal from Srinagar via Islamabad to Jammu, but this route is being superseded by the Jhelum valley route.[19]

During Maharaja Ranbir Singh's period, the perishable commodities of fruits like grapes and apples assumed a commercial significance when a wine distillery and wine manufactory were founded in Kashmir for manufacturing wine from grapes and apples.[20] However, the extent to which these products were commercialized can be seen in Table 6.6, which gives the total sales and total expenditure incurred from AD 1882 to 1900.[21]

So far as other agricultural products like saffron, water chestnuts and oil seeds are concerned, our sources do not figure out the volume of saffron and water chestnuts exported during the period under study.[22]

The forest produce, particularly wood, was in great demand in India for the construction of railways, but due to the absence of technical knowhow and modern means of transport, it could not be exploited on the desired scale.[23]

The cash value of oil seed exported from 1886-93 is as under:

TABLE 6.7: CASH VALUE OF OIL SEEDS EXPORTED FROM 1886-93

Kind of Oil Seed	*1886-7*	*1887-8*	*1888-9*	*1889-90*	*1890-1*	*1891-2*	*1892-3*
Linseed	1,766	660	627	6,201	18,528	5,479	1,335
Mustard and rape seed	9,114	13,893	35,673	81,189	13,491	99,624	59,769
Til	12,140	35,283	16,000	47,160	82,941	29,644	1,07,024

Source: W.R. Lawrence, *Valley of Kashmir*, Oxford University Press, London, 1895, p. 388.

The value of exported wood was as under:

TABLE 6.8: VALUE OF EXPORTED WOOD FROM 1886-93[24]

1886-7	*1887-8*	*1888-9*	*1889-90*	*1890-1*	*1891-2*	*1892-3*
1,85,914	2,89,333	2,53,765	48,282	43,890	2,02,124	49,696

Source: W.R. Lawrence, *Valley of Kashmir*, Oxford University Press, London, 1895, p. 388.

Shawl and Silk Trade

The shawl and silk industries also provided employment to Kashmir's population. The shawls of Kashmir were highly praised not only in India but in the royal courts of France, England, and other countries of the world.[25] Shawl was the second important source of revenue after land and continued to be an article of great economic importance even during the early Dogra rule. When Gulab Singh ascended the throne there were 7,000 shawl looms with 17,000 weavers working on them. Apart from this, there were also 3,500 *karkhandars* who were in-charge of separate units of this prominent industry.[26] The pale blue shawl presented by Maharaja to the Prince of Wales and development of special institutions for classification of Kashmiri shawls by the successor states of Mughal India depicts that this shawl was one of the most important material representation of Kashmir to the outside world.[27] It emerged as a universal symbol of aristocracy. The Kashmiri merchants were seen in Yarkand, Khotan and Central Asia for the purpose of attaining sufficient quantities of raw material. During the rule of Maharaja Gulab Singh, the Kashmiri merchants showed great determination and monopolized the wool trade of Chinese Turkistan and established warehouses there.[28] Similarly the merchants from France and British India came to Srinagar with the purpose of commissioning shawls for export.[29] The presence of French agents in Srinagar testified by travel accounts like Charles Baron Hugel left a great impact upon the shawl Industry.[30] The intervention of French agents led to a great transformation in the design of shawls in the mid-nineteenth century. The annual output of shawls reached 50 lakh in 1850 and there were about 30,000 to 40,000 weavers who were engaged with this industry. The shawls which suited the French market were manufactured. The income of the state from shawl industry was Rs. 7 lakh from Gulab Singh's reign till 1869. The demand increased and the shawl industry got a filip. But the question arises here why the impact lasted for such a short time and why only after a decade the industry received a death blow. The need is to analyse the other side of the French impact.

Due to the French intervention, the cheaper methods of shawl making became possible because of the several imitations of the shawl industry in France.[31] This marked the beginning of the decline of the shawl industry. The decline also set in because of the presence of some flaws in the system of administration that was controlling the shawl industry. The government adopted a system of grain control which was meant to supply cheap grains to the city of Srinagar for the purpose of distributing it amongst the population. Majority of the population were shawl *baafs* but in reality it never benefitted them. There used to be a *karkhandar* (owner of shawl factory) under whom there were a number of *shawlbaafs*. The shawl weavers received a certain amount of Shali from the *karkhandar* at arbitrary prices. Rs. 37 was taxed on each *karkhandar* for every *shawlbaaf* under him.[32] The state controlled the shawl trade through the institution of *Dagh-i-Shawl* which imposed heavy duties upon these shawls that resulted in heavy damage of this shawl industry. The class that got severely hit by this heavy taxation were the *shawlbaafs*. Ironically, out of the earnings of Rs. 7 they had to pay Rs. 5 as tax. Many writers have described their miseries and squared conditions in which they worked. It seemed that the state of penury for the *shawlbaafs* was for lifetime because they were banned from leaving the valley or to change their employer.[33] This cunning attitude of the state towards this industry contributed to its decline.

In the year 1847 the weavers assembled and put their demands before Gulab Singh. They demanded either they should be given permission to migrate to Punjab or their working conditions should be improved. Gulab Singh promised to do the latter but his promise was never put into practice.[34] The result was that a large number of weavers migrated to Amritsar in the hope of better working conditions.[35] Rest of the weavers who stayed back again petitioned and demanded reduction in the *shali* price and several other taxes. But their demands were rejected by the Pandit Raj Kak Dhar. Disheartened by the attitude of Raj Kak Dhar the *shawlbaafs* raised the banner of revolt in 1865.

In 1867 when the Maharaja realized that the number of shawl weavers migrating to Punjab was increasing day by day, he introduced some measures like he ordered his officials to allow the weavers to purchase eleven *kharwars* of *shali* in a year.[36] Maharaja remitted Rs. 11 from the tax in 1868 and also set up a department known as *Darogh-i-Shawl* with the purpose of addressing the grievances of the weavers. In 1867 Ranbir Singh sent a proposal to the Punjab Government demanding the appointment of an agent in London who would organize the sale of Kashmiri shawls. The Maharaja's proposal was accepted by the Punjab Government and a warehouse of Kashmiri shawls was established in New Street, London.[37] In 1868 a tax amounting to Rs. 30,000 was also remitted on the shawl weavers.

There was a significant rise in the export of shawls to Europe in the mid-nineteenth century. The value of exports in 1850 was Rs. 171,709 which reached up to Rs. 459,441 in 1861-2.[38] However the revolt of 1865 has a great blow to the exports falling up to Rs. 254,498.[39] The final blow to the exports came due to the Franco-Prussian War of 1870 which damaged the main market of Kashmiri shawls, particularly in France. In 1871 the shawl weavers dwindled from 27,000 to 24,000. The shawl industry also received its death blow from the Shia-Sunni conflicts, in which Shias were mostly affected. Most of the Shias left the valley and the industry suffered badly. The Maharaja tried his best to rehabilitate the Shias and gave them Rs. 3 lakh in relief. The Maharaja also abolished the price of *shali* sold to the *shawlbaafs*. He also reduced the tax on shawl weavers from Rs. 35 to 20. However, all these efforts proved to be failures when the valley was engulfed by a devastating famine in 1877. The famine took the lives of a substantial number of a population that was engaged with this industry. The industry lost its significance and people engaged with this opted for other occupation.

The Maharaja established its monopoly over many products that fetched significant amount of income to the state owing to his claim of master of the whole land. Lawrence, the settlement officer in Kashmir recorded: 'when I started my settlement work, everything was taxed. Fruit trees, birch barks, violets, hides, silk, saffron, hemp, tobacco, water chestnuts and paper were treated as state monopolies and farmed out to Hindu pundits'.[40] The state entrusted officials with the work of collection of share from such products. Saffron which was considered as the most lucrative crop of Kashmir was monopolized by the state. The cultivator's after hard toil in the fields were left with only half of the produce and a large portion went to the coffers of the state. In some case more than half was taken by the state and the cultivator had to be contend with ¼ of the produce.

Another good source of revenue to the state was the silk industry. The industry was in a good position during the Sikh rule and continued to be in the tempo of development during Gulab Singh's period. Gulab Singh appointed Hakim Abdul Rahim in-charge of this industry but there were still many loopholes that needed to be overcome. In 1871 N.G. Mukherjee writes, 'before 1869 the Silk Industry was ill-organized and there was no change from many years'. Moreover, the dearth of adequate statistical data hinders us from determining the actual quality and quantity of seed production as well as rearing output and reeling output. But it seems that the industry was somewhat in a better condition, which is testified by an incident which took place in 1855 when all the silkworms in Europe were caught by a horrible silkworm disease. However, 1,562.5 lbs. of Kashmiri silkworm seeds were found disease-free by an examination conducted by two Italian Experts M.M. Orio and Consono. This quantity of seed was packed in boxes made of wood and taken to Italy by the end of November.[41] One can assume that a region that could export 1,562.5 lbs. of seed for foreigners must have kept a good quality for the local consumption. During Gulab Singh's period, the total tax realized by the Government was Rs.1,30,000. Maharaja Ranbir Singh who ascended the throne in 1857 gave a new lease of life to this industry by establishing 127 rearing houses for the purpose of rearing silkworms.[42] For conducting the silk business, a department was also setup.[43] For the expansion of the silk industry Rs. 30,000 were sanctioned.[44] Ranbir Singh established its monopoly over the industry in 1871 and appointed Babu Nilamber Mukherjee as its supervisor.[45] Mukherjee introduced new methods of breeding silkworms and European techniques of reeling of silk, which improved the quality of silk significantly. In the year 1859-60 the total output of the cocoon reeling was 19 maunds. The Department purchased another 32,00,000 lbs from the villagers for a sum of Rs. 6,00,000. If we believe Charles Bates, these 3,20,00,000 were procured from about 35,000 villagers earning an income of Rs. 11 each. The rearers got a sort of relief as it was equivalent to two months' wages of the cultivators.[46] Maharaja Ranbir Singh took many initiatives like sanctioning of Rs. 3 lakh for the reorganization of the industry, ordering imported reeling appliances and machinery from Europe, awarded gold and silver medals to the most successful sericulturalists and most importantly exempted rearers from *begar*. The total yield of silk in 1871 was 70 *kharwars* amounting to Rs. 2 lakh, which gave a profit of Rs. 9,000. In the year 1872, the production reached 400 *kharwars* and government realized a revenue of *chilki* Rs. 96,000. In 1873 the production increased to 516 *kharwars* which was worth *chilki* Rs. 1,68,221 and the government got a total profit of *chilki* Rs. 40,156 after deducting all the expenditures incurred.[47] In 1874 three silk factories at Cherapora in Anantnag, Haftchinar in Srinagar and Raghunathpur in Nasim Bagh were set up.[48] Silk of good quality and soft fibre was produced in these filatures and was exported to London at the rate of 23 to 24 shillings a pound. However, the famine of 1877-8 gave a great setback to this industry like the shawl industry. The state policies were also responsible for its decline as per the testimony of Lawrence. The exemption from *begar* made the *kirmkashas* a privileged class in the society who misused their power and were looked upon by the common masses with hatred. A disease of the silkworm called Pebrine gave a final death blow to this industry. The government couldn't control the disease and the industry was almost wiped out. In 1869 there were 127 rearing houses, out of which only two survived, one at Raghunathpur in Srinagar and another at Shirpora in Anantnag.

Paper continued to be a source of income during the early Dogras as in the case of the Sikhs. When Gulab Singh took the reins of the government in 1846, he issued regulations for the full protection of this industry and during his time Kashmir continued to produce superior quality of paper which was known for its durability and excellent quality throughout India. As already discussed in the previous chapter, industry got a severe setback during the last years of Sikh rule but still only after one year of Gulab Singh's rule, paper worth Rs. 15,000 were exported by the state to Punjab. Ranbir Singh also showed good interest in this industry and in 1864 a sample of Kashmiri paper was sent for display to an exhibition held in Lahore. The visitors appreciated the quality prepared in Kashmir and the ruler of Kashmir received praises from one and all. It was during Ranbir Singh's rule that paper from Kashmir made its entry into all the government offices of native states where it was used to keep records and to maintain manuscripts. The demand multiplied also due to the establishment of papier-mâché on a sound footing that consumed a lot of paper. In order to meet local demand as well as the export demand, the Maharaja ordered for the establishment of more units of paper industry in Jammu province. The state had already 32 units of industry at Nowshera and its environs in the Kashmir province. Each unit provided employment to at least people, so in general a considerable number of people would have been employed in this industry. The government introduced virtual monopoly on this industry in 1875 and the paper manufactured was mostly consumed in the state for official usage and the rest surplus if any was sold to the merchants. A bundle of paper consisting of 24 sheets cost Rs. 3. However, during the last years of Ranbir Singh's reign, the industry received a setback and its revival became impossible due to the arrival of large quantity of machine-made paper in the market.

The state also established its control on the sale of *kuth*, tea and salt. The state also brought stones used for construction purposes under its jurisdiction by farming them to the contractors in return of a stipulated amount.[49] The state also collected a tax on the boatman in the shape of *nawia*. In 1852 Maharaja Gulab Singh formed this tax to a contractor, namely, *Lachmanju* at Rs. 1,05,000.[50] He was informed to collect this tax from the boat owners even if they remained unhired throughout the season. The dwelling boats were also brought under this taxation as per the testimony of Saraf. Similarly, another source of income to the state was *chobi farosh* (tax imposed on timber and wood). It too, like the boat tax was farmed out to contractors for Rs. 1 lakh. Rs. 91,000 was annually collected as a license tax on trade called *baj*. A tax at the rate of 5 per cent was also imposed on the department of mint. About Rs. 75,000 was collected annually from the royal mint. [51] The brick kilns were also subjected to taxation known as *chorna puzi* during the early Dogras at the rate of Rs. 50,000 per thousand baked bricks and the state claim from this source was Rs. 25,000 annually.[52] The people also had to pay a tax on marriage known as *Zar-i-Nikah* at the rate of Rs. 3 towards the state. The state collected Rs. 5,000 annually from this tax.[53] However, this tax was abolished when Maharaja Ranbir Singh ascended the throne of the state.[54] A tax known as *Gadaharaj* was imposed on the peasants for the maintenance of a charitable kitchen. Initially its income was used for the construction of the Gadhadar temple located opposite to the Shergadi Palace but with the passage of time the whole revenue appropriated under this head was used for the maintenance of chartable kitchen. During Ranbir Singh's rule the people of Ladakh were also subjected to this taxation and government earned Rs. 12,000 annually from this taxation.[55] The state also imposed a tax in cash on the movement of metals within the state. On each metal worth Rs. 1,000, Rs. 2 was charged. The tax on metals amounted to Rs. 12,000 annually.[56] The state didn't stop here and extracted from peasants many taxes in kind. On every hundred *kharwars* peasants had to pay 4 *traks* for the maintenance of sepoys, one anna per head on every sheep or goat, further the villages with land produce of 500 *kharwars* or more had to give an extra tax in the form of two or three sheep or goats, one pony and one blanket,[57] in rural areas it was mandatory for peasants to deposit 1 *seer* of *ghee* annually and in the honey producing region of Lar and Wardwen and other villages one-half during last years of Sikh rule and Gulab Singh's reign and later on two-third was taken by *kardar* as government share. Even the scavengers had to deposit towards government some skins annually. Moreover, bakers, butchers and boatmen had also to pay a sort of tax out of their earnings with no return of social services from the government.[58] The naturally grown products were also brought under the domain of taxation. A considerable amount of income was generated by taxing the *singharas* (water chestnut). The state amassed an income of *chilki* Rs. 4,000 by taxing the reed that was extracted by people from the Anchar lake and used in mat-weaving and thatching of houses. It is said, Gulab Singh in 1850 for his lust for money imposed a 'capitation tax' on all the individuals of the village practicing any labour, trade, profession or employment at the rate of Re. 1 to Rs. 2. It was collected on a daily basis. The income from these taxes amounted about Rs. 1,10,000 which was realized through *muqaddam*.[59]

For manufacturing shawls, the *pashm* (wool) of the domesticated goat and *asli tus* (the finer wool of the wild goat) were imported from Chanthan, Yarkand, Khutan, Tibet, Chinese Turkistan, and some other parts of Central Asia.[60]

The shawl manufacturing had to undergo a long apprenticeship before acquiring the shape of the finished product. First, the women would pick the coarse hairs from the imported wool. In this process, ⅓ of the weight was lost and the remainder was packed in layers with rice flour slightly moistened with oil and was subjected to pressure under a stone for about 48 hours, whereby it was cleaned and spun into thread by women.[61] After the process of cleaning and spinning of raw material was over it was then taken to *karkhanas* or factories, where the weavers used to weave it into shawls on wooden looms.[62] The workshops for manufacturing shawls existed in many parts of the valley but were mostly found in the city of Srinagar with its primitive technology.[63] However, the number of weavers working in the *karkhanas* varied according to the size of the workshop and the number of looms available there. Charles Girdlestone, who visited Kashmir in the 1870s, says, 'The most crowded workshop contained about sixty people of all ages but all males in ill-ventilated rooms.'[64] There was another system of manufacturing shawls commonly known as *sadabaf*, where a weaver used to spin *pashmina* in his own house and embroider the shawl with needles. *Sozankari* (needlework) has been a very important subsidiary industry of Kashmir. By and large needle-work was done on shawls with coloured threads of *pashmina* and some times of *tila* (brocade thread). This industry provided work to a sizeable section of Kashmiri peasants and artisans.[65]

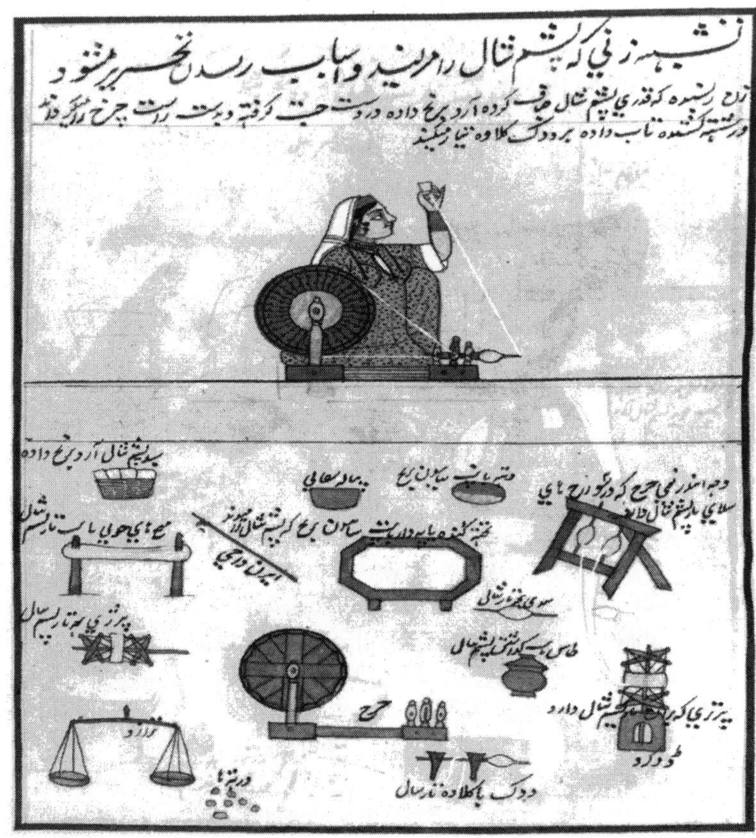

Illustration 6.1: Lady processing *pashmina* wool with traditional tools.
Source: Harbans Mukhia's Collection of Pictures from India Office Library, London.

In the former case the shawl was embroidered on the loom itself.[66] These shawls were made in different sizes and colours. Generally, the quality of a shawl depends on the fineness of its threads, harmony of colour and precision of workmanship. However, the best shawls were manufactured in Srinagar and its adjoining areas.[67] The shawls manufactured in Anantnag and Shahabad were inferior to those of Srinagar. The village workman did not have those facilities which were available to the urban artisans who worked in close touch with top businessmen and exporters. Moreover, the village artisans were

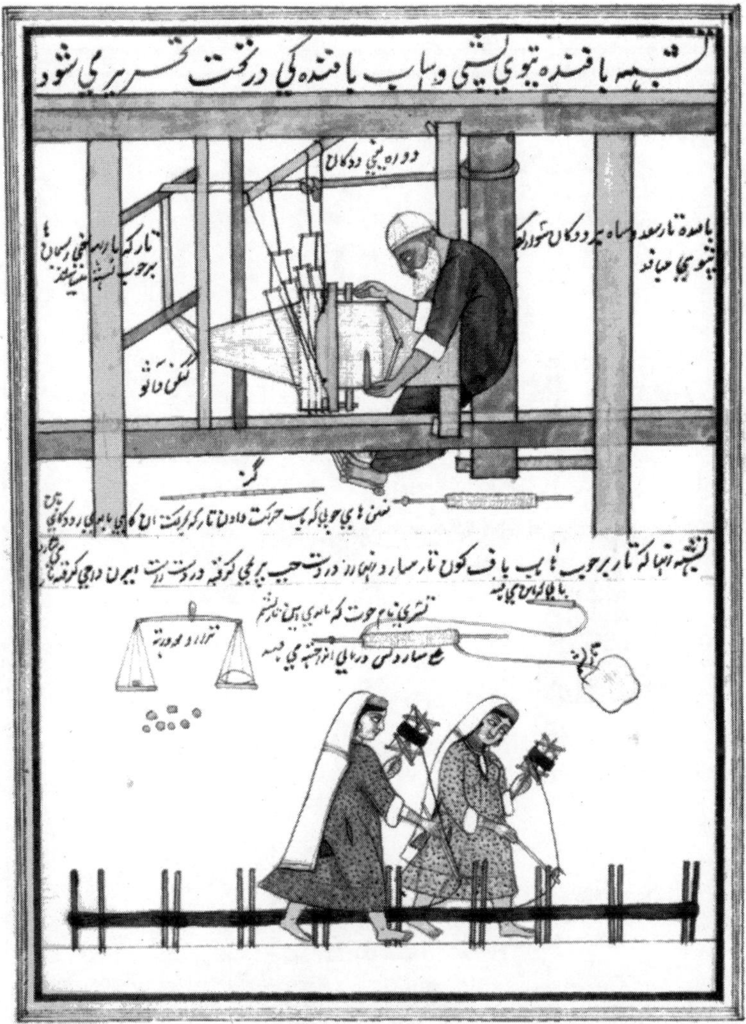

Illustration 6.2: The process of shawl making on wooden loom.
Source: Harbans Mukhia's Collection of Pictures from India Office Library, London.

essentially either landed or landless peasants who pursued the profession of shawl-making only to subsidize their income. As such they did not possess a rich tradition of workmanship which was the privilege of

Illustration 6.3: A Kashmiri Pandit merchant providing *pashmina* wool to ladies for processing. *Source:* Harbans Mukhia's Collection of Pictures from India Office Library, London.

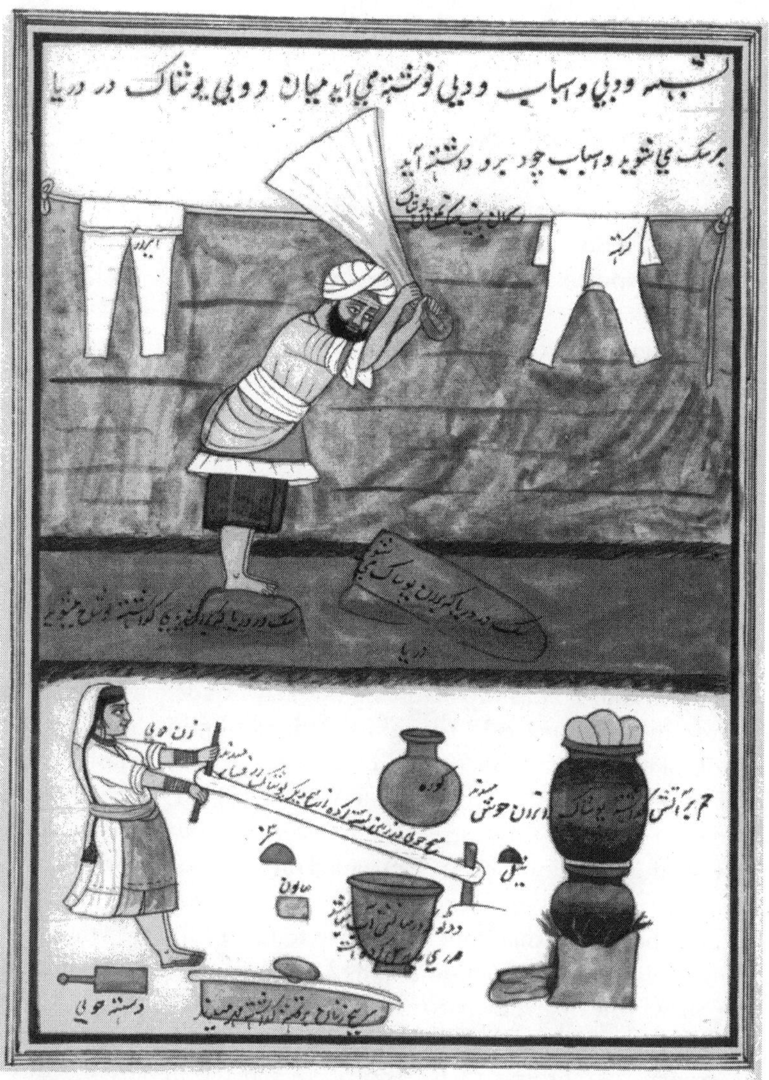

Illustration 6.4: A washerman washing manufactured clothes before they could be put on sale. *Source:* Harbans Mukhia's Collection of Pictures from India Office Library, London.

the urban craftsmen.[68] Generally, shawls were woven on the wrong side and were then rolled on a wooden beam, from which it seldom turned perfect. The shortcomings were removed by hand. After this work was over, the shawls were passed into the hands of a local washerman, who took the responsibility of removing the dirt and giving them a true shape for sending them to the market.[69]

In 1870s the price of the best shawls varied from Rs. 350 to Rs. 1,800, the square ones fetched Rs. 200 to 1,200.[70] From 1862 to 1870, the export value of shawls averaged between Rs. 25 lakh and 28 lakh .[71]

The figures mentioned in the above paragraph reveal a steady decrease in the export of shawls. There were several reasons for this decline. In the twenty years preceding 1871, Europe, which provided a brisk market for Kashmiri shawls, was shaken by no less than five wars, each involving two or more great powers of the world. These wars—the Crimean War, the Italian War of 1859, the Danish War, the Austro-Prussian conflict and the Franco-Prussian War—speeded up the tension which proved harmful for trade throughout the period.[72] They put a stop to the shawl trade in Kashmir. No reports were available about the international market, and there was a general impression that no dealing involving the shawl trade may have been entered into. To quote F. Younghusband, 'Kashmiri shawls in the middle of last century (nineteenth century) used to be very fashionable in Europe, but the Franco-Prussian War of 1870-1 seems to have sealed the fate of the industry.' The fashion went out and was never revived, and the famine of 1877-9 wiped off a number of weavers, so that now very few were left to carry on the industry.[73]

Another factor that appears to have restricted the growth of the industry was fiscal obstruction. In 1852, the total taxes collected from Dag Shawl (the Shawl Department) amounted to Rs. 7,50,00.[74] The manufacturers had not only to pay stamp duty but also custom duty on export.[75] According to R. Thorp, 47.8 per cent was the duty annually levied on the individual weaver.[76] John Irwin says that ad valorem duty of 25 per cent was charged on each shawl and its assessment and collection were farmed out to a corrupt body of officials, whose illegal exactions were said to have amounted to a further 25 per cent of the value.[77] According to R.H. Davis, till 1868,

Rs. 30 were annually demanded from weavers.[78] In 1868 this demand was reduced to Rs. 23 but still the impost of 20 per cent was levied per head.[79]

As R. Maclagan observes,

> From annexed reports, it is painfully evident that owing to the narrow-minded and suicidal policy of the Kashmir ruler, an enormous decrease in the trade between Punjab and Kashmir has taken place. The duty levied amounts almost to prohibition, and to make matters worse, the Maharaja endeavours to force trade through a certain channel. Such a policy could not fail to affect the trade disadvantageously.[80]

Consequently, the taxes charged were no less a burden for the weaver population, who showed a lack of interest and, consequently, production declined. The worst feature of the industry which appears to have given due allowance to its decline, was the condition of the workers. The nearest and most important evil oppressing the weavers was the utter lack of hope of ever-rising from their depressed condition. The more oppressive burden weighing on the weavers was the insecurity of employment. The badly constructed houses and workshops undermined their physical condition.

What care could be given to children's education when their parents worked in *karkhanas* for more than 12 hours a day? And how could life be shared under one roof when members of the family were kept away from the home all day by their work and barely met except when it was time to go to bed? [81] Surveying the multitude of deleterious influences affecting the health of weavers we can readily draw conclusions about their physical condition. Lack of care during the first years of life; insufficient and poor food; unhealthy housing conditions; insufficient clothing in severe winter; insufficient protection against the vagaries of weather; a lack of medical assistance and nursing care in sickness; and, finally, the premature employment of children in occupations proved detrimental to their development.[82] These were the common causes of the generally stunted physical condition of workers. Moreover, most places of work were arranged without any consideration for workers' help, quite apart from the fact that industrial occupations and overwork were in themselves harmful to health. Charles Girdlestone very rightly remarks, 'The occupation of shawl weavers is hereditary, more from compulsion than choice, for the son seems to have no option but to follow in his father's footsteps.'[83] The weavers were paid very small wages, which were calculated according to the number of sticks of *pashm* thread prepared by each. One who could work the stick in woof and warf one thousand times was reputed to have performed work worth one stick. Accordingly, the daily wages of weavers averaged between two and six annas.[84] In 1847 the shawl weavers abandoned the work and made representation to the Maharaja for their inadequate wages.[85] In 1854, when Maharaja Gulab Singh felt that the *karkhanas* were emptied by the exodus of shawl weavers, he decided to pay 2½ annas more than their usual wages, but only when the shawls were in great demand. Otherwise, this increase of 2½ annas was liable to reduction during years of lean demands. This was opposed by weavers and finally an increase of 1¼ annas was made in their wages.[86]

The *kitabwals* or *ustad* who kept account of wages of weavers and taught patterns earned from 6 to 8 annas a day.[87] He received 2 annas for his general supervision work, including account keeping. In addition to that, he was paid 1 anna and 3 pice per square shawl and 1 anna per striped and per flowered piece.[88] For coloured pattern the weavers got 2 pies.[89] These wages were not paid in coin but in kind. They were provided with paddy which was their staple food.[90]

Silk

Though the silk industry was of long-standing in Kashmir during the period under study, the industry appears to have been neither promising nor paying. Maharaja Gulab Singh entrusted the charge of the silk industry to Hakim Azim, his court physician.[91] The scattered references regarding the production of silk are not sufficient to generalize that the industry witnessed some advancement during Maharaja Gulab Singh's reign.[92]

In fact, it was during Maharaja Ranbir Singh's time that the silk industry was reorganized. A filature was imported from Europe with different kinds of silkworm eggs, and a department was established for undertaking developmental activities. In different parts of the valley 127 resale houses were established.

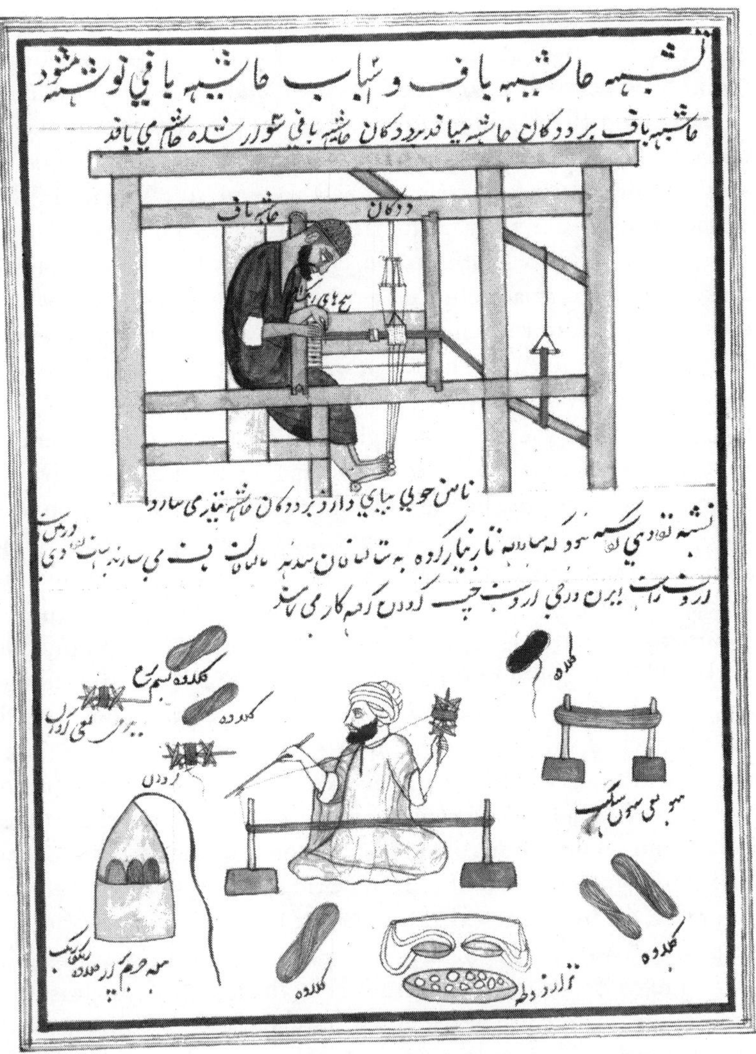

Illustration 6.5: A shawl weaver making borders of shawls on wooden loom. *Source:* Harbans Mukhia's Collection of Pictures from India Office Library, London.

However, the industry was not fully equipped to protect itself from different calamities, both natural and man-made. In AD 1878 all the silkworms died due to disease.[93] Though the supervision of industry was entrusted to Babu Nilamber Mukherjee, improvement in the reeling of silk and improvement in its production remained a farfetched thing. No doubt in 1881, Prakash Joo was able to procure some seed through Johnson, who had gone to visit Yokand in this connection.[94] Again, the symptoms of disease appeared and the worms died. From 1882 to 1890, various experiments were carried out to make this industry a going concern, but unfortunately, the whole concern was left in the hands of silk rearers who did not possess the managerial skill to ensure its progress.[95]

The number of rearing houses shrank and only two survived, one in Cherpura and the other in Raghunath Pora.[96] In 1889, attempts were made to import seeds from Italy and France on the advice of Sir Adward Buck, Secretary to the Government of India. In the same year, Sir Thomas Wardle's services were obtained to give the industry some amount of strength, but till the end of the nineteenth century, the industry remained merely in an experimental stage and not a commercial enterprise. Originally, all the processes in the production of raw silk were conducted in the peasant household.... The farmers and their families grew the mulberry trees, reared the silkworms in sheds attached to their houses, and reeled the silk on traditional instruments.[97] As a consequence of the outbreak of silkworm disease in Europe the experiments which were carried out one after the other in Kashmir could not set the industry at once to the task of meeting a large foreign demand both for silkworm eggs and silk. No doubt, it was taken up by an increased number of peasants, but that did not help the expansion of industry.[98] In spite of all these measures, silk rearing remained a household industry in the hands of peasants. The rude methods employed by the peasants could not change the character of industry. Unsanitary conditions prevailed in the homes of peasants engaged in silk rearing. This consequently proved harmful for the insect.[99]

The officials employed from time to time never cared to see whether or not the instructions were faithfully implemented. The price of cocoons was never remunerative enough to ensure the success of the industry.[100] Besides, the external backwardness of silkworm rearing also affected the working of industry. The state never inculcated among the peasants the idea that mulberry was more paying. There was no moral influence, and the peasants used it more for fuel than for leaf preservation.[101] Another reason for its under-development was the policy followed by the state. Whatever little amount was annually realized was taken away by the Maharaja and the basic interest of the industry was ignored due to a lack of proper investment. To quote Lord Curzon, 'The Maharaja and his brother both strongly declaimed in the Darbar assembled to meet me in Jammu in spring 1903 against the handing over of the industry to private enterprise.' It was a losing concern under the state because no profit was invested.[102]

Problem of Transport and Communication

For a considerable period of time, the territories of Kashmir were separated from Punjab by rocky mountain barriers in a way that cut them off from developments in plains. As a result, communication was difficult and scanty even within the valley. Within valley river transport was the best means of carrying men and commodities.

This life of forced seclusion was not conducive to the development of trade, which could have contributed to the economy of a region as a whole.

The chief means of carrying on trade was human labour, 'Man's back was considered superior to pack ponies.'[103] Porters, mules, donkeys, horses, bullocks and boats were employed for carrying goods from one place to other.[104]

The important commercial lines which connected Kashmir with the outside world were Poonch route, the Murree route, the Pirpanjal route, the Kashmir Yarkand route and the Muzzafarabad route.[105] The first among these routes which connected Srinagar and Deval via Baramulla was covered by boat up to Baramulla and thence forward from Baramulla to Rawalpindi by cart.[106] The second one was the most popular route which led from Srinagar to Bhimber and thence to Gujarat. About 30 miles of distance from Bhimber to Gujarat was covered by cart.[107] The third route passed through Uri and reached Thana Mandi which lay at a distance of 70 miles from Bhimber.[108]

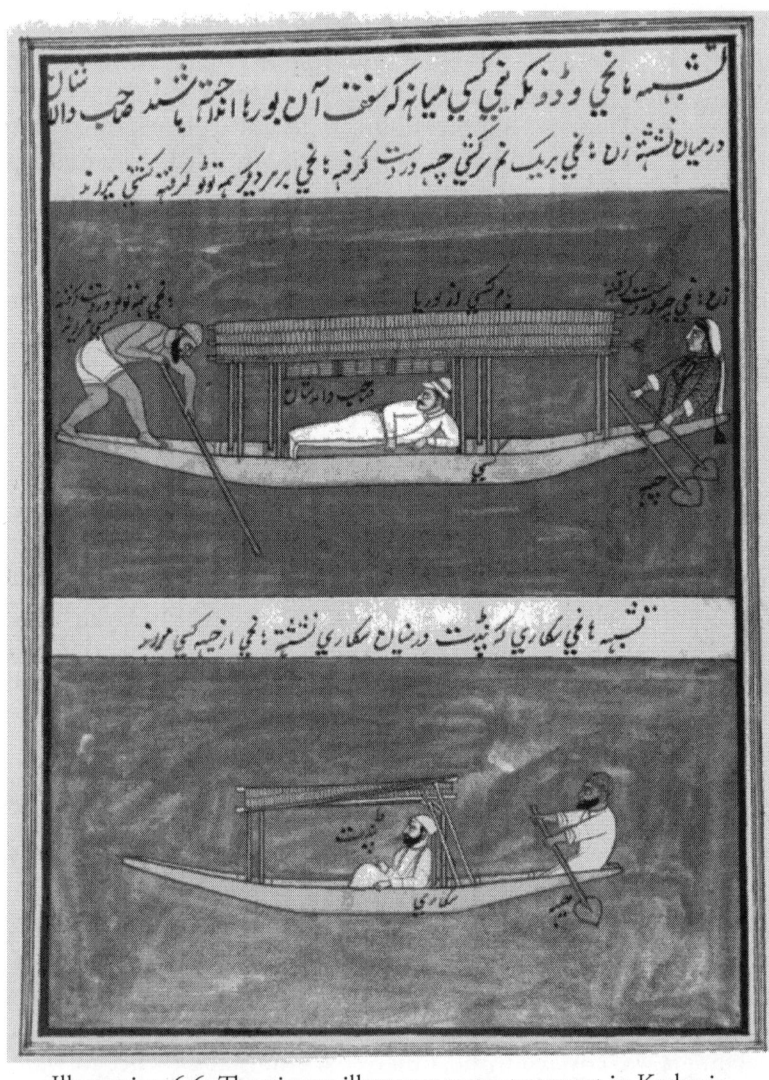

Illustration 6.6: The picture illustrates water transport in Kashmir.
Source: Harbans Mukhia's Collection of Pictures from India Office Library, London.

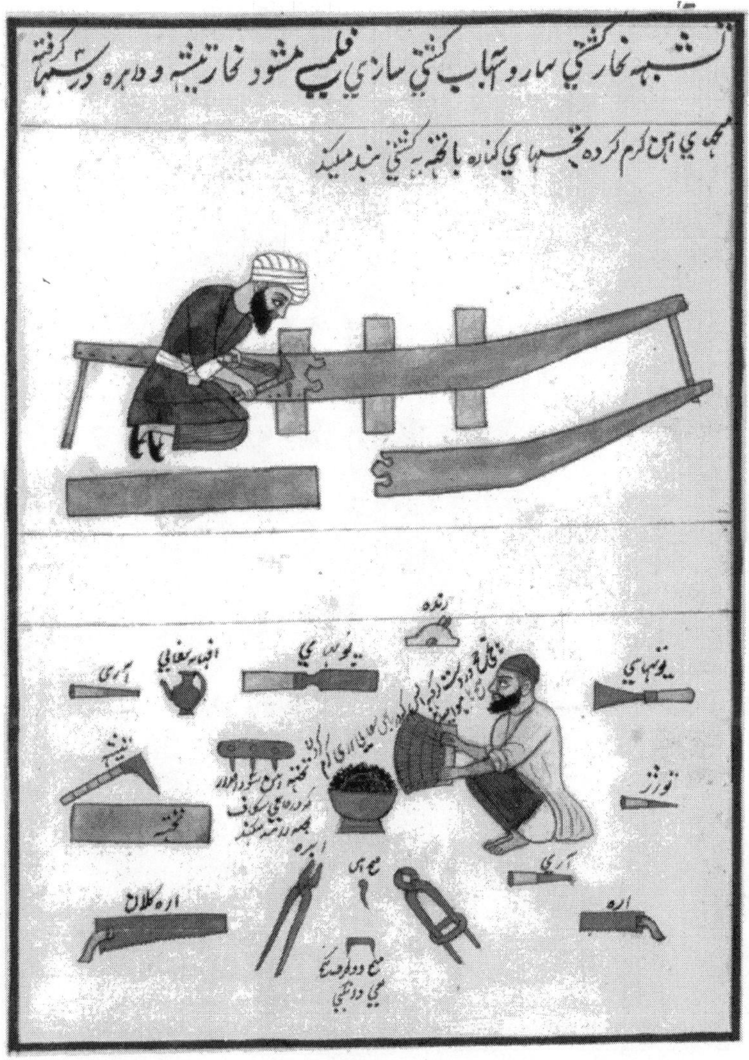

Illustration 6.7: Boat making for river transport in Kashmir.
Source: Harbans Mukhia's Collection of Pictures from India Office Library, London.

Illustration 6.8: Soil being carried to different places through river transport. *Source:* Harbans Mukhia's Collection of Pictures from India Office Library, London.

Jammu was reached from Srinagar by a route which crossed Banihal pass.[109] The other routes which connected Kashmir with Punjab were from Amritsar to Jammu and thence to Banihal pass, from Amritsar to Srinagar by Akhnon and Bodtul pass.[110] The fourth route which connected Kashmir with Yarkand passed through Kargil and Leh.[111] The fifth one crossed through Baramulla and Muzaffarabad and Peshawar.[112] This was the principal route because Jammu was near to Amritsar, the then Emporium of the Punjab, and partly because it remained open for more months during the year than other routes. But the route itself was not good. Horses could pass along with great difficulty.[113] The major portions of the carriage were completed by men and pack bullocks. All the roads connecting Kashmir to the rest of the world were dangerous and in poor condition. The depredations of robber tribes Koonjid and Kirgiz beyond the Karakoram range hampered trade on the Kashmir-Yarkand route.[114] Even during the winter months, these robbers did not spare the armed caravans of traders. The Yarkand government also did nothing to secure the merchants against the usual plundering on this route. The Yarkand Government formerly levied a duty on all merchandise brought to Yarkand market and in return used to protect traders from all types of violence within its territories. After the invasion of Kashghar by Jahangir Khoja of Andeejan, the king of Kokan prevailed on the then Chinese government to relinguish its right to duty levied on Yarkand traders from Kokan in his favour. The Chinese government, however, to escape the disgrace of such concession extended the exemption from levy of duty by the Turkish Chinese government to traders from all other directions. The Government of all countries trading with China, Yarkand and other parts of Central Asia made arrangements through their *akaskal*, i.e. the head representative of traders. The Kashmiri *akaskal*, however, could not make such arrangements in regard to the Kashmiri merchants. The Maharaja did not take immediate notice of it, as a result trade declined due to insecurity.[115] Though Maharaja Gulab Singh was compelled to send one Koodus Joo, a Kashmir trader, to the *akaskal* at Yarkand to arrange for the levy of duty for him at that place, so that these traders were protected on this Kashmir-Yarkand route, but Koodus Joo returned without much success. Nothing could be done, according to the *akaskal*, until the

Maharaja guaranteed the safety of caravans from Kirgiz robbers.[116] During Maharaja Ranbir Singh's time, Mr. Aziz Joo, a Munshi at the court of the Maharaja, was sent to Yarkand with this object, but the Munshi was stopped at Yarkand *chowki* of the police for six months and afterwards turned out of Yarkand with disgrace. Nothing was done to ensure security for traders on this route.

The routes which connected Kashmir with the Punjab were almost practically unusable. They remained closed for more than six months due to snow.[117] Only the Baramulla route used to remain open for most of the year. But it presented a lot of difficulty because the route was in poor condition. Now, whatever amount of trade could pass through these scanty and unfrequented roads with inadequate transport facilities was restricted by the fiscal obstructions. The Maharaja and his officials demanded a heavy amount of duty. These custom duties were annually farmed out to contractors who were among the Maharajas' favourites.[118] During Maharaja Gulab Singh's time Pratap Shah of Rawalpindi was the contractor for custom and paid to the state Rs. 20,000 a year.[119]

During Maharaja Ranbir Singh's period, the Jammu-Banihal route was the main channel by which all the articles from Punjab with the exception of salt were imported to Kashmir.[120] Though duties on this route had slightly been lowered, those on Akhnoor route, Bhimber and Muzaffarabad had been raised in no less than 38 cases.[121] No doubt large reductions were made on the direct route from Jammu to Leh by Sooroo but this was the worst and the least frequent route in the Maharaja's territories.[122]

Hence, trade and industry did not register much improvement. The developmental activities in the matter of roads and transport could have easily opened up the country and brought it into direct contact with the world market.

Thus, the combination of a number of factors, such as geographical barriers, lack of proper incentives, exploitation of the artisans, heavy burden of taxes on trade and industry, insecurity of the roads, difficulties in transport, technical stagnation, and state monopolies, all proved detrimental to the growth and development of trade and industry in Kashmir.

NOTES

1. Mirza, *Akhbarat*, vol. I, f. 113.
2. Mirza, ibid., ff. 1, 27, 36. Foreign and Pol. Weekly, July 1863, file nos. 73-75, NAI. See also M.I. Khan, *History of Srinagar*, pp. 57-8.
3. Capt. Cunnigham, *Memo*, Foreign Dept. Sec. 31 March 1848, file nos. 66-77, NAI.
4. Lawrence, *Valley*, p. 23.
5. Capt. Cunnigham, *Memo.*
6. Ibid. R.H. Davis, *Report on Trade*, pp. 47-9. Foreign and Pol. A, July 1863, file nos. 73-5, NAI.
7. Lawrence, *Valley*, op. cit., pp. 390-4.
8. Mirza, *Akhbarat*, op. cit., vol. I, ff. 1-2.
9. R.H. Davis, op. cit., Appendix A., pp. 1-30. *Majmu-i-Report of Jammu Kashmir-va-Tibet*, 1873-75. See also *Memorandum on Central Asia and its Trade with Hindustan* by *Capt. T.G. Montigomerie to the Secretary to Govt. of Punjab*, no. 173, 20 July 1861, NAI.
10. Lawrence, *Valley*, p. 23.
11. Ibid.
12. R.H. Davis, op. cit., pp. 47-2. The Foreign and Pol. A., July 1863, file nos. 73-5, NAI. Lawrence, *Valley*, pp. 390-4.
13. Lawrence, *Valley*, op. cit., pp. 390-4.
14. Mirza, op. cit., vol. IV, p. 88.
15. Ibid., See also Lawrence, *Valley*, pp. 390-4.
16. R.H. Davis, op. cit., Appendix A, pp. 1-3. *Majmu-i-Report of Jammu, Kashmir-va-Tibet, 1873-75*. See also, *memorandum on Central Asia and its Trade with Hindustan by Capt. T.G. Montigomerie to the Secretary to Govt. of Punjab*, no. 173, 20 July, 1861, NAI.
17. *Administrative Reports of the Period from 1882 to 1900*, State Archives at Jammu and Srinagar.
18. Lawrence, *Valley*, op. cit., pp. 390-4.
19. *Report on the Financial Condition of the Kashmir State. 10th August 1891. In Accordance with Instructions Received from the Government of India*, pp. 6-10.
20. Pandit Bhag Ram, *Annual Administrative Report of Jammu and Kashmir*, 1893, Government Rambir Press, Jammu, 1894, pp. 130-1.
21. M. Suraj Bal, *Administration Report of Jammu and Kashmir, 1898-1900*, Government Rambir Press, Jammu, 1901, pp. 303-23.
22. Lawrence, *Valley*, p. 383.
23. Sir R. Temple, *India in 1880*, London, 1881, pp. 296-9. See also *A Note on Jammu and Kashmir State*, pp. 41-5.

24. Lawrence, op. cit., p. 388.
25. Charles Girdlestone, op. cit., pp. 29-30.
26. D.N, Dhar, *Kashmir: The Land and its Management,* Kanishka Publishing House, Delhi 2004, p. 145.
27. Chitralekha Zutshi, *Languages of Belongings, Islam, Regional Identity, and the Making of Kashmir*, Oxford University, 2004, p. 44.
28. Ibid., p. 82.
29. Ibid.
30. Ibid.
31. Ibid.
32. Robert Thorp, *Cashmere Misgovernment* ,op. cit., p. 50; Bates Charles, *Gazetteer*, op. cit., p. 54.
33. Bates, *Gazetteer,* op. cit., p. 54.
34. Anthony Ames Frank, *The Kashmir Shawl and its Indo-French Influence*, Antique Collectors' Club; 1st edn., 1986, p. 35.
35. Chitralekha Zutshi, *Languages of Belongings*, op. cit., pp. 83-4.
36. Ibid., p. 65.
37. *Persian Records*, file no. 399.
38. Trade Reports of Jammu and Kashmir State.
39. Thorp Robert, p. 51.
40. Ajit Bhattacharjea, *Sheikh Mohammad Abdullah—Tragic Hero of Kashmir,* New Delhi: Lotus Collection, 2008, p. 13.
41. Mohammad Ismail Parey, 'History of the Silk Industry in Jammu and Kashmir (1846-1947)', Ph.D. thesis submitted to Kashmir University, 1983, p. 30.
42. Lawrence, *Valley of Kashmir*, op. cit., p. 367.
43. Ibid.
44. Wilson Andrew, *Abode of Snow,* William Blackwood and Sons, Edinburgh and London, 1876, pp. 364-5.
45. Sukh Dev Singh Charak, *Life and Times of Maharaja Ranbir Singh*, Jay and Kay Book House, 1985, p. 140.
46. E.F. Neve, *Beyond the Pirpanjal: Life Among the Mountains and Valleys of Kashmir,* Fisher Unwin London, London, 1912, p. 58.
47. Bates, *Gazetteer,* op. cit., p. 67.
48. G.M.D. Sufi, *Kashir*, The University of the Punjabi, Lahore 1949, pp. 575-6. The spinning-wheels we saw here were worked by hand, but at the larger filature at Raghunath Pora, on the shore of the Dali, we were told they are worked by waterpower. The silk appeared to be of remarkably good quality, with a soft and fine fibre, and, from a correspondence on the subject shown to us, some samples which had

been sent to London were pronounced by Messrs Durant and Co. H.W. Bellew, *Kashmir and Kashghar. A Narrative of the Journey of the Embassy to Kashgar in 1873-74*, Trubner and Co., London, 1875, p. 83.

49. Younghusband, *Kashmir*, op. cit., p. 78.
50. *Gazetteer of Kashmir and Ladakh*, op. cit., p. 114.
51. P.N.K. Bamzia, *A History of Kashmir: Political, Social, Cultural, From the Earliest Times to the Present Day*, New Dehli: Metropolitan Book Company, 1962, p. 160.
52. Muhammad Yusuf Saraf. *Kashmiris Fight for Freedom*, Feroz Sons Ltd., Lahore, 1977-9, p. 286.
53. *Gazetteer of Kashmir and Ladakh,* op. cit., p. 115.
54. *Annual Administration Report of the Jammu and Kashmir State for the Year 1939-40*, op. cit., p. 23.
55. Saif-ud-din, op. cit., vol. II, 1848.
56. Ganesh Lal, *Siyahat-i-Kashmir*, op. cit., p. 35.
57. Saraf, *Kashmiris Fight for Freedom*, op. cit., p. 281.
58. Lord Birdwood, The Struggle for Kashmir, *International Affairs*, vol. 28, no. 3, July 1952, pp. 300-3.
59. G.M.D. Sufi, op. cit.,vol. II, p. 782.
60. Mirza, op. cit., vol. I, ff. 93, 96. R.H. Davis, op. cit., pp. 48-9, and Appendix XXIV. Foreign Sec. Sept. 1872, file no. 59, NAI. Charles Girdlestone, op. cit., p, 30.
61. Foreign and Pol. A., 31 March 1848, file nos. 66-70, NAI. All the peasants of Kashmir were engaged by the state officials for cleaning this wool without wages. Mirza, op. cit., vol. I, ff. 93-6.
62. Charles Girdlestone, op. cit., p. 28.
63. In 1847 there were 6,000 workshops in the valley of Kashmir. *R.G. Taylors Regulations*, (*Ain*) *Foreign Secret Correspondence*, dated 28 January 1848, NAI.
64. Charles Girdlestone, op. cit., pp. 28-9. R. Thorp, however, mentions that the number of workmen ranged from 20 to 300. T. Thorp, *Kashmir Misgovernment*, op. cit., p. 62.
65. C.H. Bates, *Gazetteer*, op. cit., p. 54, see also M.I. Khan, *History of Srinagar*, op. cit., p. 56.
66. Charles Girdlestone, op. cit., pp. 28-9.
67. Ibid., p. 28.
68. Ibid., pp. 28-9.
69. Ibid., pp. 28-30. See Foreign and Pol. A., 31 March 1848, file nos. 60-70 (Capt. Cunnigham's *Memo on Kashmir*), NAI.
70. Charles Girdlestone, op. cit., p. 28.

71. Davis, op. cit., see Appendix CCV-CCXX.
72. W.K. Farguson and G. Brun, *A Survey of European Civilization*, Houghton, Mifflin, Boston, 1947, p. 738.
73. Youghusband, *Kashmir*, op. cit., p. 211.
74. Mirza Saif-ud-Din., *Akhbarat*, op. cit., vol. I, f. 24.
75. Ibid.
76. R. Thorp, *Kashmir Misgovernment*, p. 63.
77. John Irwin, *The Kashmir Shawl*, H.M. Stationery Office; 1st edn., 1 January 1973, London, p. 9.
78. Davis, op. cit., p. 73.
79. Girdleston, op. cit., p. 29.
80. 'Memorandum of R. Maclagan, Secretary to the Government of Punjab', *Davis, Report,* Appendix. E.
81. Charles Girdlestone, op. cit., pp. 28-30.
82. Ibid., see also C.E. Bates, *Gazetteer*, p. 33. Hassan, op. cit., vol. III (Urdu tr.), p. 572. Sir R. Temple, *Journals kept in Hyderabad, Kashmir, Sikkim and Nepal*, 2 vols., 1859-71, W.H. Allen & Co., 13, Waterloo Place, Pall Mall, S.W. London, 1887, p. 276.
83. Girdlestone, op. cit., p. 28.
84. Ganesh Dass, *Sayahatnama*, op. cit., p. 33.
85. Mirza Saif-ud-Din, *Akhbarat*, op. cit.,vol. I, f. 21.
86. Ibid.
87. Girdlestone, op. cit., p. 29.
88. Ibid.
89. Ibid.
90. Saif-ud-Din, *Akhbarat*, op. cit., f. 30.
91. G.M.D. Sufi, *Kashir*, op. cit., vol. II, p 575.
92. Ibid.
93. Pt. Anand Koul, *Geography of Jammu and Kashmir State*, Thacker, Spink & Co., Calcutta, 1925, p. 58.
94. Ibid.
95. Lawrence, *Valley*, p. 368.
96. Ibid. See also S.T. Wardle, *Kashmir, its New Silk Industry*, W.H. Eaton, The Moorlands Press, London, 1904, p. 35.
97. *Dewan Krishen Lal's Account of Kashmir*, op. cit., Foreign Sec., 31 March 1848, file nos. 66-77.
98. Wardle. op. cit., pp. 9-10. See also H.M. Lefroy, *Report on an Inquiry into the Silk Industry in India*, Superintendent Government Printing, Calcutta, 1916, pp. 40-1.
99. Wardle, op. cit., p. 237.

100. Chaudhri Khan Bahadur, *Census of India*, Superindent of Census Operations, Madhya Pradesh, 1921, vol. XXII, pt. I, pp. 178-9. India 1923. See the portion devoted to Kashmir tables.
101. Manmohan Wazir, *The Silk Industry of Kashmir*, p. 96. See also Tara Chand Wazir, *My Life Story, the Lesson it has Taught me 77 Years in Retrospect*, vol. I, p. 293. Shri Tara Chand Wazir has worked in many capacities. He was Senior Sericulture Asset. in Sericulture Department of Kashmir from 1916 to 1924, Deputy Director (1924-8), Director (1931-41), Chief Director Sericulture (1942-8). The unpublished Autobiography is typed and available with his son Shri Man Mohan Wazir.
102. Wardle, op. cit., p. 237.
103. Major K. Mason, *Routes in Western Himalayas Poonch, Kashmir and Ladakh*, Published (under the Direction of the Surveyor General of India, Calcutta, Dehradun 1922, vol. I, pp. 1-2.
104. *General Report on Kashmir Railway Survey*, 1890, Jammu Archives. The Kashmir Railway was surveyed in 1890 with James Arthur Anderson from Public Works Department (PWD), in-charge of the survey. Also from the PWD the following Executive Engineers were posted in 1890: James Arthur Anderson, Boswell Parkinson Milsom and Paget Patrick Dease.The record of the Institution of Mechanical Engineers records that Herbert Septimus Harington was deployed to the 'Kashmir Railway Survey' as 'acting as Engineer-in-Chief'. Unfortunately the date of this is not given. The broad gauge (BG) of line 16 miles (26 km) was opened in March 1890 and named the Jammu-Sialkot Railway, later becoming the Jammu and Kashmir Railway (Native State Section) being a branch of the North-Western Railway (NWR) from Wazirabad, Punjab, to Jammu through Sialkot.
105. David Ross, *Land of Five Rivers and Sand Sind*, Chapman Amp Hall. London, 1883, p. 147. R.H. Davis, op. cit., Appendix XXIV. Lawrence, *Valley*, op. cit., p. 383. See also *Imperial Gazetteer of India*, vol. XV, *From Kashmir to Kotayam*, op. cit., p. 132.
106. Major K. Mason, op. cit., vol. I, pp. 1-18, 33-8, 144-6 for details see pp. 234-93.
107. Ibid., pp. 1-7.
108. Ibid. See also Lawrence, *Valley*, op. cit., p. 383.
109. Ross, op. cit., pp. 139-40. Major K., op. cit., pp. 33-8. See also Davis, op. cit., Appendix XXIV.
110. *Imperial Gazetteer of India*, op. cit., vol. XV, p. 74.
111. Chaudhri Khushi Mohamad, *Preliminary Report of Ladakh Settlement*

of 1908 under the supervision of Diwan Alim Chand G.C., Superintendent Ranbir Prakash Press, Jammu 1908, p. 2, *Assessment Report of Kargil Tehsil*, 1911, p. 35. Major K. Mason, op. cit., vol. I, pp. 234, 293.

112. Major K. Mason, op. cit., vol. I, pp. 75-80.
113. Ross, op. cit., pp. 139-40.
114. Davis, op. cit., Appendix XXIV.
115. Davis, op. cit., pp. CXCIV-CXCVI.
116. Ibid.
117. Ross, op. cit., pp. 139-40.
118. *Copy of a letter from T.D. Forsyth to Esq. C.B. Commissioner and Superintendent Jullunder Division to T.H. Thornton Esq. D.C.L. Secretary to Government of Punjab*, Foreign and Pol. A., July 1863, file nos. 73-5. NAI.
119. Ibid.
120. *Translation Copy of a Petition Submitted fry Tara Chand, from Lahore to the Secretary to the Punjab.* Govt. Foreign and Pol. A., February 1867, file nos. 26-7, NAI.
121. Ibid.
122. Davis, op. cit., Appendix XXIV.

CHAPTER 7

Conclusion

In the foregoing pages we have analysed some chief aspects of Kashmir's Rural Economy, viz., agricultural production, the land revenue system, the position of the revenue assignees and grantees, the position of the peasantry in the rural society and the pattern of trade as the secondary sector of Kashmir's economy and society, in so far as it was related to the rural economy. Kashmir's agriculture was clearly primitive in its application of tools and techniques. The reasons for this are not far to seek. The climate hindered double cropping patterns; the region's isolation from the rest of the subcontinent gave them a degree of unchangeability that is far more marked than in other part of India. The ruling class, at various levels, smugly perpetuated this relative stasis by, on the one hand, taking no initiatives to improve upon the existing technology and, on the other hand, by exploiting the peasantry to the point of leaving them utterly resourceless to attempt improvement on their own.

No doubt, the majority of the population depended on agriculture in Kashmir. That, too, was a highly stratified society, with the social structure perpetuating intense exploitation of the peasantry. But this stratification and exploitation did not provide any momentum for economic development and resulted in a large degree of stagnation for society. Professor Harbans Mukhia has argued that in ancient and mediaeval Indian history, the high fertility of land and the low subsistence needs of the peasantry eliminated those acute and prolonged conflicts from society, which caused fundamental changes in the entire socio-economic organization in western Europe. But this still does not satisfactorily explain the history of Kashmir. It is true that the fertility of land in the valley of Kashmir was very high and the subsistence of the peasantry very low, though perhaps a shade higher than in the main land due to climatic factors. But the steady deterioration in the condition of the peasantry did not lead to any change in the production system. Nor did the change occur as a result of action from above at the level of the state or the intermediaries.

The reason for the production system not undergoing any change from above was the apathy of intermediaries and the state for developmental activities, because the intense exploitation met their timely needs. The form of payment and the amount that the peasant was obliged to make were based primarily on the arbitrary demands of the revenue machinery.

The frequent assessments of revenue failed to bring either a settled advantage or a basic transformation in the economic relations of various classes connected with the land revenue administration. The landed intermediaries acted in an oppressive manner and gradually transformed into a western type of landed proprietors.[1] Besides, their demand for *begar* from the peasants resulted in the system of periodic migration of labour from Kashmir in search of a living, causing in turn a labour-shortage in Kashmir itself. They uprooted the Kashmiri peasant from the sphere of his subsistence economy and forced him to cater to their own needs. This played a decisive role in the emergence of the wage labourer. From the second half of the nineteenth century down to the first half of the twentieth century, *begar*, or forced labour system, predominated all over Kashmir, supported by the machinery of the state. The Dogra intermediaries compelled the peasants to work on road building, transportation of goods, and the construction of administrative and private buildings for their own use.

Because the rate of revenue extraction was high and the methods of collection were strict, the state sapped whatever initiative and capital the peasantry might otherwise have had. Deprived of all resources above the barest subsistence, and at times even below it, they could not afford to increase productivity from their own lands and labour. For generating even the nascent capital for investment in the development of agriculture, commercial activity would otherwise have been a suitable alternative for the peasants of states like Kashmir, which produced commercial fruit crops in abundance. But the success of such a system depended on well developed regional and wider markets as well as the means of communication and transport, all of which were absent, and the state evinced no interest in developing them.

On the other hand, the monopoly of the state in the trade of agricultural and non-agricultural products, with the consequent depression of prices paid to the peasants, often brought him to such levels where it was impossible for him to make a reasonable living.

The technological and economic stagnation of Kashmir in this period was thus the chief bottleneck in the region's social and economic development. The social context of the stagnation lay precisely in the high degree of exploitation of the peasantry.

The exploitative nobility, comprising the *chakdars*, the *jagirdars*, the *pattadars*, and the *muafi* holders, were the main source of political and economic support for the Dogra Raj. They found that renting land to peasants was more advantageous, which also provided them with a socio-economic basis for the absenteeism among the landlords.

The productive resources of Kashmir's land and labour were inadequately utilized in the first instance, so that the landlord's exploitation of the peasant, based as it was on limited production, perpetuated the backwardness of Kashmir's economy both for the peasant and the landlord.

Though a land settlement was undertaken in 1889 to give some relief to the peasantry and to ensure a redistribution of land, neither the revenue machinery nor the landed aristocracy extended their cooperation to settle the agrarian problems, for it tended to delimit the opportunities for prerequisites and speculation. Thus, the land settlement of 1889, with all the best intentions, failed to register any progress either in the redistribution of land or in improving productivity. The history of Kashmir during the second half of the nineteenth century provides us with a classic illustration of the elite in a backward society holding back the society's progress lest a change undermine its position.

Thus, while the neighbouring regions of Kashmir were entering the modern world through various stages of internal and external turmoil, Kashmir retained most of the characteristics of a mediaeval economy and society until the end of the nineteenth century, and even to this day, though mercifully the winds of change have also been blowing over the past couple of decades.

NOTE

1. Harbans Mukhia, 'Was There Feudalism in Indian History?' *The Journal of Peasant Studies*, vol. 3, no. 3, April 1981, pp. 292-3.

Bibliography

I. Primary Sources

A. Sanskrit and Persian Manuscripts and Printed Texts

Ain Pratap Code Part II. Ain no. 5, Jammu Archives.

Ali, Sayyid, *Tarikh-i Kashmir* (Persian Ms.), Research Department Library at Kashmir University, Srinagar, Kashmir.

Anonymous, *Baharistan-i-Shahi*, Persian Ms., Research Department Library, Srinagar, Kashmir. Though it describes the history of Kashmir from the earliest times, the information from the beginning of the Sultanate in Kashmir up to 1614 is more valuable.

______, *Tarikh-i-Kalan*, Persian Ms., Punjab, State Archives, Patiala. It is a detailed account about the Socio-economic and political condition on Kashmir under the Sikhs (1819-46).

______, *Tuhfat-ul-Ahbah*, Persian Ms., Research Department Library, Srinagar, Kashmir. It deals with the ancient history of Kashmir briefly but gives a detailed account of the religious and political activities of the Sultans of Kashmir.

Dhar, Ramju, *Kaifiat, Intizam Mulk-i-Kashmir*, Persian Ms., Research Department Library Srinagar, Kashmir. This manuscript gives a short account of the revenue system of Kashmir from Emperor Akbar down to Maharaja Ranbir Singh's reign.

Fazl, Abul, *Ain-i-Akbari*, Persian, 3 vols. The original Persian text was translated into English in three volumes. The first volume, translated by Heinrich Blochmann (1873) consisted of Books I and II. The second volume, translated by Col. Henry Sullivan Jarrett (1891), Asiatic Society of Calcutta as a part of their *Bibliotheca Indica* series, vol. II, 3rd edn., 1978. Besides being an important source of Indian history *Ain-i-Akbari* provides us a detailed information on Kashmir's topography, the life of the people, the administrative system and the land revenue administration of Kashmir as a sarkar of the Mughal Empire.

Jahangir, *Tuzuk-i-Jahangiri*, 2 vols. English translation by A. Rogers and H. Beveridge, London, 1909-14.

Kalhana, Pandit, *Rajatarangini*, English translation by M.A. Stein, 2 vols., London, 1900. It is the first historical record of Kashmir. It is a rich storehouse of information on political, social, economic and cultural conditions of Kashmir from earliest times upto 1149-50.

Lal, Ganeshi, *Sayahatnama* (Persian), Punjab Government Record Office, June 1846, rpt. 1955. English tr. V.S. Suri, Chandigarh, 1976. It is a brief but valuable account of Kashmir recorded by Ganeshi Lal during his visit to Kashmir in the 1840s.

Mirjanpuri, Muhammad Khalil, *Tarikh-i-Kashmir*, Persian Ms., Research Department Library, Srinagar, Kashmir. It is a history of Kashmir from the earliest times upto Maharaja Ranbir Singh's reign. It was written under the orders of Raja Kak Dhar, one of the high officials of Maharaja Gulab Singh. It provides information on the political, economic and social problems of Kashmir from 1840 to 1885.

Nath, Dewan Amar, *Zafar Nama-i-Ranjit Singh*, Persian Ms., ed. Sita Ram Kohli, University of Punjabi, Lahore, 1928. It is a detailed history of Maharaja Ranjit Singh and his political activities.

Raja, Jona, *Rajatarangini* (Sanskrit), English tr. J.C. Dutt. under the title *Kings of Kashmira* (3 vols.), printed by S.K. Sham, Calcutta, 1898, rpt. Atlantic Publishers & Distributors, Delhi, 1993. It is the earliest contemporary history of the Sultanate in Kashmir.

Ram, Dewan Kripa, *Gulab-Nama*, Persian text, 'Lahore', 1865, English translation by S.S. Charak, Jammu, 1977. It is an official biography of Maharaja Gulab Singh written by his Prime Minister under the orders of Maharaja Ranbir Singh.

———, *Gulzar-i-Kashmir*, Persian text, Lahore, 1877. The original manuscript is available in the National Archives of India, New Delhi. This book is a mine of information on Kashmir's agricultural and non-agricultural products. It throws a flood of light on technology which was used in carrying out agriculture and trade. It also gives detailed information about the various professions of Kashmir's population.

Saif-ud-Din, Mirza, *Akhbarat*, Persian Ms., 13 vols., Research Department Library, Srinagar, Kashmir. It is a huge collection containing reports sent by Mirza Saif-ud-Din, the news writer of British Government at the court of Maharaja Gulab Singh. He used to send these reports to

British authorities at Lahore. Besides providing information on social and economic aspects of Kashmir under Maharaja Gulab Singh, it also gives detailed information on Anglo-Kashmir relations from 1846 upto 1856.

Saifullah, Mir, *Tarikhnama-i-Kashmir*, Persian Ms. The copy of this manuscript is available with the family of late Prof. Z.L. Jalla of Kashmir University of Srinagar. It provides a brief but interesting information on the socio-economic aspects of Kashmir under the Sikhs and the Dogras.

Shah, Peer Hassan, *Tarikh-i-Kashmir*, Persian Ms., 3 vols., 1885. Research Department Library, Srinagar, Kashmir. Vol. I has been translated, into Urdu by Moulvi Mohd. Ibrahim, State Government Press, Srinagar, 1885, published from Srinagar in 1967. It is a detailed history of Kashmir from the earliest times down to the close of the nineteenth century. Besides political history it deals with the life of some saints of Kashmir. It is by for the most important and comprehensive work on the geography of Kashmir.

Singh, Mahan, *Tarikh-i-Kalan* (unpublished Persian manuscript, Punjab Archives Patiala M/1004.

B. Archival and Other Documents

The following documents have been consulted at the National Archives of India, New Delhi; Punjab State Archives, Patiala; Jammu and Kashmir State Archives at Srinagar and Jammu.

Ahmed, Mir, *Dastural-Amal-i-Kashmir*, Persian Ms. M/829, Punjab States Archives, Patiala. Besides dealing with the political aspects of Kashmir's history it is source of information on land revenue system of Kashmir under Afghan and Sikh rulers.

Arzi Submitted by Hill Chiefs of Kashmir to Henry Lawrence, Foreign and Secret Consultations, 26 December 1846, file no. 1225, National Archives of India. *Copy of a letter from T.D. Forsyth C.B. Commissioner to T.H. Thronton Secretary to Government of Punjab*. Foreign and Political Department, Section A., February 1867, file nos. 26-7, National Archives of India.

Capt. Cunnigham's Memo., Foreign and Political Department Secret Consultation, 31 March 1848, file nos. 66-77, National Archives of India.

Chief Secretariat Political and General Department, file no. 76 of 1896 (unpublished document), Jammu Archives.

Chief Secretariat, Political and General Department, 1876, file no. 76, Jammu Archives.

Darwin, Charles, *The Formation of Vegetable Mould through the Action of Worms and other Invertebrates with Observation on their Habits*, London, 1881.

Diary of P.S. Melvill, Punjab Government Records, Lahore, 1911-15, Punjab State Archives, Patiala.

Diary of R.G. Taylor, Punjab Government Records (1847-49), vol. VI, Punjab Government Press, Lahore 1911-15.

Farman regarding *jagir*. With cash and kind in Martand and Devasar *illaqa* in favour of Pandit Raja Kak Dhar, 1905 Samvat (with the family of Sham Sundar Lal Dhar in Boulevard) at Srinagar.

Farman, Regarding Jagir with Cash and Kind in Martand and Devasar in Favour of Raja Kak Dhar, 1905.

Foreign and Political Consultation, 30 December 1848, file nos. 452-3, National Archives of India.

Foreign and Political Department A., July 1863, file nos. 73-5, National Archives of India.

Foreign Department Secret Consultation, December 1846, file nos. 1266, National Archives of India.

Foreign Department Section E, December 1890, file nos. 196-211, National Archives of India.

Foreign Department Section E, file nos. 295-306. National Archives of India.

Foreign Department Section E, October 1836, file nos. 235-300, National Archives of India.

Foreign Dept. Sec. 31 March 1848, file nos. 60-77, unpublished, National Archives of India.

Jammu and Kashmir State Council Proceedings, 26 October 1904, Jammu Archives.

Karvai-Jalsa-Council Aliya Riyasat Jammu-va-Kashmir (Urdu and Persian), Jammu and Kashmir State Archives, Srinagar.

Khalsa Durbar Records, Punjab State Archives, Patiala, Bundle no. 5, vol. XIII.

Khalsa Durbar Records, vol. XIII, no. 3, Punjab State Archives, Patiala.

Lal, Dewan Krishan, *Account of Kashmir*, Foreign Department Section, 31 March 1848, file nos. 60-8 (unpublished document), National Archives of India.

Lawrence, H.M., *Transfer of Government to Maharaja Gulab Singh*, Section E, 28 January 1848, Section C, file nos. 33-44, Jammu Archives.

Lawrence, John, *Condition of Kashmir*, Secret Committee, 31 March 1848, file nos. 66-77, National Archives of India.

Lawrence, W.R., *Report on the Position of Cultivating Classes in Kashmir*, Foreign Department Section E, February 1890, National Archives of India.

Letters from Sir Hentry Hardinge to Queen Victoria, Foreign and Political Department, 18 February 1846, National Archives of India.

Levy of Cesses in Reassessment of Jagirs in State and Validity of Pattas Granted. Chief Secretariat, Political and General Department, file no. 76 of 1896, Jammu Archives.

List of Ruling Princes, Chiefs and Leading Personages in Jammu and Kashmir State and Gilgit Agency (Government Publication), Delhi, 1939,

Nicholson's Letter Containing Information of Kashmir Foreign and Sec. C., December 1846, no. 1266, NAI.

Patta Granted to Pandit Raja Kak Dhar Regarding Grant of Jagir in Hamal Ilaqa, 1866, Srinagar Archives.

Patta Regading Grant of Jagir of Kava Chak illaqa on Hereditary Basis in Favour of Pandit Raja Kak Dhar, 1863, Photostat copy at Srinagar Archives.

Patta Regarding Grant Of Jagir in Nunar Ilaqa in Favour of Pandit Raja Kak Dhar, January 1857.

Patta Regarding Grant of Jagir in Nunar illaqa in Favour of Pandit Raja Kak Dhar, 1857, Jammu Archives.

Patta Regarding Grant of Jagir of Kava Chak Illaqa on Hereditary basis in the Name of Pandit Raja Kak Dhar, 1863.

Petition of Dewan Lachman Dass against the Cash Settlement, Chief Secretariat, Political and General Department, 1896, file no. 2, Jammu Archives.

R.P. Nisbets Letter to the Secretary Government of India, Foreign Department 29 January 1890, file no. 15, National Archives of India.

Rules Regarding Grant of Waste Land for Cultivation as Sanctioned by His Highness the Maharaja Sahib Bahadur, Jammu, 1917, Jammu Archives.

The Letter from H.M. Lawrence to Gurrie. See nos. 1240-1, 8 December 1846, Jammu Archives.

Wingate, A., *Preliminary Report of Land Settlement in Jammu and Kashmir, 1888-89* (unpublished), Jammu Archives, 1889.

Wynne, H.L.P., *Report on Kashmir*, 1872, For. Pol. A, file nos. 343-9. January 1873, National Archives of India.

C. Administrative, Assessment and other Reports

A Note on Jammu and Kashmir (published by Jammu and Kashmir State), Ranbir Government Press, Jammu, 1928.

A Note on Jammu and Kashmir, Jammu, 1928, Jammu Archives.

Administrative Report of Jammu and Kashmir (*1921-22*), Jammu, 1923 (Government Publication).

Assessment Report of Kargil Tehsil, Jammu, 1911, Srinagar Archives.

Assessment Report of Pratap Singh Pora Tensil, Ranbir Government Press, Jammu, 1917.

Bal, M. Suraj, *Administration Report of Jammu and Kashmir, 1898-1900*, Ranbir Government Press, Jammu, 1901.

_____, *Administrative Report of Jammu and Kashmir State, 1898-1900*, at Ranbir Government Press, Jammu, 1901.

Big Landed Estates Abolition Act, 1950, Srinagar 1950.

Big Landed Estates Abolition Act, XVII *of Samvat* 2007, Jammu 1953.

Browning, *Punjab Government Records* (*1847-1849*), vol. IV, Allahabad, 1911.

Census of India 1921, vol. XXII, pt. I, Jammu, 1923.

Copy of a letter from T.D. Forsyth to Esq. C.B. Commissioner and Superintendent Jullunder Division to T.H. Thornton Esq. D.C.L. Secretary to Government of Punjab. Foreign and Pol. A. July 1863, file nos. 73-5, NAI.

Cunnigham, Capt., (*Memo on Kashmir*), Foreign and Sec. C, 31 March 1848, file nos. 60-77, National Archives of India (NAI).

Davis, R.H. , *The Report on Trade and Resources of Countries on Northwestern Boundary*, Government Press, Lahore, 1862.

_____, *Report on Trade and Resources of the Countries on the North Western Boundary*, Government Press, Lahore 1862.

Diary of A. Cocks, Punjab Government Records (*1847-1849*), vol. IV, Allahabad, 1911.

Ganganath, Wazir, *Report on Jammu and Kashmir State*, 1943, Jammu Archives.

General Report on Kashmir Railway Survey, 1890, Jammu Archives.

_____, *Annual Administration Report of Jammu and Kashmir State* (*1890-91*), at Ranbir Government Press, Jammu, 1892.

_____, *Annual Administration Report of Jammu and Kashmir* (*1891-92*), at Ranbir Government Press, Jammu, 1893.

_____, *Annual Administration Report of Jammu and Kashmir* (*1892-93*), at Ranbir Government Press, Jammu, 1894.

——, *Annual Administration Report of Jammu and Kashmir State, 1894-95*, at Ranbir Government Press, Jammu, 1896.

——, *Annual Administration Report of Jammu and Kashmir State, 1895-96*, at Ranbir Government Press, Jammu, 1897.

——, *Annual Administration Report of Jammu and Kashmir State, 1898-1900*, at Ranbir Government Press, Jammu, 1901.

Lal, Dewan Krishen, *Account of Kashmir*, Foreign Deptt. Secret Correspondence, 31 March 1848, National Archives of India.

Lawrence, W.R., *Assessment Repent of Awantipur*, Ranbir Government Press, Jammu, 1920.

——, *Assessment Report of Awantipura Tehsil*, Jammu, 1920.

——, *Assessment Report of Baramulla Tehsil*, Ranbir Government Press, Jammu, 1905.

——, *Assessment Report of Handwara Tehsil*, Jammu, 1921.

——, *Assessment Report of Handwara Tehsil*, Ranbir Government Press, Jammu, 1922.

——, *Assessment Report of Ich, Nagam Tehsil*, Jammu, 1891.

——, *Assessment Report of Mirbahri*, Jammu, 1898, Jammu Archives.

——, *Assessment Report of Pratap Singh Pora Tehsil*, Jammu Archives.

——, *Assessment Report of Uri-Tehsil*, Jammu, Ranbir Government Press, 1898.

——, *Impact of New Settlement on the Cultivator of Kashmir*, 1909.

——, *Report on the position of cultivating classes in Kashmir*. Foreign Deptt. Sec. E. Feb. 1890, Jammu Archives.

Majmui Reports (in Urdu) for the years from 1887 to 1891, Ranbir Government Press, Jammu and Kashmir Archives in Srinagar.

Maxwell-Lefroy, H., *Report on an Enquiry into the Silk Industry in India*, Calcutta Superintendent Government Printing, 1917, vol. II, National Archives of India.

Mohamad, Chaudhri Khushi, *Preliminary Report of Ladakh Settlement of 1908 under the Supervision of Diwan Alim Chand G.C. Superintendent*, Ranbir Government Press, Jammu, 1908.

Note on the Review of the Six Tehsils of the Valley, Jammu and Kashmir Government, Jammu, 1900.

Preliminary Report of Land Settlement, Jammu, 1908.

Ram, Dewan Anant, *Majmui-i-Report* (Urdu), 1877-8, Ranbir Government Press, Jammu Archives.

——, *Majmui-Report Jammu-va-Kashmir and Tibet* (Urdu), 1873-5, Jammu Archives.

Ram, Dewan Kripa, *Majmi Report on Jammu and Kashmir* (Urdu), 1872-5, at Ranbir Government Press, Jammu Archives.

Ram, Pandit Bhag, *Annual Administration Report of Jammu and Kashmir State (1889-90)*, Ranbir Government Press, Jammu, 1891.

———, *Annual Administration Report of Jammu and Kashmir State (1894-95)*, Ranbir Government Press, Jammu, 1896.

Report of British Empire Exhibition Jammu and Kashmir, London, 1924.

Report of British Entire Exhibition, Jammu and Kashmir, Fleetway Press, London, 1924.

Report on the Financial Condition of the Kashmir state, 10 August 1891 in Accordance with Instructions Received from the Government of India.

Review of the Working of the Land Reforms with Special Reference to Big Landed Estates Abolition Act in Jammu and Kashmir, 1952.

Steedman, E.B., Report on the Revised Settlement of the Jhang District of the Punjab 1874-1880, Lahore, 1882.

Techno-Economic Survey of Jammu and Kashmir State, NCAER, Delhi, 1969.

Translation Copy of a Petition Submitted by Tara Chand, from Lahore to the Secretary to the Punjab Government, Foreign and Pol. A., February 1867, file nos. 26-7, NAI.

Wingate, A., *Preliminary Land Settlement Report in Jammu and Kashmir*, unpublished report in Jammu Archives, 1888-89.

Wreford, R.G., *Census of India, 1941*, vol. XXII, Jammu, 1943.

D. Travel Accounts

Adams, A.L., *Wanderings of a Naturalist in India*, Edmonston and Douglas, Edinburgh, 1867.

Biscoe, Tyndale, *Kashmir in Sunlight and Shade*, London, 1922.

Brinkman, Arthur, *Wrongs of Kashmir*, London, 1868.

Bruce, G.C., *Kashmir*, London, 1915.

Douie, Sir James, *The Punjab Northwestern Frontier Province and Kashmir*, Cambridge University Press, 1916, rpt. New Delhi, 1994.

Forester, G., *Selections from Travels and Journals*, Bombay, 1909.

Girdlestone, Charles, *Memorandum on Kashmir*, Foreign Department Press, Calcutta, 1873 and Fleetway Press Ltd, London, 1873.

Grevis, P., *This is Kashmir*, Cassell & Company Ltd., London, 1954.

Griffin, L.H., *The Punjab Chiefs*, Chronicle Press, Lahore, 1865.

Hugel, C.B., *The Punjab and Kashmir*, Jammu, 1972, 2nd edn.

Jacquemont, Victor, *Letters from India*, London, 1936.

Knight, Capt. William Henry, *Diary of a Pedestrain in Kashmir and Tibet*, New Burlington Street, London, 1863

Knight, E.F., *Where Three Empires Meet*, London, 1905.

Kokino, A. Petro, *Three Weeks in a Houseboat*, Longman's Green, London, 1920.

Korbel, J., *Danger in Kashmir*, Princeton University Press, 1954, rpt. 1966, Srinagar, 1954.

Lambert, C.A., *A Trip to Kashmir and Ladakh*, H.S. King Collection, London, 1877.

Milne, J., *The Road to Kashmir*, London, 1929.

Moorcraft, W. and Trebeck, *Travels in Himalayan Provinces of Hindustan and Punjab, in Ladakh and Kashmir*, 2 vols., London, 1841.

Moorcraft, W., *Tour Diary*, Ms. EURD – 265, available in Jammu University Library.

Neve, A., *Thirty Years in Kashmir*, London, 1913.

Neve, E.F., *Beyond the Pirpanjal*, Church Missionary Society, London, 1915.

Ross, David, *Land of Five Rivers and Sind*, Chapman Amp Hall, London, 1883.

Singh, Maharaja Pratap, *Diary of an Inspection Tour to Gilgit*, Jammu, 1896.

Thorp, R., *Kashmir Misgovernment*, London, 1870.

Vigne, G.T., *Travels in Kashmir, Ladakh, Iskardu, Countries Adjoining the Mountain Courses of Indus and Himalayan, North of Punjab*, 2 vols., Henry Colburn, London, 1842.

Younghusband, E., *Kashmir*, Edinburgh, 1909.

E. Gazetteers

Bates, C.E., *Gazetteer of Kashmir and adjacent Districts of Kishtwar, Badrawah, Jammu and Nowshera, Punch and the Valley of Kishan Ganga*, Office of the Superintendent of Government Printing Press, Calcutta, 1873, rpt. Light & Life Publishers, New Delhi, 1980.

District Gazetteer of Jhang, 1883-4, Punjab State Archives, Patiala.

Gazetteer of Kashmir and Ladak, compiled under the Quarter Master General in India, the Intelligence Branch, Superintendent of Government of Calcutta, 1890.

Imperial Gazetteer of India, vol. XV (from Karachi to Kotayam), Oxford, 1908.

Lawrence, W.R., *Imperial Gazetteer of India*, Provincial Series, *Jammu and Kashmir*, Calcutta, 1909, rpt. Rima Publishing House, Delhi, 1985.

F. Contemporary Historical Works

Andrew, Wilson, *Abode of Snow*, William Blackwood and Sons, Edinburgh and London, 1876.

Bellew, H.W., *Kashmir and Kashghar. A Narrative of the Journey of the Embassy to Kashgar in 1873-74*, Trubner and Co., London, 1875.

Brailsford, H.W., 'Kashmir Today through Foreign Eyes', Bombay, 1948.

Chand, Munshi Hukam, *Tarikh-i-Multan*, Lahore, 1884.

Cunningham, *A History of the Sikhs from the Origin of the Nation to the Battles of the Sutlej*, New Delhi: Low Price Publications, 1977.

Douie, James, *Punjab Settlement Manual*, Superintendent, Government Printing, Punjab 1899 and 1930, New Delhi, rpt. Daya Publishing House, Delhi, 1985.

Drew, F., *The Jammu and Kashmir Territories*, Edward Stanford Edition, London, 1895.

Fauq, M.D., *Rahnuna-i-Kashmir* (Urdu), Lahore, 1912.

Griffin, L.R., *Punjab Chiefs*, Lahore, 1805.

Harding, Charles, *Viscount Harding*, Clarendon Press, Oxford, 1900.

Hugel, Charles Baron, *The Punjab and Kashmir*, John Petheram, London, 1845, rpt. Asian Educational Services, Jammu and Kashmir, Jammu, 1972.

Hunter, Guy, *Modernizing Peasant Societies*, Oxford University Press, London, 1968.

Husband, Francis Young, *Kashmir*, Adam and Charles Black, London, 1909, rpt. New Delhi: Asian Educational Services, Delhi, 1996.

Joo, Mahad, *Various Trades in Kashmir (1823–24)* (unpublished document), Jammu Archives.

Khasta, Hargopal Kaul, *Guldasta-i-Kashmir* (Urdu), Lahore, 1883.

Lawrence, W.R., *Valley of Kashmir*, Oxford University Press, London, 1895.

Nicholson, A.P., *Scrapes of Paper: India's Broken Treaties, Her Princes and Her Problem*, Ernest Benn Ltd., London, 1930.

Ray, S.C., *History and Culture of Kashmir*, 2nd edn., Delhi, 1970.

Ross, David, *Land of Five Rivers and Sind*, Chapman Amp Hall, London, 1883.

Stein, M.A., *Ancient Geography of Kashmir*, Baptist Mission Press, Calcutta, 1899.

Stein, M.A., *Ancient Geography of Kashmir*, Calcutta, 1889.
Temple, S.R. *India in 1880*, London, 1881.
Temple, Sir R., *India in 1880*, London, 1881.
———, *Journals Kept in Hyderabad, Kashmir, Sikkim and Nepal*, 2 vols., 1859-71, W.H. Allen & Co., London, 1887.
The Northern Barrier of India, London, 1877.
Wakefield, William, *The History of Kashmir and Kashmiris*, Sampson Low, Marston Searle & Rivington, London, 1876; rpt. Seema Publications, Delhi, 1975.

II. Secondary Sources

Ali, M. Athar, *The Mughal Nobility under Aurangzeb*, Aligarh, 1970.
Amarnath, *Zafarnama-i-Ranjit Singh*, (Punjabi trans. by Janak Singh), ed. Kirpal Singh, Patiala, 1983.
Bahadur, Chaudhri Khan, *Census of India*, Superindent of Census Operations, Madhya Pradesh, 1921, vol. XXII, pt. I, pp. 178-9. See the portion devoted to Kashmir tables.
Bamzia, P.N.K., *A History of Kashmir: Political, Social, Cultural, From the Earliest Times to the Present Day*, New Dehli: Metropolitan Book Company, 1962.
Banerjee, A.C., *The Khalsa Raj*, Abhinav Publications, New Delhi, 1985.
Banga, Indu, *Agrarian System of the Sikhs*, Delhi, 1978.
Bawa, S.S., *The Jammu Fox: A Biography of Maharaja Gulab Singh*, Southern Illinois University Press; London and Amsterdam, Feiffer and Simons, London, 1974.
Beg, M.M.A., *Zara-i-Islahat* (Urdu), Jammu & Kashmir Government Press, Srinagar, 1950.
Bhattacharjea, Ajit, *Sheikh Mohammad Abdullah—Tragic Hero of Kashmir*, New Delhi: Lotus Collection, 2008.
Big Landed Estates Abolition Act, XVII, Jammu, 1953.
Birdwood, Lord, 'The Struggle for Kashmir', *International Affairs*, vol. 28, no. 3, July 1952.
Charakh, Sukhdev Singh, *Life and Times of Maharaja Ranbir Singh*, Jammu: Jay Kay Book House, 1985.
Dhar, D.N., *Kashmir—The Land and its Management*, Kanishka Publishing House, Delhi, 2004.
Dhar, O.N., 'Land Reforms in Kashmir', *Indian Affairs Record*, vol. III, no. 4, National Archives, Delhi 1954.

Farguson, W.K. and G. Brun, *A Survey of European Civilization*, Houghton, Mifflin, Boston, 1947.

Frank, Anthony Ames, *The Kashmir shawl and its Indo-French Influence*, Antique Collectors' Club; 1st edn., 1986.

Goswamy, B.N. and J.S. Grewal, *Mughals and Jogis of Jakhabar*, Simla 1967.

Gupta, Hari Ram, *History of the Sikhs: The Sikh Loin of Lahore*, vol. V, Munshiram Manoharlal, New Delhi, 1991.

Habib, Irfan, *Agrarian System of Mughal India, 1526-1707*, Bombay, 1963.

Howard, Albert and Gabrielle L.C. Howard, *The Development of Indian Agriculture*, Humphrey Milford, Oxford University Press, London, Bombay 1929.

Howard, Albert, *An Agricultural Testament*, Brand Albatross Publishers and Oxford University Press, London, 1972.

Howard, L.E., *Earths Green Carpet*, Cambridge University Press, London, 2012 (rpt.).

Hunter, Guy, *Modernizing Peasant Societies*, Oxford, London, 1969.

Hussain, Fazal, *Kashmir-aur-Dogra Raj* (Urdu), Gulshan Publishers, Srinagar, 1979.

Irwin, John, *The Kashmir Shawl*, H.M. Stationery Office; 1st edn., 1 January 1973, London.

Jalali, J.L.K., *Economics of Food Grains in Kashmir*, Lahore Mercantile Press, 1931.

Kapoor, M.L., 'A Study in Socio-Economic Life of People during Maharaja Pratap Singh's Period, 1885-1925', unpublished Ph.D. thesis approved by Jammu University in 1972.

Khan, M.I., *History of Srinagar*, Aamir Publications, Srinagar, 1978.

Kosambi, D.D., *An Introduction to the Study of Indian History*, Popular Book Depot, Bombay, 1956.

_____, 'Origins of Feudalism in Kashmir', *Journal of Bombay Royal Asiatic Society*, 15th Anniversary, Bombay, 1957.

Koul, Pandit A., *Geography of Jammu and Kashmir*, 2nd edn., Srinagar, 1980.

Koul, Pt. Anand, *Geography of Jammu and Kashmir State*, Thacker, Spink & Co., Calcutta, 1925.

Koul, S.N., *Kashmir Economics*, Srinagar, 1954.

Koul, S.R., *Biography of Maharaja Gulab Singh*, Srinagar, 1923.

Latif, S.M., *History of Punjab*, Delhi, 1964.

Lefroy, H.M., *Report on an Inquiry into the Silk Industry in India*, Superintendent Government Printing, Calcutta, 1916.

Mam, Phool Pyari, *Maharaja Gulab Singh*, an unpublished Ph.D. thesis approved by Kashmir University in 1981.

Marx, Karl, *Notes on Indian History*, Foreign Languages Publishing House, Moscow, 1988.

Mason, Major K., *Routes in Western Himalayas Poonch, Kashmir and Ladakh*, published under the Direction of the Surveyor General of India, Calcutta, Dehradun, 1922.

Nargis, D., *Tarikh-i-Dogra Desh*, Jammu, 1963.

Nargis, Dewan Narsingdas, *Maharaja Ranbir Singh* (a vernacular biography) Jammu, 1921; rpt. Jammu, 1983.

Nicholson, A.P., *Scraps of Paper, India's Broken Treaties, Her Princes and Her Problem*, London, 1930.

Palit, D.K., *Jammu and Kashmir Arms*, Dehradun, 1972.

Panikkar, K.M., *Gulab Singh, the Founder of Jammu & Kashmir State*, London, 1930.

Parmu, R.K. *History of Muslim Rule in Kashmir*, Peoples Publishing House, Bombay, 1969, Delhi, 1969.

_____, 'History of Dogra Rule in Kashmir 1846-1947', unpublished Manuscript. Office of the Director History Unit, Jammu and Kashmir, Srinagar (type copy).

Powell, Baden, *Land Systems of British India (1841-1901)*, The Clarendon Press, London, 1892; rpt. Oriental Publishers, Delhi, 1967.

Rai, Satya Mehta, *Partition of Punjab*, Asia Publishing House, Chandigarh, 1965.

Raina, A.N., *Geography of Jammu and Kashmir State*, India Book House, Bombay, 1971; rpt., National Book Trust, Delhi, 1977.

Sapru, A.N., *The Building of Jammu and Kashmir State, an Achievement of Maharaja Gulab Singh*, Lahore, 1931.

Saraf, Muhammad Yusuf, *Kashmiris Fight for Freedom*, Ferozsons Ltd., Lahore, 1977-9.

Sharma, D.C., *Kashmir Agriculture and Land Revenue System Under the Sikh Rule 1819-49*, Rima Publications, Jammu, 1986.

Sharma, R.S., *Indian Feudalism*, University of Calcutta, Calcutta, 1965.

Sharma, T.R., ed., *Ranjit Singh Ruler and Warrior*, Chandigarh: Publication Bureau, Panjab University, 2005.

Singh, Fauja, *Some Aspects of State and Society Under Maharaja Ranjit Singh*, New Delhi, 1982.

Singh, R.L., *India: A Regional Geography*, National Geographical Society of India, Varanasi, 1971.

Sufi, G.M.D., *Kashir*, 2 vols., Punjab University, Lahore, 1949.

Suri, Sohan Lal, *Umdat-ut-Tawarikh*, Daftar II, English trans. by V.S. Suri, Punjab Itihas Prakashan, Chandigarh, rpt. Amritsar, 2002.

Techno-Economic Survey of Jammu and Kashmir State, NCAER, Delhi, 1969.
The Jammu and Kashmir Yearbook, a Master Document on Jammu & Kashmir the People and Their Life, Government Press, Jammu, 1972.
The Medieval History Journal 1600-1900, vol. 11, no. 1, Sage Publications, New Delhi, 2007.
Wardle, S.T., *Kashmir, its New Silk Industry*, W.H. Eaton, The Moorlands Press, London, 1904.
Whitcombe, Elizabeth, *Agrarian Conditions in Northern India*, University of California Press, Berkeley, 1972.
Zutshi, Chitralekha, *Languages of Belongings: Islam, Regional Identity, and the Making of Kashmir*, Oxford University, New Delhi, 2004.

Unpublished Thesis

Mohammad Ismail Parey, 'History of the Silk Industry in Jammu and Kashmir (1846-1947)', thesis submitted to Kashmir University for award of Ph.D. degree), 1983, p. 30.

Index